Routledge Revivals

A LAST VINTAGE

A LAST VINTAGE

ESSAYS AND PAPERS
BY
GEORGE SAINTSBURY

Edited by

John W. Oliver : Arthur Melville Clark : Augustus Muir

Personal Portraits by

David Nichol Smith
Dorothy Margaret Stuart
Helen Waddell

First published in 1950 by Methuen & Co. Ltd.

This edition first published in 2018 by Routledge
2 Park Square, Milton Park, Abingdon, Oxon, OX14 4RN
and by Routledge
711 Third Avenue, New York, NY 10017

Routledge is an imprint of the Taylor & Francis Group, an informa business

Publisher's Note
The publisher has gone to great lengths to ensure the quality of this reprint but points out that some imperfections in the original copies may be apparent.

Disclaimer
The publisher has made every effort to trace copyright holders and welcomes correspondence from those they have been unable to contact.

A Library of Congress record exists under ISBN: 51006437

ISBN 13: 978-1-138-55461-0 (hbk)
ISBN 13: 978-1-138-56349-0 (pbk)
ISBN 13: 978-1-315-12174-1 (ebk)

A LAST VINTAGE

Uniform with this book

GEORGE SAINTSBURY : The Memorial Volume

A LAST VINTAGE

ESSAYS AND PAPERS

BY

GEORGE SAINTSBURY

Edited by

John W. Oliver : Arthur Melville Clark : Augustus Muir

Personal Portraits by

DAVID NICHOL SMITH

DOROTHY MARGARET STUART

HELEN WADDELL

METHUEN & CO. LTD. LONDON

36 Essex Street, Strand, W.C.2

First published in 1950

CATALOGUE NO. 5277/U

PRINTED IN GREAT BRITAIN

PREFACE

THE volume of George Saintsbury's writings published in 1945, his centenary year, was given so agreeable a welcome that its three editors, Dr. John W. Oliver, Dr. Arthur Melville Clark and myself, were encouraged to bend again to the gathering of those of his essays and papers that lay still uncollected. The far-scattered class which make up 'that brotherhood of men who sat at the feet of Professor George Saintsbury in the University of Edinburgh' (and some thousands of us still survive) are not the only ones who can be called Saintsburians: there are those who take pleasure in recalling the apocalyptic comments of Saintsbury the journalist in periodicals of the 'eighties and 'nineties; there are those who have studied with profit his copious literary criticism and history; there are those who joyfully acclaimed the mellow but none the less vital essays that came from him in the days of his autumn flowering at Bath; there are those who revere him as their master in the appreciation and lore of wine, second only in the long tale of vinology (or should I say œnology?) to Saint Urban himself: all of which goes to show that George Saintsbury was a man with a robust plenitude of talents. And these talents he burnished and used with that prodigal and jubilant industry of his. Those who knew the man will remember the joy with which he accepted the gift of life and how he went at every new experience, whether it were a book of modern verse or a bottle of Château Latour, with a clean palate, an open and ordered mind, and an elated curiosity. Some reflections of that spirit will, we hope, be caught in these pages.

Mr. Christopher Saintsbury, his surviving son, has not only given his approval to the making of this book but is also surrendering the royalties so that a sum of money, added to the royalties of the previous volume, may be handed over to the University of Edinburgh to form a suitable memorial in the department where his father filled the Chair for twenty years. For this act of generosity and for valued help we take pleasure in recording our thanks.

We count it a fortunate thing that we have been able to include Dr. David Nichol Smith's tribute to Saintsbury. On the evening of 23rd October 1945, the Merton Professor of English Literature in

Oxford delivered it as the Centenary Oration to the Saintsbury Club: a club which had been founded fourteen years previously by André L. Simon, Colonel Ian Maxwell Campbell, the late Maurice Healy K.C., and others, to pay their dues of honour to the man who had given them and all kindred spirits his *Notes on a Cellar Book.*

We are grateful both to Miss Helen Waddell and Miss Dorothy Margaret Stuart: the one for her study of Saintsbury the bookman, a study so rich and vivid and affectionate; the other for her picture of the man as she knew him in the days of his retirement at 1, Royal Crescent, Bath—a unique picture in words that might have been written as a companion-piece to the portrait by Sir William Nicholson that hangs today in the Common Room of Saintsbury's old college in Oxford.

Mr. W. M. Parker, by contributing a bibliography (which he modestly describes as a 'check-list'), has provided a useful tailpiece to this our final collection of George Saintsbury's essays and papers.

AUGUSTUS MUIR

CONTENTS

ACKNOWLEDGMENTS

GRATEFUL acknowledgment must be made to the editors and publishers who have given permission to reprint the essays and studies included in this volume: to the editors concerned for articles from *The Times Literary Supplement, Wine and Food, The Dial, The Kensington News, The Criterion, The Glasgow Herald, The Athenæum;* to Messrs. Constable and Co., Ltd., for the study of Marryat's novels in their edition of *Jacob Faithful* and for the introductory essay to Miss Helen Waddell's translation of Prévost's *Manon Lescaut;* to Messrs. David Nutt for the study of Montaigne and Florio; to Messrs. Sampson Low, Marston and Co., Ltd., for 'A Note on Criticism' from the Introduction to *Essays on English Literature* by Edmond Scherer; to Messrs. Chatto and Windus for *A Moment to Spare;* to the Syndics of the Cambridge University Press for Miss Helen Waddell's tribute; to Messrs. Hodder and Stoughton Ltd., for articles from *The Bookman;* to Messrs. John Lane, The Bodley Head Ltd., for 'A Sentimental Cellar' from *The Yellow Book;* to Sir John Murray for articles from *The Fortnightly Review;* to Messrs. Macmillan and Co., Ltd., for extracts from *Macmillan's Magazine;* to the Royal Society of Literature for *Andrew Lang in the 'Seventies and After;* to Mr. John Hatton, Spa Director, Bath, for *Bath in Literature.* Thanks for help generously given are due to Mr. J. E. Scott, to Miss Dorothy Margaret Stuart, to Miss Mair Davies, to Mr. Oliver Rottmann of the English Library, Cambridge, and to Miss K. Mary Smith of the Bodleian Library, Oxford.

A CENTENARY TRIBUTE

BY DAVID NICHOL SMITH

(Delivered at the 27th Meeting of The Saintsbury Club, held at the Vintners' Hall, London, 23rd October, 1945.)

THIS evening we celebrate the centenary of the birth of George Saintsbury at Southampton on 23rd October 1845. We celebrate also the anniversary of another event in his long life, a fiftieth anniversary, for it is fifty years almost to the day since he entered on that period when he attained to his full stature as a man of letters. He had been leading the uncertain life of a journalist, a political as well as a literary journalist, when by his appointment to the chair of Rhetoric and English Literature in the University of Edinburgh he was enabled to devote himself entirely to his favourite studies, to write the books which he wanted to write, and to become a very great professor.

I remember well the year of his appointment. David Masson had retired in the summer of 1895, and we who had been Masson's pupils viewed the choice of a successor to him with some anxiety. Three of the many candidates were understood to be hard in the running—Saintsbury, W. E. Henley, and Walter Raleigh, then a young professor in the University of Liverpool. As it is a Regius chair, the appointment was in the hands of the Secretary for Scotland, who was then Lord Balfour of Burleigh, a man known to take his duties very seriously. He interviewed these three candidates, but he was slow in making up his mind, and he was not a man to have his mind made up for him by others. July passed, and the new session was to begin in October. August passed; and not till about the middle of September was it announced how his choice had fallen. He took a risk, for so far Saintsbury's only academic experience was as an undergraduate at Oxford, and one of his latest publications had been a chapter in the Fur and Feather Series on 'The Cookery of the Grouse'. That Balfour of Burleigh thought that he was taking a risk I have had on good authority.

Within two or three weeks Saintsbury arrived in Edinburgh, ready to begin the exacting work of a Scottish university session, but without a single lecture written. A fortnight later, actually on

15th October, he gave his inaugural lecture. A student of Masson's could not fail to be struck with the precise and rapid utterance of the new professor as he expounded his views on the functions and the scope of the office which he had just assumed. That lecture was carefully written and was ready for publication. It has been reprinted in the excellent memorial volume which appeared a few days ago. As I read it, fifty years after having heard it, the whole scene comes back to me vividly. But that was only his inaugural lecture. In the following twenty weeks or so he was expected to give over a hundred lectures, and he gave them. He spoke them from the stores of his knowledge and the wealth of his experience with only a few notes. Not being written, these lectures could not be repeated, though the subjects could not be new year after year. The truth is that Saintsbury never indulged in mere repetition. He has written on the same subject frequently, but always differently. I do not say that he always improved on what he had already written. But whatever he writes he always gives what he is thinking at the time, adjusting it to his immediate purpose.

Now you must bear with me if I appear to bring myself in too often in what I am now to say. But when your Honorary Secretary invited me to speak to you this evening he made a special point of my long acquaintance with Saintsbury, and had I not known him I should not have ventured to be speaking to you now.

He had not been long in Edinburgh before I met him. I was recommended to him as a young man who would do a little piece of work for him. It was to revise the dates in the index to his forthcoming volume on *Nineteenth Century Literature*, and it turned out to be a heavier piece of work than either of us had expected. I cannot think that the inclusion of these dates in that index was his own idea, and I suspect the publishers. But it was then that I began to gather the evidence which in time led me to the conclusion that the only dates in which he could be trusted to be minutely accurate were the dates of vintages. In these I understand he was impeccable.

And I am glad to remember that not only did he give me my first paid job but I retaliated by giving him his first routine job as Professor outside his lectures to his classes, for I had written a post-graduate dissertation on which he had to report, as he did very speedily, and very kindly; and from that time I never received from him anything but kindness. There were to be many years in which I did not see much of him, but I saw him from time to time, in Edinburgh and Oxford, and we occasionally corresponded.

As a correspondent it was his invariable habit to answer by return of post. Not for a day would he let me be one up on him. I never received a long letter from him, and I never heard of any *man* who did—one, I mean, of these long easy-going letters with

> All the floating thoughts we find
> Upon the surface of the mind.

His letters give the impression that he has other things on hand, as indeed he had. He thought little of them, and left instructions that none were to be published. But every letter of his that I have seen has a quality which may remind us of what he himself has said about letter-writing—'The more the spoken word is heard in a letter the better, and the less that word is heard the worse'. Short as his letters might be, in their wit or unexpected turns of phrasing, in their allusiveness or their precision, I can hear him speaking.

And when I called on him during the years of his professorship, I always felt that there was a limit to the time that he had to spare. As soon as I had gone, I knew that he would be down again at his desk. For these were the days of his big books. He took it to be one of the duties of a professor to speak to a much wider audience than his immediate students, and to take every opportunity that his chair afforded him of contributing to the general advance of English studies. The days of the big book seem now to be passing, if they are not already past. Our Victorians liked to write monumental treatises (and so did their contemporaries in other countries)—works of great scope, embodying great learning, and giving a comprehensive view of their subject. Nowadays we seem to have lost that ambition. We plan composite books, with several contributors. We find it easier to confine ourselves to one aspect of a subject. If we scheme big books in our young days, the chances are that we shall write only a fragment of them. How many of us have been asked by our uncles or older acquaintances how we were getting on with our *magnum opus?* It was always a *magnum opus*. That is a question which I should never think of asking any of my young friends. But Saintsbury was an old Victorian in planning on a large scale, and fulfilling his ambitions.

First in time among his big books is his *Short History of English Literature*, which, in view of the extent of ground which it covers, the freshness and the confidence of its judgements, and the remarkably short time in which it was written—less I believe than a year—I am inclined to consider his greatest *tour de force*. With its completion he had cleared the way for another project, one which had been long in his mind, his great *History of Criticism*—not a history of English criticism only, but of all European criticism from the days of the Greeks and Romans. It was our first and is still our only history of criticism in all its main phases. That work was no sooner finished than he turned to his *History of English Prosody from the Twelfth Century to the Present Day*. English Prosody is a very controversial subject, but it does not seem to me to matter whether or not we accept Saintsbury's theory of the structure of English verse. No one has ever propounded a theory which everyone accepts. But no one I think can browse in this book without finding that the zest with which Saintsbury studied the forms of English poetry is contagious. Then came a book on *English Prose Rhythm*, tracing the changes throughout the centuries in the modulation of our best prose. These big books all belong to the twenty years of his professorship at Edinburgh. When he retired from his chair at the age of seventy he had accomplished the heavy tasks which he had imposed upon himself. He had written his big books. And he would not have been Saintsbury had he not written much else. He had been, for example, the chief contributor to the *Cambridge History of English Literature*. He had edited, again for example, a collection of the Caroline Poets. And no sooner had he retired than he solaced himself with a book on the eighteenth century which he called *The Peace of the Augustans*—the book of his which has been selected for inclusion in 'The World's Classics'. To some of us it may seem that the title was well chosen, though not of purpose, to mark the end of his strenuous labours.

The seventeen years which followed were to have their own tale of work. Another big book remained to be written, the *History of the French Novel*, and then he was free for what had come easy to him since his journalistic days—the essay, or preface, or introduction, about a particular book or author. He lived now in Bath, at the corner of the Crescent, in a small set of rooms which were chosen because they were on the ground floor; when I saw them I thought them rather dark, certainly very crowded, and perhaps dusty. These were troubled years. Here his wife died, after long patient nursing on his part. But he could now relax and write only what he wanted and when he wanted; and it was here that he gave us what in this company I may call the triumphant proof of his relaxation, the book which has brought us together this evening. His *Cellar-Book* I have always understood is the real founder of the Saintsbury Club. Not it alone of course, but we all know how it took us by surprise, and how it widened the circle of his readers. It struck the note for his *Scrap Books*, those jumbles—and that they are jumbles is part of their attraction—of reminiscences and observations provocative, wise, and always independent. He trailed his coat for the pussyfoots, but they would not tread on it. He paraded his Toryism, his distrust of what is called progress, his belief that 'nearly all the supposed new things, bar mere mechanism, are old'. Here was his last chance to say what he had left unsaid, and he snatched at it with glee. 'I did want to say what I have said here', he tells us. For any one who did not know Saintsbury, there is no surer way to learn what sort of man he was in his later years than to read these *Scrap Books*. In the careless ease with which playfulness jostles with conviction we detect his sense of the recognition which he had won. If it was during the days of his professorship that he grew to his full stature as a man of letters, it was in his retirement that he attained to the full measure of his fame.

During these years I had the luck to be his colleague in the examination of a Cambridge candidate for the degree of Ph.D. There had to be a viva, but as Saintsbury could not go to Cambridge the Cambridge man had to go to Saintsbury. The viva was arranged to be held in his rooms in Bath, and I was told to come in time for lunch. Bristol milk, and then we sat down to a chicken, which Saintsbury himself carved. With one flick of the knife the wing seemed to fall off. I have never seen a chicken carved with greater skill, and Saintsbury was then eighty-three. He was in excellent form, as sprightly in his talk as a young man on a holiday. We talked of many things—of his London days, and Merton College, and of a contemporary man of science who had the misfortune to believe that this life was the end of everything for him. Then came the business of the day. He had to prepare his room for the viva. 'We must have a table', he said, remembering his experiences at Oxford where a table, a very extensive table, is a regular part of the equipment. The only table that came handy was a circular table, about two feet in diameter. We sat down on one side, and the candidate was ushered in and sat down on the other. Saintsbury asked him a few questions, and I followed, and any doubt that either of us might have had was dispelled. The viva was over. But Saintsbury could not let that young man go at once after so formal a meeting. 'Will you have a glass of port?' he said. So all three of us had a glass. The young man left, and we had to record our verdict. Saintsbury volunteered to write the report and wrote it straight off, but I have to add that I transcribed it. A day or two later the young man learned in Cambridge that he had been ploughed. I was told afterwards that he was disappointed. Was it a hoax to offer him that glass of port? Now I put this question to you. If any of you as a young man had been offered the choice of a glass of port with Saintsbury or a Ph.D., which would you have chosen?

When Saintsbury drafted the report, I remarked on its excellence. He smiled and said 'Well, I think I can still do these things, but I am not so quick now'. There was no sign of any slackening in the pace that afternoon. Nor had I ever known him more at his ease, and more genial. That was our last meeting. He died at Bath a year or two later, at the age of eighty-seven. The papers announced that the funeral at Southampton would be strictly private, but we in Merton, knowing his affection for his old college, of which he was an honorary fellow, asked his son if we might be represented, and his son replied by telegram—'Merton, yes'. It fell to me, as Sub-Warden of the college at that time, to be its representative. Not without several inquiries I made my way to the grave in the Old Cemetery, Southampton, which seemed to be strangely quiet. When the funeral party arrived there were about six of us in all, mostly relatives who had continued to reside in his native town.

Now why is it that we honour the memory of Saintsbury? You in this Club have your own answer, and it is very like the answer which is given by those who know him best as a judge of books. We honour him because of his enjoyment of what is good, his zest in the discovery of what is good, his independence in proclaiming what he believes to be good, or not so good. 'I have never yet given a second-hand opinion of any thing, or book, or person', he says at the beginning of his *Cellar-Book*. That is a proud boast, and none of us will challenge it. You confirm it; and it is certainly true of his judgements of books and their authors. The work of the critic and the literary scholar takes many forms, and no man can be equally good in all. For some of them Saintsbury had no great liking or aptitude. As I have already hinted he was not much interested in dates. Once when I pointed out to him that a date on which he had founded part of his argument was probably wrong—in other words that what he had taken to be the literary vintage of 1682 was probably the vintage of 1678—he replied, 'I daresay you're right, but you know I have a godless indifference in points of this sort', though he added that 'the facts were certainly worth stating'. As an editor of texts he was what we might call old-fashioned, and I think that his eyesight, as well as the rapidity with which he always worked, unfitted him for the minuter problems which are the occupation of our modern textual critics. But when he speaks of a poem as a poem, or of any work as the artistic embodiment of its writer's purpose, he suffers no lets or hindrances. Hazlitt once said that when an artist leaves behind him any work which is a model in its kind, we have no right to ask whether he could do anything else, or how he did it, or how long he was about it. Saintsbury could not have wholly subscribed to that, though of all the great English critics Hazlitt in his happier moods, unclouded by personal dislikes and bitterness, was, I think, the one to whom he was most akin. An historian who set himself in book after book to trace the changes in the art of literature could not have subscribed to such sweeping limitations. But when I read his histories I invariably find that what interests me most is not the tracing of movements and tendencies, which is essential in a history, but the appreciations of individual authors. There Saintsbury always seems to me to be at his best. He brings to the surface what may have been only latent in our minds, he gives a sharp focus to what we may have seen only dimly, or he makes us realise what we may not have suspected. We may not always agree with him, but having the courage of his opinions he invites us to have the courage of our own. Not the least of the lessons which he taught to his students at Edinburgh, and still teaches to his readers everywhere, is to think for themselves, and for that, and for the validity of his judgements, and for the light which they shed, we honour the memory of George Saintsbury.

THE LAST YEARS

BY DOROTHY MARGARET STUART

NO man ever hated publicity, or what is now called 'writing up', with a more hearty hatred than did this great Englishman; but he was undeniably 'good copy', and 'good copy' he remains more than a decade after his death. Did not Mr. Robert Lynd imagine 'a young critic a hundred years hence eagerly enquiring what manner of man was George Saintsbury'? Much has been written on the subject, much more than he himself would have wished, for the most part faithfully, in no instance with malice: yet if that young critic should try to reconstruct a true and lively image from certain of the published materials, the result could hardly fail to be a figure hopelessly out of drawing against a background wholly out of perspective. In the modest hope that these notes may be of some service to him—or to other interested enquirers less remote in time—I have accepted an invitation to put on record a few of my own memories and a portion of my own knowledge concerning 'G. S.'

Let us begin at the beginning, rather in the fabled manner of G. P. R. James.

On a certain August morning in the year 1926 a youngish and slightly nervous pilgrim (feminine gender) 'might have been observed' descending from a taxi-cab at the main portal of 1, Royal Crescent, Bath. The step from a paper to a flesh-and-blood acquaintance is always a perilous one; and there can be no regression. Add that the person to be visited for the first time was venerable in every sense of the term and it will be understood why the pilgrim's hand trembled a little as she rang the bell and set echoes clanging in the hollow depths of the old house.

The paper-acquaintance had begun in the previous year, and had flourished exceedingly. Both parties were devotees of the goddess whom George Saintsbury loved to call 'Divine Nonsensia', and this cult served to create a second bond fully as strong as that already created by a common love of literature and of all the gracious gaieties of life. How characteristic it was that 'G. S.' did not say to his new correspondent, 'If you should find yourself in Bath, do come and see *me*,' but, 'There is in my little dining-room here a rather fine Rossetti drawing, never engraved or published; if you should find yourself in Bath, do come and see *it*.'

So, ostensibly to see the Rossetti drawing, I took my courage firmly in both hands and went.

After being admitted to a bleak entrance hall—graced by a cast of the head of the Apollo Belvedere on a mock-marble column—I was led through an interminable, dim and tortuous passage to the suite of chambers occupied by my host. I had seen only one likeness of him, belonging to the close of the Edinburgh period. It showed an engagingly ugly old gentleman with a scholar's stoop, wearing a straggly beard and an Inverness cape. As I followed my guide I hastily assembled my ideas as to what the reality might be. 'Short, anyhow,' I said to myself, perhaps a little regretfully, 'He is almost certainly *short.*'

I entered the large, light, book-encumbered room looking out on the Crescent Fields, and a figure in a black skull-cap rose from behind a table by the window. It seemed to go on rising longer than the supposed short person had any right to do. As a matter of sober history, Saintsbury stood five feet eleven inches without shoes; and even his curious high-shouldered stance could not make him appear other than tall. It is strange that a disciple who visited him at Bath should have described him as 'a little old man', and his habitat as 'a basement'.

Many passers-by used to glance up to get a glimpse of the picturesque figure at the chaotic writing table. One noble (and witty) lady, who often did this, said that he reminded her of 'an old astrologer casting a horoscope'. When he was told that another lady had remarked that she liked to see the 'Dear Old Gentleman' sitting there, he feigned indignation. 'Is thy servant a D.O.G.?' he wrote to me, after citing the remark. Little more need be said about his personal appearance—concerning which he nourished as few illusions as Charles II did about *his*—but the recent reminiscence-writer who spoke of him as 'bald' was wrong. Under the skull-cap which suited his quaint *allure* so well he had a thick crop of white hair still touched with golden brown behind the ears. I remember that he was slightly disconcerted when my modern lack of enthusiasm on the subject of beards brought into sudden relief the barrier of years dividing us. 'And yet,' he said, lightly touching his own, 'The Unreasoning Eye of Affection once said it was a pretty colour.'

One little vanity alone he had—his hands, which were and remained really beautiful. He had a trick of sitting with them clasped round a flexed left knee while the right leg was stuck straight out, a youthful attitude which—contrasted with his otherwise venerable air—seemed to me in a sense symbolic. He was indeed compounded of boyishness and melancholy, vehemence and gentleness, whimsy and profundity. After this long digression let me return to our first encounter. There was no lady available to act as hostess and so, after shaking hands, he said with the utmost seriousness, in his beautifully-modulated and curiously *young* voice, 'I have prepared for you—as David Copperfield did for Mrs. Micawber—two wax candles, a bottle of lavender water and a packet of mixed pins. You will find them in the room on the other side of the passage.' Find them I did, set forth upon a typical Victorian dressing-table; but before I departed in quest of them I was inspired to say, 'I am sorry I have not brought my cap with me in a whity-brown paper parcel.' Never was a happier inspiration. As my host said himself long afterwards, 'It did the trick': and it marked the beginning of a joyous friendship lasting and deepening to the day of his death nearly seven years later, punctuated by many pilgrimages to Bath, and kept vivid between-times by a constant and voluminous correspondence. It has been stated that Saintsbury in his last days was 'almost sightless'; that was not so. His sight, never strong, deteriorated towards the end, but his oculist said in 1932 that his eyes 'would last his time'—and they did. He was always able to read what he really wanted to read and write what he really wanted to write. I can bear witness to the enormous range of his interests, embracing practically every subject from modern criticism to modern cricket. The last letter he wrote to me, less than a week before his death, began with an allusion to 'that accurséd body-line bowling'. He liked and admired several writers of what was then (1926–33) the younger school; and he certainly did not feel himself to be neglected, undervalued or forgotten. 'I have lived so long,' he said to me delightedly, 'I have lived so long that the young men have come back to me.' Of his own early childhood he sometimes vouchsafed charming glimpses. His home was in Pembridge Villas, Notting Hill, and at the age of four or five (he was born, remember, in 1845) he used to accompany two considerably elder sisters over Campden Hill to Kensington High Street by way of Holland Walk. Their destination was often a small shop down a short flight of steps where the Misses Saintsbury used to buy embroidery silks and Berlin wool. The proprietor's name was 'Derry'; 'Toms' as yet was not. Saintsbury asked me once if the Kensington High Street of to-day resembled the pictures of it in the advertisements; 'for,' he added, 'if it *does*, I hope you cross yourself every time you go there.'

In an illustrated magazine of the year 1850 I unearthed a coloured fashion-plate showing a small boy wearing a peaked straw cap with a tassel, a tight-waisted, full-skirted coat of snuff brown frogged with military braid, and pale pink boots. This I bore with me on my next visit to Bath, demanding to know if such had been the garments of my illustrious friend in that year of grace. He looked gravely at the picture. 'Yes,' he said at last. 'Yes. Something like that; but I *think* the boots were *blue.*'

No account of George Saintsbury would be complete which omitted all mention of his passionately (and, alas, archaically) chivalrous attitude towards women. It pervades his writings and it pervaded his conversation. 'All but the very *worst* of *you,*' he once said to me, 'are so *much* too good for all but the very *best* of *us.*' In a lighter vein he was prodigiously *galant* (though not in the florid Victorian manner) and quite capable of carrying on a gay flirtation at long range with a lady whom he had never seen, but whose portrait pleased him. This was my mother. When I showed him the portrait he ceremoniously removed his skull-cap. 'You must tell her,' he said, 'that I could not stand covered before her.' As an instance of his rare and beautiful kindness I permit myself to record here that during the first six weeks after her death in 1932 (less than a year before his own) he did not leave me for a single day without some sign or word from him, even if it were only a few lines on a post-card of an Oxford College.

Among the writers of my generation whose friendship gave him much pleasure was a woman writer from Northern Ireland, as charming as she is learned. We never met during his lifetime, but in the very year of his death we were introduced by the late Lord Rennell at an English Association dinner. Later I said to her (perhaps foolishly) that it was odd that 'G. S.' who had spoken of each of us to the other, should never have tried to bring about a meeting between us. 'My dear,' she answered, as wittily as wisely, '*He never mixed his drinks.*'

This brings me to the two subjects, wine and food, upon which the true Saintsbury disciple would certainly wish me to say something. Unfortunately there is not much that I can say. In Bath there were no opportunities for gastronomic refinements or subtleties, and 'good plain' was the highest standard attained. My host stuck pretty constantly to the chicken-and-champagne formula of 'the Lady Mary of Lady Maries'; only on one occasion did medical advice decree that he should substitute whisky-and-soda for champagne, and then he insisted, gently but firmly, that his guest should have a baby-bottle of the more frivolous drink all to herself. It has been said that he was 'wineless' during those last years; that was not so, whether the word be interpreted as meaning 'not possessing wine' or 'not permitted to drink wine'. On the shelves of the big corner cupboard in his library one caught fascinating glimpses of bottles of many sizes, shapes and colours, and from these shelves he would bring 'elevenses' for himself and me, usually sherry. Once or twice we had *Danziges Goldwasser* instead, and it amused him to tilt the flask to-and-fro so that I might see the flimsy lambent flakes of gold-leaf swimming inside. I remember that one of his tributes to Divine Nonsensia was the idea of 'a goose the size of a wren'. Such a creature, he maintained, would be equally agreeable as an entrée or as a pet; but I cannot recollect what wine we agreed should be drunk with it, if it were served in aspic or on toast.

After what I have recorded in these random notes I trust that Mr. Lynd's enquiring critic will realize that bleak poverty was not among the burdens of George Saintsbury's old age. The absurdity of the suggestion will be obvious to anyone who reflects that the retirement-pension of a Regius Professor in the University of Edinburgh cannot justly be described as meagre, or who recalls the sum of the respectable (if not considerable) private fortune sworn for probate on the death of this Professor in particular. The real and cruel deprivation of his closing years (apart from family bereavement too sacred and too personal a subject to be touched upon here) was the dispersal of his fine library and the consequent necessity of 'making do' with what must have seemed to him an exiguous number of inadequate books. This dispersal was dictated by the fact that on leaving Edinburgh he had—as he told me himself—'literally nowhere' to put some fifteen thousand books, many of them in folio.

No one who enjoyed the privilege of being admitted to the inmost circle of his friends is likely soon to forget George Saintsbury. He was in courage indomitable, in kindness unwearying, in faith invincible. To his life's close he possessed the gift of winning and holding the strongest personal affection. Such affection it was that delivered him—as he once wrote to me—from the 'grey set life and apathetic end' too often the portion of the very old.

For these things—his courage, his faith, the touch of Springtime that lingered even in the winter of his days—let us who loved him be grateful always. *Bene semper vale, dilectissime doctor.*

THE MAN OF BOOKS

BY HELEN WADDELL

GEORGE SAINTSBURY was born on 23rd October, 1845, at Southampton: he died at Bath on 28th January, 1933, and was brought for burial to the place of his birth. He had lived within twelve years of a century: like Dryden and like Dr. Johnson, the builder-oak of the criticism of his time. As insular in one sense as the Venerable Bede (for though a great walker he was no traveller), he had like him the *potestas orbis terrarum*, at any rate of the lands the Romans knew. And like him too, 'in every generation he speaks familiarly'. There is no fashion so dead as that of the day before yesterday, and the yesterday between 1914 and 1918 was a gap that few men of seventy could bridge. But something in his integrity, the magnanimity and ripeness and obstinacy of his mind, his quick ironic concern for the new world about him, his awareness—in the phrase which he used to illumine the darkness of Swift—of 'the accepted hells beneath', his faith in a *civitas Dei* that honourable men might still inherit: these made his name a stronghold, an assurance that some things could not be shaken. 'That choleric and heavenly temper of thine', wrote Peter of Celle to John of Salisbury, 'is gayest in thine afflictions, puts forth leaves in the frost': and those who saw him in the Augustan twilight of the house of his last inhabiting, a solitary indomitable figure with straggling grey hair and black skull-cap, gaunt as Merlin and islanded in a fast-encroaching sea of books, came out from him with some understanding of Boethius' definition of eternity—'whatsoever comprehendeth and possesseth the whole fulness of life here and now, to which naught of the future is lacking, and from which naught of the past hath flowed away.' The miseries of old age and the slow oncoming of death had no dominion over that free spirit.

It was his habit to commend Gibbon as one who could regard his subject from a vantage-ground of twenty centuries: but for himself, the centuries were not so much a vantage-ground, as a continuation of his own experience. He read, in Milton's phrase, 'as if alive in every age'. Whether the book before him is Petronius Arbiter's *Satyricon* or Norman Douglas's *South Wind*, he speaks of it as its contemporary. It might seem impossible that a man of his extreme idiosyncrasy and vigorous prejudice should have been the most catholic critic of his time, most profoundly the 'Understander' whom Ben Jonson in preface after preface invoked in vain. Yet this High Churchman and High Tory refused to join the chorus of censure on the 'scrannel pipes' outburst in *Lycidas:* 'The supremacy of expression and phrase and verse remains—the discord and declension, even to those who find them such, are in the sentiment only.' The 'fits and squalls of moral darkness' in Hazlitt never overshadowed for him 'the abiding intellectual light', though it is plain that he becomes embarrassed by 'a kind of shabbiness' in Hazlitt's handling of his affairs: and he was the first to rehabilitate Leigh Hunt, in spite of all those shifts and meannesses against which, as a *Times* reviewer once put it, 'the King of critics might have roared a noble indignation'. 'The man could write': the neck-verse saved many a hanging. If it did not wholly save Sterne, it was because he offended in the one particular that turned Saintsbury's ink to vitriol. Not frank indecency he could dismiss that in his beloved Rabelais as 'a time-deodorised dunghill by the roadside, not beautiful, but negligible'. But the snigger he could not away with: and if Sterne is damned, it is because a 'perfect literary artist' has crystallised the snigger in English prose.

He had indeed to defend himself more than once for his catholicity,

> Je voudrais boire tout le vin
> Et baiser tout le monde.

For the critic's baptism, he wrote, *manet oceanus*: and the Unpardonable Sin to him was 'enquiring of a work of art whether it has done, not what the artist meant it, but what the critic wanted it, to do. . . . The religion of literature is a sort of Pantheism: you never know when the presence of the Divine *may* show itself, though you must know where it has shown. And you must never forbid it to show itself, anyhow or anywhere.' Like his favourite Longinus, his final test was the literal *transport*, the taking of a man out of himself: and it might be with the resistless sweep of:

> All night the dreadless Angel, unpursu'd

or the jogging homeward trot to

> The table-flap, the mutton-bone, and Mary.

In either instance, the man has done what he set out to do.

'Wordsworth can . . . write the most detestable doggerel and platitude. But when anyone who knows what poetry is reads—

> Our noisy years seem moments in the being
> Of the eternal silence,

he sees that, quite independently of the meaning . . . there is one note added to the articulate music of the world . . .' He leaves Wordsworth, he goes straight into the middle of the eighteenth century, and he sees Thomson with his hands in his dressing-gown pockets biting at the peaches, and hears him between the mouthfuls murmuring:

> So when the shepherd of the Hebrid Isles
> Placed far amid the melancholy main,

and there is another note, as different as possible in kind and yet alike, struck for ever. . . . 'In this matter, as in all matters that are worth handling at all, we come of course *ad mysterium*. Why certain combinations of letters, sounds, cadences, should almost without the aid of meaning . . . produce this effect of poetry on men, no man can say. But they do.'

Saintsbury, said his critics, 'writ no language'. It was one of the many contradictions in him—contradictions that made his very existence extremely delightful to his friends—that he whose main preoccupation was form in verse or prose, and whose first essay, *Baudelaire*, preached his lifelong and unpopular doctrine of style before subject, should himself write like the scour of a river in spate, allusion tumbling on allusion, parenthesis rammed within parenthesis, reckless to reject the straws and faggots that his headlong thought swept up on its course. But this very unselfconsciousness, this possession of the man by the subject, had its rewards. The range of his style is enormous. There was an adroit and mischievous gravity. of which his writings on Shakespeare are sufficient evidence: 'The uncertainty of the poet's birthday is one of the best known things about him'. . . . 'But the nature of commentators abhors a vacuum.' There was an extraordinary balance and epigraphic quality, seen at its height in the preface to his *Specimens of English Prose Style*, on the writers of the early eighteenth century: 'They were unrivalled in vigour, not easily to be beaten in sober grace, abundantly capable of wit, but as a rule they lacked magnificence. . . . Addison's renowned homilies on death and tombs and a future life have rather an unrivalled decency . . . than solemnity in the higher sense of the term.' Here, his style has itself this unrivalled decency: but on poetry, it can at times reach to magnificence. On Dryden: 'the inimitable ring which distinguishes his verse from all others—the ring as of a great bronze coin thrown down on marble.' On Shakespeare's Sonnets, after a characteristically contemptuous handling of the theories, biographical and other, which account for them: 'All these theories and others are possible: none is proved: and for the literary purpose, none is really important. What is important is that Shakespeare has here caught up the sum of love and uttered it as no poet has before or since, and that in so doing he carried poetry—that is to say, the passionate expression in verse of the sensual and intellectual facts of life—to a pitch which it had never previously reached in English, and which it has never outstepped since. The coast line of humanity must be wholly altered, the sea must change its nature, the moon must draw it in different ways, before that tide-mark is passed.' His own tide-mark is reached in his criticism of Donne: 'But it is not here (in satire) that we find the true Donne: it was not this province of the universal monarchy of wit that he ruled with the most unshackled sway. The provinces that he did so rule were quite other: strange frontier regions, uttermost isles where sensuality, philosophy, and devotion meet. . . .' 'Behind every image, every ostensible thought of his, there are vistas and backgrounds of other thoughts dimly vanishing, with glimmers in them here and there into the depths of the final enigmas of life and soul. Passion and meditation, the two avenues into this region of doubt and dread, are tried by Donne in the two sections respectively, and of each he has the key. Nor, as he walks in them with eager or solemn tread, are light and music wanting, the light the most unearthly that ever played about a poet's head, the music not the least heavenly that he ever caught and transmitted to his readers.'

For Saintsbury, there was no poet, and hardly any writer, like Donne. And the spiritual and sensual kinship between these two men, the poet and his first discoverer, had its counterpart in the circumstances of their lives. Both were of a high pride and in their youth of towering ambition, and both were checked and frustrated of what they had judged to be their vocation, courtly diplomacy for one, 'Academe' at Oxford for the other. Both were denied security and reputation through the best years of their manhood, and found in place of them a passion and mastery and exultancy in living that glows to the last twilight of their day: and in the end, when they had come to their strength without it, they had honour in all men's mouths. Saintsbury's five times repeated failure at Oxford to obtain a Fellowship cost him something more than the initial sharpness of humiliation—leisure for an absolute exactness of scholarship, even though it was more than made up for by his depth and range: moreover, a loss that touches mediævalists more nearly, it cost us his *History of the English Scholastics*. But the losses were outweighed by the gains. He married young: he had Prospero's island of enchanted lawn at the beginning of his life instead of at the end, and all his years were transfigured by it: and he was supremely his own master. No fellowship could have cramped him into a Pattison or a Casaubon: but it might have cost us the absolute Saintsbury. He could hardly have read more than he did: and his reading might not have been so continuously shot through with the richness of living. Ironically enough, when at fifty he accepted the Chair of Rhetoric and English Literature at Edinburgh, it cost us his *History of Wine*. Here again, there is a heavy credit side. The twenty years in Edinburgh are the years of the *opera Maiora*, the *Short History of English Literature*, the editing and part writing of the *Periods of European Literature*, the *History of Criticism*, the *History of Prosody*, the *History of English Prose Rhythm*. *The Peace of the Augustans* finished in Edinburgh, his *History of the French Novel*, begun in Edinburgh, finished in Bath, have the mellowness of his Indian summer: and its twilight was lit with the gay lanterns of the *Cellar Book*, and for good discourse, the small but weighty *Trivia* of the three *Scrap Books*.

The world fell in love with them: but the reader who knows these only, knows no more than the surface of his mind. 'Of mighty mould, part hero and part saint of learning, he knew, when time came, how to use harbour, inn, and evening hour: but *after* he had crossed ocean and climbed peak: and it is the traffics, discoveries, and ascents, that count—the vast and austere efforts of his manhood, not the ungirt pastimes and pleasantries of age. Posterity would lose without the *Scrap Books*, yes: but their value is that they are by the historian of Criticism and of Prosody.'[1]

His last will and testament recorded his wish that no biography should be written of him, and no letter published. It was, and even his modesty must have known it, to deny himself a surer immortality than the scholar's, a life in men's minds that would have persisted

[1] Professor A. Blyth Webster in the *Saintsbury Memorial Volume* (Methuen 1945).

when his vast learning had become a legend like that of Gerbert or of Scaliger. For as a letter-writer he ranks with Walpole and with Lamb, and his letters are to his graver works as the *Colloquies* of Erasmus to his studies in Lucian and Cicero: quintessential. But the refusal, in an age crazed for personal publicity, is a gesture so characteristic of him that it uplifts the heart. This is the man we knew: not the Johnsonian Saintsbury who loved to fold his legs and have his talk out: not the Meredithian Saintsbury, emerging from his cellar with a bearded Hermitage reverently and triumphantly bestowed: but the solitary scholar who was his own best company, 'Lord not only of Joyous Gard but also of Garde Douleureuse', reading, reading, reading through the small hours in the familiar chair with the two tall candlesticks behind it. And their light falls, not on his face, but on the open book.

ESSAYS AND PAPERS

EARLY TWENTIETH CENTURY LITERATURE

WE have all heard of the 'naughty 'nineties': there has perhaps been quite enough reproof and vindication of the decade and its preface of the later 'eighties from that point of view. But it was, I think, pretty clear to fairly critical eyes, and it ought to have become clearer still as those eyes profited more and more by what Dryden calls, in one of those bronze phrases of his,

> The firm perspective of the past,

that any 'naughtiness' there may have been gave not at all the substance of the doubt that might fairly be entertained about that period, but was only one of its accidents. When the historian of English literature in the twentieth century writes his due chapter of antecedents, the fault which he will most probably find with this part of our time is—and certainly it is a *maxima culpa*—the fault of Pose. Now pose has always been a sort of measles of literature, affecting youth chiefly though by no means only; and like all diseases it sometimes becomes epidemic and malignant at particular periods. But I cannot remember in experience or in history any time at which it was more prevalent or multi-form than in the last ten or fifteen years of the nineteenth century. During the earlier time of that century it had, except in the curious sub-group of which Beddoes, Darley, Wade and a few more were poetical members for the first division, and the 'Spasmodics' for the second, chiefly confined itself to the mildest of all its forms—imitation of great ones: Byron, Tennyson, Dickens, Carlyle and latterly Swinburne were all thus wrongly worshipped. But Swinburnian *pastiche*, as a busy reviewer of those days can testify, did not really go very far. Parodies, of course, were innumerable, but there is no pose in them. The most delightful serious example—dear for nearly half a century:

> Where the cocoa and cactus are neighbours,
> Where the fig and the firtree are one—

is American, not English.

Moreover, as must be obvious, pose of imitation, though exceedingly boring, is not exactly mischievous. Pose of revolt, unless it is actuated and directed by positive genius, can be mischievous also—and indeed can combine the two characteristics in a very deadly manner. The poses which grew up under the *fin de siècle* impetus (who was it, by the way, who first thought of that calamitous expression?) made a 'party in a parlour' which, though the very opposite of 'silent', too frequently seemed to put in candidature for being 'damned'. There was the pose of naughtiness already referred to; the pose of violence; the pose of paradox; the pose of neo-Bohemianism; the pose of platitude inverted; the pose of distorted form; the pose of attempted mixture of science and literature; the pose of cosmopolitanism; divers minor and more or less individual poses of imitation of things and persons that had not been considered worthy of imitation, and poses of denigration of persons and of things that had been so considered. But though the particular attitudes of the particular pose might vary, the general characteristic, apart from the fortunate exceptions already excepted, undoubtedly *was* pose. Perhaps indeed, after an unusually intense and long-continued activity of literature, one of two things is pretty certain. There will either be an acquiescence in comparative mediocrity, such as that which followed the period from Spenser to Milton, or some kind of struggle for *tours de force* to hide the diminished supply of force itself. It was the obvious duty of the twentieth century—to apply a slightly mixed and also slightly vulgar but vigorous and relevant metaphor—to 'get its pose off its stomach'. Nor were the conditions, albeit not very cheerful at the moment, wholly discouraging. There is something characteristic, and not entirely though it may be partly ridiculous, in the remark of the younger of those two Latin tragedians whose work unfortunately we have in barest fragments: 'I thought it best to have something in my genius for time and age to mitigate,' said Accius to Pacuvius. And these persons certainly provided that 'something' bountifully.

It is perhaps scarcely taking too much upon oneself or one's own craft for a critic to say that at such a time criticism has her work specially cut out for her. Not criticism of the foolish old 'Judex-damnatur-cum-nocens-absolvitur' kind: for it is at least doubtful whether such criticism ever did any good at all, and in the particular state of things just described it was almost certain to do harm. The people who did not pose and did not admire posing did not want such criticism; and the posers and their admirers would merely take it as proof that they had 'shocked the *bourgeois*', which was just what they wanted to do. The ironical or *persifleur* critical mode was more suitable—in fact, had admirable opportunities and was sometimes absolutely necessary; but this kind has its dangers. It is not the easiest thing in the world to do well; it is peculiarly apt to go off through the touchhole when it is done badly; and it is quite certain that a very large number of people do not really enjoy it—are more or less puzzled by it, and sometimes find the puzzlement passing into positive dislike. Yet nothing—except the mere passage of time, which in its own peculiar way heals all things if only by destroying some—could do so much in the way of 'mitigation' (the Romans were not a humorous folk, or young Accius might have used the word as Swift or Thackeray would) as criticism. It would have, of course, to be criticism varied in kind, even the Judex *v.* Nocentem sort being, on very rare occasions, perhaps allowable; while the kind of *persiflage* is much more often so. But criticism in general—the faithful and fairly lively representation of what the work really does look like to a tolerably healthy, intelligent and well-trained mind other than the author's—could hardly have better scope than at such a time; there being, of course, besides the exceptional torchbearers always to be kept in mind, plenty of sound honest stuff produced besides the pose-work to supply the mill with better grist. To this, in such a retrospect as the present, it will be better to turn attention.

The general plea that one sees advanced for literature, as for other things, in the first quarter of the twentieth century is, I believe, that it has accomplished nearly, if not quite, as great a liberation from convention as the corresponding period of the nineteenth did; the subsequent periods of the nineteenth itself having re-established the tyranny of this odious thing in a degree equal to, if not worse than, that which it previously enjoyed. Those who have attained unto the Higher Scepticism may, indeed, ask if there is anything at all special in this: if it is not merely the operation of the eternal flux and reflux in a particular department of life or the functions of life. And unamiable individuals may go on to ask whether a convention of revolt is less conventional than one of imitative obedience—whether, indeed, convention and unconvention are not really the same thing. But these questions, though not irrelevant, are somewhat extraneous to the present one. That question (by itself and stripped of all previous and dependent questions), 'What has been the general character of these twenty years and more of English literature?' is quite enough for anyone to answer at one time, and may even seem more than enough to anyone who is acquainted with literary history at large. That firm perspective of the past whereof we spoke before is hardly available yet. But at least one can say that the rather yeasty state of literature which was so prominent thirty and even twenty years ago has to a great extent, though by no means entirely, worked or fermented itself out. What the quality of the matured vintage of this 'twenty' will be as a century one can hardly say yet. The literatures of centuries as they take longer to come into existence so they take much longer to be appreciated than the gifts of Bacchus. But some of us may take a good omen from the fact that, while the wines, or some of them, of 1820 were among the very best of their century, those of 1920 already seem not unfit to challenge a similar position.

In poetry, oldest and greatest of all forms of letters, I do not understand that the most sanguine eulogist and herald of youth claims—unless 'the sun is in his eyes'—any absolute and proved mastership as yet attained by anyone who did not publish before 1900. I use, of course, mastership not in the sense in which one speaks of proficients of more or less excellence, but in that in which one speaks of Shakespeare or Shelley. On the other hand, there is claimed, perhaps with justice, a very much greater amount of proof of the above-mentioned proficiency itself. We certainly have poetry now from poets compared to whose work the earliest work of Wordsworth and Coleridge, of Shelley and Tennyson is rubbish, though it does not follow that any of them will produce something better than 'Tintern Abbey' or 'The Ancient Mariner', than 'Alastor' or 'The Lotos-Eaters'. But undoubtedly the main feature of the period has been the abundant adventure in what is called 'free verse'. I do not much admire the term, for I cannot acknowledge any 'slavery' in metre or in rhyme. But one may admit (if it were of any importance I myself have very elaborately admitted) that irregular rhythm—destitute of the atmosphere which rhyme supplies and the *contour* given by metre—may be beautiful, admitting this for the simple reason that it has been so in the past. Yet it may be doubted whether the conditions of this form or forms have as yet been sufficiently elaborated. It is quite clear that this kind of freedom is certain to indulge itself in mere anarchy at first. As to what some people seem still to think and do more than seem to say—that metre and rhyme will be superseded—one may be rash enough to pronounce this impossible, because both answer to persistent physical demands for the outline and the atmosphere above referred to. But there undoubtedly is room for ametric and unrhymed but symphonically rhythmed verse, and for hybrid kinds between this and other forms in which these two decades have experimented already and which they may perfect further.

Poetry, however, is a matter the history of which is always a history of miracles; and miracles are things better dealt with in the past than in the present or in the future. Prose fiction is less 'kittle' to deal with, and the present writer happens to be in a rather exceptionally competent position to deal with it. For he happened to begin reviewing novels (with a pretty fair knowledge of what they had been before) in large numbers just when their palmy time, from the late 'forties to the early 'seventies of the last century, was ceasing, and ceasing rather hurriedly. 'The old three-decker' was a delightful institution; it deserved its delightful funeral hymn. It had a glorious history. But like other glorious three-deckers it was subject to dry-rot, and the dry-rot had set in pretty unmistakably. To come still closer to facts and change the metaphor, in the language of the same poet, you might say of the average novel bridge-builder of that day,

Each bridge that he makes either buckles or breaks

at the second volume. Immoral reviewers, I believe, never read their second volumes at all; moral ones, I know, sighed and groaned —not to say lost their tempers—over them. Some even wished that it might be the custom to print them in blank or 'dummy'; for in that case there would have been no trouble of reading, and the volumes would have made most useful notebooks. On the other hand, those more-than-three-deckers or Santissimas Trinidades, the novels in parts, though they could be as great in quality as they were in bulk, were rather intolerable when they were only great in the latter and encouraged certain vices of their own—forgetfulness or even complete absence of plot, inconsistency of character, and the like. And when the individual strength of the novel-producers began to die off, as it did about the time mentioned, things became rather doleful, and the Mr. Toobads of the time used to tell us that the novel had had its day and would soon cease to be.

But few things, if any, that have been cease to be; they only undergo changes. That the change of the three volumes into one more or less coincided with the appearance of a new blossoming of romance in the hands of Stevenson, who is dead, and some others who are happily alive is worth noting, of course, though the connection was certainly not causal. The at-last-achieved popularity, after long neglect, of George Meredith probably had a little more to do with the contemporary growth of the 'problem' or 'analytical' novel. At any rate, both kinds took to the six-shilling (war-made seven-and-six) standard very kindly. Whether here again (with the few exceptions already several times glanced at) the *sommités* have been as lofty and as numerous as between 1845 and 1870 we need not inquire. And it is, of course, easier in more respects than those of time and trouble to write one volume than it is to write three, even if the print is something smaller and the pages more crowded in the single one. Perhaps the average novel—even the better-than-average—is less re-readable than it was sixty or seventy years ago; but the average, and even the less-than-average, is, probably not merely because of its shortness, more readable once. It is a drawback, no doubt, that it is as a rule so anxiously and almost tremblingly modern; and this modernity threatens it with something like the fate of the novel of the Regency, which even the present writer finds it difficult to read now, though he can read those of most other times, from Xenophon's to Marcel Proust's. And it may be urged by the devil's advocate that something of this readableness is due to mere craftsmanship—that thing so different from artistry, though very well in its way. But this very confinement to things actual or supposed to be actual, with the increased attention to some kind of technique, has its negative advantages. One may get rather tired of the bachelor-girl in the flat and the amateur detective who (with an assistant something like the old 'zany' of the travelling quack) 'makes a hare' of Scotland Yard; but they are better than the Cambridge undergraduate who, in a novel, I think of the 'seventies, 'had a few holidays because of the death of the Greek Professor'.

In respect of some at least of the more ambitious and successful representatives of the twentieth century (first quarter) novel, it will be exceedingly interesting to critics of the future to see how they *stand*. For most of them, I believe, have been written much more in accordance with a definite scheme, in intention always, and no doubt in result not seldom. This 'scheme' is not (again as I understand it) identical with the old 'plot', though that old plot sometimes, as in the case of *Tom Jones*, comes near it, whether from above or below does not here matter in the least for our present purpose. It is pretty certain that the best stories of the past have not as a rule been constructed in such a fashion. But then the best stories of the past have as a rule been so constructed that you care very little, or not at all, what plan, scheme, purpose, or anything of that kind the author had before him. 'Never mind your significance, old man!' our reckless forefathers and some of their unblushing descendants have said and still say. 'Give us story! Give us character! Give us (if you can) conversation vividly true to nature, not of our time only, and, in moderation, description ditto. Go on as long as you can hold us; or stop as soon as you know you are likely to let us slip.' This requirement may be deplorably apolaustic, may even, as things apolaustic will so often, sink to the verge of immorality. But it is a requirement that the human race has apparently been making from the time of the Odyssey, which is probably the first 'best story' of the Western World at least, whatever the reader may think choicest of the times before 'significance'. One may doubt *in petto* whether the human race at large does not make it still. But only the Future can safely judge the Past, and even the Future had better be careful.

As regards branches of literature which have always approached nearer to the scientific than fiction in verse or prose—history, philosophy, and miscellaneous kinds—the past quarter of a century will no doubt hold its own, subject to the doom which, except in the rarest cases and by virtue of purely literary excellence, awaits these mixed kinds. To those who really appreciate this excellence time does not matter in the least. Ancient and modern are all the same. For the *vis formæ* is not only *superba* but *eterna*. When the force is only in the matter it may not exactly lose all its power, but certainly finds that power what the financial people call 'a wasting asset'. At a library committee once a good-natured representative of science gibed a colleague who had taken under his wing a new edition of a thirteenth-century text, 'What's the good of that?' 'Well,' said the other, 'it may be much good or little; but such as it is it will keep its goodness for another half-dozen centuries, while you'll be discarding as out of date the parcel you have got before you possibly next session, and certainly before half a dozen years are over.' And the man of science, being a good-natured man, acknowledged the hit. Nevertheless, there is no doubt that, in spite of some efforts to separate history from literature, and in spite also of a mighty superfluity of biography, you might fill not bad bookshelves or even cases in this sort from the period. And although the War—that terribly magnified and intensified as well as veracious thunderstorm of Caleb Balderstone—interfered with many things, the two decades have seen fair continuance of the apparently humble but really invaluable task of recovering and making accessible the treasures of the past—a task which was so long neglected in England, and which the nineteenth century was almost the first to take seriously.

Lastly, let us come—perhaps I should say come back—to that most abused but hardy branch of letters, criticism. Parasite in both senses, plague, disgrace, discipline again in more senses than one, tonic or whatever else it may be called or thought, it is not, perhaps, too sanguine or too flattering to see in it, at the present time, with allowance for things to be allowed for, symptoms healthy rather than otherwise—healthier pretty certainly than they were five-and-twenty or twenty years ago. Foolish denigration of things past, foolish exaltation of things present, foolish expectation of things future are with us still; and the last named—least distasteful, though perhaps most pity-worthy, of the three—has again been encouraged by that omnipresent reagent 'The War' and the consequent hope of a new world. There is not a new world, there will not be a new world, there never has been a new world—at least in the sense of sudden and immediate novelty. At the bottom perhaps things never change at all. People are always thinking that things are very nice and finding that they have to pay for them; blaming other people for their own acts; quarrelling with their brothers; finding the daughters of men fair; feeling quite sure that the deluge will not come; and so on and so on and so on. But even the apparent and, so far as they go, real changes never take a very short time, in literature as elsewhere. And the great increase in careful study of past literature, as well as the active experiment in new production, which has for some time characterised our days can hardly fail to tell for good. It is true that great mistakes have been and are being made—mistakes which directly affect this good and hamper it or turn it to bad. But these mistakes are mostly due to political interference and not to purely literary agencies. And some hold that there are signs already of the disastrous ebb of really humanistic culture—the worst thing of all—turning, however slowly, to something like flood.

But, as has been more than once hinted, and perhaps even more than hinted, in this brief survey, there never was such a John Barleycorn (name of good omen and good record!) as literature. You may do the most dreadful things to it; it may look as if it had ceased to exist, and it will surprise and delight you by getting up and waving in the wind as merrily as ever. Only being, in one way if not in all, more spiritual, it will give the surprise and delight at much less regular intervals, and in even greater variation of quantity and quality of crop. Diagnostics as well as prognostics respecting it had need to be mainly Pantagrueline in order to be safe: and the only abiding motto is *Sursum corda.*

The Times Literary Supplement, 4th January, 1923.

A STUDY OF MARRYAT

TO say that Captain Marryat is forgotten nowadays would no doubt be excessive. He is reprinted—sometimes even in that singular form, betokening something between honour and dishonour, which used to be called Bowdlerising. Good critics do sometimes take notice of him: and, as they cannot help doing if they *are* good critics, make the notice favourable. There must still be a remnant of the Old Guard that thought of him something more than merely favourably. But help is probably still desirable to let him have the benefit of that slow but salutary reaction from a certain disease of the last thirty or forty years which seems at last to be taking place. The learned call this disease *Chthesophobia*, or 'horror of yesterday'.

The symptoms of this fell complaint have been various, but they have generally turned on an inability to recognise as agreeable, or meritorious, or even tolerable, anything which does not display the features, submit to the conditions and meet the demands of the present day. Marryat's ships are queer old hulks without so much as a steam—much less an oil—engine of the most rudimentary kind in them, and without any screws to hand except those one drives with screwdrivers. Instead of sinking each other not so much at sight as out of sight, they come close together and the crews indulge in vulgar 'rags' on each others' decks. The separation of classes is awful: and there is actually flogging of those who don't and, which is worse, of those who do deserve it. There is much too much rum drunk: though, by the way, Marryat himself is not very partial to rum. There is not so much as mention of a submarine or an aircraft-carrier. Turning to land matters, the boys fight at school—a disgusting habit. The girls, when they are ladies, are much too submissive to the men, and when they are not, display in the treatment of them the same undue 'class'- feelings which offended before. The technique is lamentable: and though there can hardly be said to be a deficiency of 'pattern', it isn't the pattern we want and like. The 'values' are wrong.

All which, without any apologies to those who may have uttered it or who may have been influenced by it, is simply rubbish.

There might be some small danger in attempting to cure it, get rid of it, or turn it to useful stuff, by pointing out that even were all of it true, the books provide most interesting and trustworthy illustration of that wonderful naval effort which for a quarter of a century played *Britannia contra mundum*; made it possible for the Army to win the last round of that game, and as long as history is history will be a more and more notable part of our English record. One could add that the social 'illustration' generally is not inconsiderable. But in the good old phrase we 'have no care' and need have no care to take this line, which is only one of several and often treacherous side-paths leading away from the highroad of literary criticism. 'Are Marryat's novels good novels?'—of their own class, of course—and 'Is Marryat a good novelist?', which, albeit most closely allied, is not a wholly identical question, though the difference is not quite the same as in that other pair which has puzzled some: 'Is this a great piece of poetry?' and 'Is the author a great poet?' One can, however, answer cheerfully, 'Yes! both.' Marryat's novel-romance-stories are good novel-romance-stories—very good sometimes; never or hardly ever very bad. And he is a good novelist-romancer-story-teller, though for the reason given in the last few words, and perhaps for others, to be called so with certain qualifications and limitations.

The most important of these others we may perhaps take at once.

There are several touchstones, dividing lines of good and bad, or whatever term be preferred—which affect novels; but there is one of pre-eminent importance though common to the other kinds of 'fiction' or creations in the lower depth, that is to say drama, poetry which is not *merely* poetry, and (some would add) history. The question which best applies this test is, 'Are the people in this story live people, and are the things done what live people would do?' If the answer is 'Yes', the book is saved offhand: though it may be placed in lower or higher divisions of the Heaven of human creations. If 'No', it must be shut out, though of course again there are several —indeed many—mansions in the corresponding Inferno. Whether there is also a Purgatory for such books is a very subtle question which, fortunately, we need not discuss here. There *have*, however, been cases which suggested it; while there have even been some suggesting both promotion from the mid region, and degradation to it. But they also are not for us.

It will be obvious to all but the meanest capacity that the enemy will have a speedy demurrer to this. Perhaps he will say, 'But who is to be the judge of "liveness"?' A person or thing may seem 'live' to you because you were contemporary with it and not to us because we were not: and in the same way an actual life may seem not living to you because it has left you behind. This is plausible: but the plausibility won't stand examination. The contents of literature are fortunately not limited to the actions and reactions of the longest single life: and our supposed judge can try his judicial powers on, in round numbers, the productions of certainly more than two thousand years, perhaps much more. Necessarily he will be able, having many more assistances, to feel modern incidents, actions and characters closer to him than ancient, and therefore clearer. But the 'certain vital marks' are quite distinguishable, in the very oldest examples, and (if they are there) should be distinguishable in the most modern. I venture to think that I can see the 'liveness', the *different* liveness, of Circe and Calypso and Nausicaa, pretty clearly. If I did not see Dido too I should be the more generous in my estimate of Virgil. And so I do at intervals all through the ages even to the present day—when they are to be seen. Guinevere is all right (I mean the original Guinevere of the French romances) and Lancelot. Except Pepys was there ever a greater autobiographer than Dante? There is hardly a not-live person in all Shakespeare's 'crowd', as we may call it without descending to slang. Liveness indeed for a time took refuge in poetry and drama mainly. Is not (one appeals to the gentlemanliness of the Prince of Darkness in apologising for any apparent pertness) Milton's Satan 'alive'? Dryden's Melantha, though less brilliantly so than her spiritual daughter Millamant, is alive. And did not Addison and (or perhaps rather) Steele, bring liveness back into prose with his essays and other stories? As for the great eighteenth century novelists, even Richardson, though in an artificial sort of way, has liveness: and others show it in ascending measure to Fielding, where it is simply in quintessence.

Towards the end of this century this liveness certainly began to die down again, a fact of which we have one most curious evidence in a single person, namely Fanny Burney who is quite alive in *Evelina* and able to contribute liveness but quite unable to do so in *The Wanderer* [1]. Perhaps a still more curious and almost uncanny piece of evidence to the same effect is the strange way in which such a creative faculty as Miss Austen's was actually held back—compelled as it were to keep its 'childfuls of Life' not 'bodiless' but 'in the gloom' till the nineteenth set them free. As for Scott, he is perhaps the best touchstone of all: and he brings us up to Marryat's own time: indeed they overlapped.

[1] People I believe have 'taken up' as they are always doing 'the penetrating wit of its heroine'. But she is quite hopeless.

But it is of Marryat himself that we are to speak, and I certainly have not the least fear of his not being able to meet the test in himself and apply the countertest to his readers. He died only a year or two after I was born: he reflected, I think, a rather older type of life than that contemporary with even his earlier books; and (which is not perhaps quite relevant) though I was born in a port and have as a small boy lunched under the star of cutlasses in the gunroom (or whatever it was) of the *Victory*, I have all my life known very little of the navy or of maritime ways generally. But except when he transgresses into land 'society', where he never strikes one as being much at home, I find him and his alive almost everywhere—quite infinitely more alive than some later novelists and novels who and which date from times when I have been myself quite conversant with the very society they depict, or would depict if they could. It may be excusable—and indeed it is here my business—to work this out somewhat in detail.

Of his life there is no need to say much. Anyone who wants the details may find them, not at too great length and told with excellent knowledge and sympathy, in my friend Mr. David Hannay's book. The naval part of it, if not of the longest and beginning too late for participation in any of the great Nelson fights, was meritorious and lively, starting with exceedingly active service under Cochrane in the north-western Mediterranean and ending, as far as the 'activity' was concerned, with some sharp business in Burmese rivers. The home part, of not quite twenty later years, was busy with literature, and with, for avocation, not very wise but very sailor-like expenditure of well-earned money on not so well-chosen matters. At the last of all he did some bookmaking, and indulged in some not too fortunate collaboration, but with that we need not have much to do. I will only say that *The Children of the New Forest* seems to me (not at all because I am a Hampshire man) to be a very good sort of children's book indeed. I remember reading it myself, with others of the most various kinds from Shakespeare to Mayne Reid and from *Robinson Crusoe* to Scott, and finding it not at all out of place in that well-varied menu. *The Little Savage* is less good, but not bad. But we should begin with the beginning, not the end.

Frank Mildmay or *The Naval Officer*, though not a very delectable book to read, is an exceedingly interesting one to study from our point of view. It is extraordinarily 'matterful', as the late Dr. Grosart used to be fond of saying. From his own experiences under

Dundonald and other captains, from the 'yarns' of comrades and from the *publica materies* of naval tradition and gossip, Marryat drew good stuff enough for two or three novels at least. But he had not as yet, or had very partially, perceived or mastered the immense difference between anecdotes told merely for their matter, and anecdotes wrought into the character and artistic presentation of special human beings, not merely acting for themselves but reacting on others. This again is at least partly due to, and more than partly connected with, the fact that there is only one character and that a pretty bad character in the book—Mr. Lieutenant and Commander Frank Mildmay himself, who, if not quite such an unmitigated young ruffian as Peregrine Pickle, is saved (to the small extent to which he *is* saved) chiefly by living half a century later; and in whom this advantage is counterbalanced by a corresponding indulgence in very nauseous moralising from which 'Perry', to do him justice, is entirely free. One feels, to do Marryat justice also, that he thought he was doing the proper thing when he made this naval officer deplore the moral lapses of a girl who, but for him, would probably not have morally lapsed at all; whom he seduced, deserted and actually plundered. But one also feels that it would have been much nicer if he had *not* thought it the proper thing. And one sees the novice when, after a long sketch of by no means bad but more or less historical matter, he winds up with an ultra melodramatic *dénouement* of discoveries, gambling, duels, unhappy deaths, and recommendations to people who go to Bordeaux to drink *vin de Beaune!* How far 'out of it' he was at this time, the last item will enable almost any properly educated reader to see. Had he done that *at* Bordeaux, one smiles to think how the Bordelais would probably have revenged Eugenia on him.

Still, this first book has a peculiar interest of its own *as* a first book. Critics with a fair knowledge of general literary history, to back a pretty long experience of books coming fresh from the press, know, or ought to know, some classifying points about these latter. If there are any instances of an utterly bad beginning turning to a good ending here I do not know them. Beginnings as yet characterless may turn to splendid after-developments. Milton is almost one of these, and Shelley and Tennyson are quite two. Uncomfortably numerous, especially in novel-writing, are those which seem to shew a certain promise, never to be fulfilled. Innumerable, of course, are those which—what shall one say?—are like the beginnings of Milton and Shelley and Tennyson but are not in the least degree followed by followings similar to theirs. But *Frank Mildmay* belongs to none of these classes. It is a piece of quite genuine and (though it may be rash to say this when one was not present at its actual first appearance and did not read it till one was familiar with some at least of its best successors) obvious novice or apprentice work. The writer has both experience and invention of life; he can tell a story; and he can make if not characters, character-*parts*. But there is a sort of coarseness in him which may worsen into brutality, and a roughness which may draw near to ruffianism; though he can tell a story, he does not know how to manage it; he tries other things that he cannot manage, and he leaves the reader with rather a bad taste in his mouth.

Now Marryat evidently saw this, set to work to correct it, and did to a very great extent succeed. He was always a little ruthless, which perhaps the traditions of the eighteenth century navy excused if they did not demand. Poor old Mr. Easy *had* to be got rid of, and the way of doing it probably hurt him very little. But there was not the slightest reason why we should be told anything at all about the end of that excellent 'super' Dr. Tod- or Tadpole in *Poor Jack*, and anyhow it need not have been made perhaps the most painful of all—the actual and practical though unpoetic equivalent of the 'broken heart' of metaphor. Still, it would hardly have done for the population of the *Arethusas* on the one side and the *Belles-Poules* on the other to be too tender-hearted. That he was aware of some of the faults of his *Naval Officer* is, I think, clear from the structure of *The King's Own*. He has tried several new dodges there. There is little or nothing of the dangerous suggestion of camouflaged autobiography as perhaps there was before; but there is quite open presentation of the captain of the *Ariadne*, to give the book a 'real' flavour at the beginning, while at the end the historic thrill of the destruction of the *Droits de l'Homme* plays something of a similar part. He has, however, extra-melodramatised this by the poisoning of Seymour; while a little earlier there is an even worse mixture—this time of melodrama with ugly farce—in the other successful attempt to murder, followed by the horse-play with the murdered woman's heart. I believe the introduction of the great Fleet mutinies at the opening has pleased some people more than it does me; but the privateer-smuggler business is not bad, and the off-cruise where Jerry and Seymour distinguish themselves is capital. It has not always been the case that editorship has been good for a man's own literary work; but directly or indirectly his captaincy of the *Metropolitan*

Magazine seems, no doubt partly because it came after these comparative failures, to have done Marryat a surprising deal of good. *Newton Forster*, his first contribution, may perhaps still be regarded as a trial piece—some people I know, though I do not, think it uninteresting, but it is much more faultless than either of its forerunners. And then in three years or a little more came his four best—*Peter Simple*, *Jacob Faithful*, *Japhet in Search of a Father*, and *Mr. Midshipman Easy*.

Of praising and, what is not always the same thing, enjoying *Mr. Midshipman Easy*, there will, I hope, be no end with me till I myself end. It was given me as a birthday present (not, I am happy to say, in an expurgated copy) when I cannot have been much more than eight, and I have read it at frequent intervals and with never-failing satisfaction till now when I am something more than eighty. It seems to me almost perfect of its kind. In the words of an old friend of mine on something else 'there is nothing to omit and nothing to deplore'. It is amusing all through, and there is also in it, and blowing over it all through, something which, if not 'better than amusement', is unfortunately not always found where amusement is—a thoroughly clean, healthy, manly and gentlemanly spirit. By his own frank confession Mr. Jack Easy was not an expert theologian and not exactly first class in the higher parts of seamanship and navigation. But he never did a shabby thing, and as far as one can see never said (after his 'rights of man' stage) a silly one: he was prompt to punch anyone's head who deserved it, and not in the least afraid of having his own punched in the process. Perhaps he drew rather freely on his papa; but other people were welcome to a share of his drawings. I have heard from experts hints of doubt as to the Spanish he learnt at the Zaffarine Islands; but the circumstances of his learning have to be considered. It may be urged that he ought to have had a sister for Gascoigne to marry; but this deficiency was hardly his fault. He must in his later days have made one of the best squires in Hampshire: and he had not been long enough in the navy to acquire some of those harmless, but sometimes slightly annoying, oddities which are occasionally displayed by retired men of both those services which Pacifists hate and good folk love. I should very much like to have known Jack: and I think I did once know a person of his later status who was not altogether unlike him, though very much older, and a soldier not a sailor in his earlier days.

The general public, I believe, have generally preferred *Peter*

Simple, and the preference has got itself registered after the usual vague manner in the form of stock descriptions of it as his 'best' book. Far be it from me to say a word against Peter as a whole:

> I would we had upon our shelves
> Ten thousand good as he,

or even half a dozen, which is more within human and literary probability. But I should like the whole or almost the whole Privilege business (the incident of the wicked uncle's being checkmated in the matter of O'Brien's appointment is good) removed—and if, as it probably would, it took Peter's papa with it I should not mind. With this removal I should have nothing but praise left for it, though I should never like Peter quite so well as Jack and though he ought not to have had that fatal conversation with the man on the taffrail. For when one turns to the rest one is almost ashamed at having found any fault at all. Peter is great—much greater than his captain—on the sacredness of conversation between two gentlemen; and he is, if not great, quite engagingly innocent and polite in his adventure with the 'nicely dressed young lady'. Nor does he ever fail on board (the prisoner adventures, which are partly borrowed, are good but not so good). O'Brien is the jewel he ought to be throughout: and the captains (not least the great liar) and the lieutenants and the crews likewise. Peter's pass-examination (a matter to which Marryat returns more than once) is well staged and spoken up to: and in fact the book is full of good things, not the least of them being Swinburne's yarns. Céleste is of course shadowy—much more so than Agnes, whose introduction scene at least is quite lively and almost adapted to the modern theatre. But she is at any rate a nice little girl, and no doubt did not become a nasty 'great' one as they called them then. When did 'great girl' go out? I do not think it passed the mid-nineteenth century.

If we take *Japhet in Search of a Father* third in order (the exact chronological succession of the four does not matter) no doubt a certain falling off may have to be confessed: in fact it is the most unequal of all the group. Edgar Poe, of whose rather curious review of a later book of Marryat's we may have something to say presently, and who, as one of his countrymen, contemporaries, and indeed colleagues said, had a monomania for detecting plagiarism, would probably have shaken his head over the copying in the title from Hannah More and her *Coelebs in Search of a Wife* and no doubt, as we may ourselves see, Marryat did latterly rather tend to 'follow' on land if not on sea. But this matters here hardly anything at all. The earliest part, after Japhet had left the Foundling, is quite good, though (or rather partly because) it contains that tantalising personage the prophetess Aramathea Judd, of whom a really remarkable character might have been made, but of whom Marryat—either not recognising her possibilities or feeling himself unequal to them—makes us lose sight at a police station after a vulgar 'rag' of which itself we are only given a sort of 'headline' account. The subsequent adventures of the two boys with the gipsies are again not bad: but after this the book tails off a good deal; though the gambling Major is fair. Marryat's attempts to follow the fashionable novel of his day were never very happy,[1] and things do not get much better when he changes for a time to the melodramatic, and the ci-devant 'Melchior' gets murdered (for I suppose it was technically murder) in endeavouring to get somebody else murdered. The actual finding of the 'father', however, is not badly managed, and the de-Quakerising of the Quaker damsel has its merits. Perhaps poor Mr. Cophagus need not have been killed: but there the old question of comparative ruthlessness, as in the other case of Mr. Easy *père*, comes in.

I believe *Jacob Faithful* has some pretensions to be at the top of the competition among Marryat's novels for favour of the 'best' kind. It has something like a prerogative vote—in the Latin rather than in the English sense—from Thackeray; and if it has but little of the sea in which its author is novelist-Admiral, it seldom quits '*the* river', which ranks next to 'the sea' at large as an English water. It has sometimes been charged against Marryat that, when he had no actual fighting to season and light up his books, he was too apt to take to melodrama. We certainly here start with spontaneous combustion and end with a man saved from shooting when the order to fire is all but given; while, earlier than the middle, we have the hero chucked overboard with every chance of being knocked on the head if he tried to get on board again. But none of these incidents is allowed too big a place; and in particular Marryat was wiser than Dickens in not attempting any elaborate defence of the spontaneous combustion business.

Again, it may have been—and to go farther, probably has been—said that Marryat had better have left women out altogether, or kept himself to 'Susan on my knee' and the already mentioned 'young lady very nicely dressed' who got Peter sent on board. He

[1] Nor is his satire on it in *Olla Podrida*.

obviously had the traditional sailors' limitations in his knowledge of them; though, oddly enough, he knew or imagined originals suggesting good working up, such as the prophetess in *Japhet*, also just mentioned, and that Eugenia in *Frank Mildmay* who, proper or improper, is so far in advance of her rather ruffianly lover. But Agnes and Céleste in his two chief books and Minnie in *Percival Keene* are little more than outline; the heroine, if you can call her so, of *The King's Own* is even less; and as for Poor Jack's first love, Janet Wilson, who makes a fool of him and nearly prevents him from making a happy man of himself, she is simply spoken of, and never seen at all. Bessy in this last book and Sarah here are pleasant sensible girls and no doubt made capital wives, but that is all. Of Amine in *The Phantom Ship*, for whom some claims have been made, more later. Mary, the other heroine here, is, with the exception of Amine, by far his most elaborate and certainly his most successful sketch. Of course, she is an outrageous flirt, and one has a pretty shrewd idea that she was not likely to cease flirting, though she was also not likely to come to actual mischief. If she did it would probably be Tom's fault. Jacob is rather a prig with her after the very first: and the Dominie had himself quite as much as herself to blame if, in the circumstances, he let his heart get so very much the better of his head. Her own head seems, bar the excessive flirtatiousness, to have had an inside worthy of the out. I have always very much liked her speech to Jacob, 'You can't help thinking kindly of a girl you've kissed', with its quite obvious and almost audible aside 'unless you're a brute as well as a prig'. But the fact is that Mary ought to have been in a station of life quite different from that in which she found herself. Her mother was admittedly a rather queer person; one wonders—but let us not be scandalous.

The rest of the book requires no extensive criticism in detail, but should have a little, such criticism being, not as some moderns do vainly seem to think, an impertinent intrusion, but a comely salute and performance of ushership. Jacob himself, one sometimes fancies, is that not infrequent and nearly always interesting *persona* in which the author puts a good deal of himself, or his own idea of himself, with characteristics strikingly different to disguise this. He is certainly, to an excessive extent, *rancunier* against Mr. Drummond, and there is perhaps rather too much not quite 'sweet' reasonableness about him. But this was probably intended in part to set off and apologise for the opposites in Young Tom. I own, though this is perhaps not sweetly reasonable, that I should have liked both better if a slight proportion (not too much) of their respective attributes had been deducted from each and transferred to the other.

The inset of the wicked uncle and the kidnapped will is good; that of Mrs. Turnbull and her follies less so. But a strong point in favour of the book, and one which, I should imagine, has had a great deal to do with its popularity, is the very considerable *variety* of its subjects, and their appeals. A kind of novelist who has been growing commoner and commoner since Marryat's time could spin three or four books out of *Jacob*. And from this partly results freedom from that curse which did undoubtedly fall on the beloved 'old three-decker', the frequent emptiness of its middle deck. The desert of the second volume had to be overstepped, honestly or by skipping, by almost every novel reviewer between 1830 and 1890. There were three volumes of *Jacob Faithful*, but the second is not a desert at all. And though the run-in at the end of the third, to change the phrases again, is certainly a rush, there is nothing extravagant in it, however one may shake one's head over the future of Tom and Mary, and fail to be rapturously envious of that of Jacob and Sarah.

Perhaps, for anyone who has been permitted by nature to mingle genuine with critical enjoyment, there is no book of Marryat's which gives his character as a novelist more obligingly than that which, if one remembers rightly, did so much good to, and was so ungraciously thanked for it by, Thomas Carlyle in one of the severest trials that an author has ever been subjected to. *Snarley-yow, or the Dog-Fiend*, is of course inferior as literature to the four which have been selected as Marryat's best. It is almost throughout an example of what the Greek rhetoricians called *rhyparography*—coarse writing, or at least writing about coarse stuff which sometimes, as in the dog's-tail business, becomes disgusting. It sometimes also outrages probability if not possibility, in more than one detail as well as the total effect of the attempt of Vanslyperken's greater fiend of a mother to murder Smallbones. Its history (not an unimportant item) is more than once queer.

And yet, somehow or other, readers—even readers who are not fond of rhyparography, who cannot help reading critically, and to whom it is not even new—find themselves reading it again with interest from cover to cover. That this reading is to some extent, as in the case of *Poor Jack*, bribed by the interspersion of the songs, may be true. Some of these songs are of the very best of their kind. It would not be easy to beat 'Susan on my knee' or 'The Captain stood on the carronade.' But perhaps 'Port Admiral you be d——d' is the pearl of greatest price. All the three ought to be illustrated, and all give charming subjects to accompany and point their verse-appeal. But the majesty of scene and action provided by Poll with her apron twisted round her arms, between the supporting but shivering figures of Bet and Sue (one's mind glances to the happier Susan on the knee poem) is unsurpassable.[1]

However, the songs come mostly (all these three do) early in the book, and their absence, though it would certainly lessen, would not destroy the pleasure it gives. The secret of this pleasure is that the man *can tell*.

Besides his display of the mysterious and invaluable gift so often displayed by the spinsters and the knitters in the sun, and so often missing in gentlemen who are acquainted with the very latest theories of novel-technique, there is something else to be noted in this book which is not quite so fully present in the quartet of 'firsts' themselves—at least in the two best of them, for both *Jacob* and *Japhet* have something. This is, if not exactly plot, something like plot—an end proposed, forwarded, and reached. In the present writer's favourite the only end except the printed 'finis' is that of poor old Mr. Easy, who has really little or nothing to do with the book after its beginning, except to pay Jack's drafts. The Privilege estate and peerage business may for some readers provide a story with an end; but for my part I rather wish it wasn't there, and to speak frankly, I don't believe Peter ever *was* Lord Privilege. But Japhet does find his father, and Jacob is satisfactorily (and much more 'conformably' than in Peter's case) provided with plentiful coin, a pleasant wife and so forth, though the real story-end (one fears it was not an end at all) is that of Tom and Mary.

In *Snarley-yow* things are completely different from all these. The interwoven fates of this hell-hound and his more disgusting if less terrible master seize you at once, hold you throughout and only let you go when the fiend and the scoundrel have ceased kicking at their several yardarms. The re-appearances of Snarley-yow are extremely well managed, and combined with those of Smallbones in a really ingenious manner, while the humours of the crew and the Dutch widow are adjusted as relieving touches quite *secundum artem*. In everything but quality of substance it really would not

[1] People have a stupid habit of calling these things 'doggerel'. Doggerel is verse which takes no liberties in prosody, and these take none.

be extravagant to call this Marryat's best book—from some modern points of view it probably is.[1]

Of Marryat as a short story-teller—his performances as such belong mainly to the period before his American journey—it is difficult to say much. I do not remember anything of his in this way which pleases me more than the story, in *The Pasha of Many Tales*, of the wind which was so strong that it blew a drowning man in ricochets from the crest of one wave to that of another, till the last landed him on the keel of a capsized boat and he was saved. There is really a great deal there that you can recommend to a friend: the great deal consisting of things of the most different kind, from the enormous audacity of the conception to the picture, not in the least impossible to the imagination, of its carrying out in fact.

Perhaps the best place to look for this and other miscellaneous work—much if not all of it the magazine matter, which he discusses as well as furnishes—is *Olla Podrida*. The bulk of it is indeed composed of a smaller 'Continental' Diary illustrating, like the bigger American one, his very odd notion of the meaning of that name. There are no doubt a few date-headed chapters or paragraphs here: and he refers now and then to 'memoranda', but on the whole we meet the same sermons on texts, instead of jottings of particular experience, in both. And the whole is made in a manner to explain and justify the American adventure itself. He finds fault with the Continental governments and so must go and see the Transatlantic.

The *Diary in America* is a very curious book, though perhaps not, to the general reader, a very interesting one. The pages of the London Library copy do not look as if they had been often turned over, unless the fingers that turned them were unusually delicate. In the first place, it is not a 'Diary' in the usual sense at all, though it may have been based upon one, and the 'remarks on institutions' which (to be quite fair) are also mentioned on the title-page, almost constitute the six volumes, the greater part of which comes actually under general headings, 'Law', 'Army', 'Religion', 'Education', 'Slavery', etc. Marryat was distinctly unlucky in his times and season, for he landed at New York in the midst of a financial 'crash' and during almost the whole of his sojourn the Canadian troubles were going on. In these he was much on our side of the frontier, and the actual share which, as a Queen's officer, he took, almost necessitated

[1] And would be more so if the story of Nancy Corbett had been more fully worked out. Marryat is rather fond of or liable to these experiments in tantalising or confessions of inability. Compare the other Nancy in *The Poacher*.

trouble on the other side. In fact, on more than one occasion, when he returned to those States, he got into situations which, if Fear and he had not been utter strangers, might have been unpleasant. But for its immense length, and a kind of pillar-to-post wandering of treatment which is rather irritating—to which must be added a constant bickering with Harriet Martineau which is more irritating still—the book would be both pleasant and instructive.

From the American book, one sees or seems to see—what indeed the unamiable reader may say might be seen or seem to be seen about other people—that Marryat had desires, ambitions, 'inklings', or whatever you like to call them, which his defects of education and the character of his early experience made it impossible for him to carry out. There is certainly no need to be unhappy about this from the selfish point of view: for no alteration of the scheme of things in this direction could possibly have given us anything better than *Mr. Midshipman Easy* and *Peter Simple;* or could even possibly have given us *them*, while it might probably have given nothing at all. But it is interesting to find him so little of a Captain Cutwater, with no ideas in his head except those connected with regions bounded by rudder, bowsprit, topgallant mast, and keel, prodigal of delight though the ideas actually connected with that region may have been to us. Let it only be added that, if there are things in his book which could not please American men, there is no ill-nature or ill-manners whatever, and that, from a very early page to the very last opportunity towards the end, the Captain is never tired of asserting that American girls are the prettiest in the whole world, with occasional italics to enforce his declaration. It is also pleasing, though sad now, to find in his pages the really poetical item that you might then distinguish the grave of a Virginian gentleman by the mint growing from his precedent juleps. The rose and briar of the ballad may have suggested this; but they can still grow; this no more.

In some ways Marryat may be said not to have made a bad thing out of his two years 'over there'. He seems to have quite enjoyed his experiences as a whole, though there are one or two sharp expressions; he received sixteen hundred pounds for the *Diary*, a transaction which, it has been suggested, was probably not very lucrative to the publishers; and he must have had more, though we do not know how much more, for the *Phantom Ship*, the whole of which seems to have been written abroad. This book has interested different people rather differently. I have myself never been able, either when I first read it in midway of life or now, to enjoy it much. I have no objection to its *diablerie*, or magic or whatever you may call its furbishing up the Legend of Vanderdecken. I admit that Amine the heroine is not merely the most ambitious but the most heroine-like of all Marryat's heroines. Her fate in the Inquisition does not of itself make me dislike the book; for though I have no foolish contempt for happy endings I grant that unhappy ones can be made effective. But it seems to me on the whole *heavy*, and destitute of the 'liveness' of which we have talked. At the same time it *is* interesting as further evidence of what was said above in connection with the *Diary* itself—that there was always more or less a kind of 'quest' in Marryat, or at least a temptation to questing. It is not his only historical novel or romance, for *Snarley-yow* had been that in a way; but it is his only romance in the sense in which that term is more generally used.

In *Poor Jack* he returned in another sense to England, home, and if not beauty such as he had found in America, the life on river if not on sea, which he knew so well and could tell of so vividly; while here as in *Snarley-yow* he was rather prodigal of capital verse of the kind which some call doggerel, but which can be famously good *of* its kind. The ruffian is not very good; Marryat was never good at ruffians except when he didn't mean to make them such; but nearly all the rest is excellent.

I am rather afraid of getting myself regarded as, if not a quack of anti-modernity, a hopeless crank of it, when I say that I put down *Masterman Ready* almost with Marryat's best work and certainly as a most remarkable example of his extraordinary *naturalezza* when he had his hand thoroughly 'in'. 'Why! the thing is a mere suggestion from the *Swiss Family Robinson!*' says the enemy. Of course it is: and that is part, though very far indeed from the whole, of the beauty of it. For a duller thing than the supposed original—except for the riding on the ostrich (which I own I always wished to do in my earlier years) and the agreeable variation in liquor effected in the cocoanut milk—has never I think been put into the hands of defenceless childhood. I remember that about the same time when I rejected the Swiss thing with scorn, I rather enjoyed Eugénie Foa's mild but (like cocoanut milk in its inception) rather refreshing *Petit Robinson de Paris*. The other has in quintessence the dull stupidity which used at one time to be associated with some things German, though others were as different as possible. Of course the people who blame it for associating things not associable are as dull as itself. I should not have minded if not merely this insult to science had been committed, but the 'family' had discovered a tribe of leprechauns who were accustomed to work a quarry of the philosopher's stone and whose queen was as exceptionally charming as Youwarkee in *Peter Wilkins*. But the book is as dull as ditchwater and as heavy as Mr. Jingle's baggage. *Masterman Ready* is bright and light, and all that it according to any reasonable specification ought to be. Once more we may say that the sea has still been a refresher of such powers as he had.

Percival Keene (in which this refresher has been once more constantly applied) has had hard measure in some competent quarters, but I have always had a certain kindness for it. Not for the hero, in whom we must, I fear, allow an unpleasant lapse or even relapse into something like the character of Frank Mildmay. It is not his fault that he is an illegitimate child, born and brought up under very unromantic circumstances; and charity may excuse him as a most mischievous one—even, or perhaps especially, when he turns a catch-word ('it'll end in a blow-up') of his ruffianly Irish schoolmaster into a fact by setting fire to a collection of fireworks which the fellow has commandeered from his scholars and stowed in an empty case under his chair. Indeed one almost says *Macte virtute* then. But there is not much virtue about Percival. He discovers precociously, and more than precociously works on, his illegitimate relationship to his captain; he himself has more than a touch of Frank Mildmay's bad blood; he is even snob enough to avoid, as below him, when he is rising in the service, a rather charming aunt—who as a girl has comforted and petted him as a child; and when we leave him with a very nice wife, 'the name and arms of Delmar' and eight thousand a year which he has not exactly stolen but worked himself into—we can't give him the other tag about *meruit* and *ferat*. But the book—the last but one of Marryat's mainly sea-books—recovers much of the freshness and liveness of his best efforts; the explosion of the schoolmaster at the beginning puts one—especially if one has known much of 'education' from the inside—into a good humour, and there is an excellent sailor man named Cross who comes in just after and continues till the very end. He is of the same type as Swinburne in *Peter*, though perhaps a little 'lower', as is the tone of the whole book. Still, he is of the type also of God's and Mr. Baldwin's if not perhaps exactly of Mr. Milton's 'Englishmen', and one is glad to shake hands with him and to thank his secondary creator. When I read this book again after some half-century's interval it was at once quite familiar and quite fresh. The fighting is plentiful and excellent.

A glance has already been given to the odd conjunction of Poe and Marryat—two writers as different in character as any you could find in the whole world of literature—through the American poet's review of *Joseph Rushbrook or The Poacher*. That it is a very unfavourable one was only to be expected. No American at that time had any particular reason to go out of his way to be kind to the Captain, and there was much in him—putting 'politics' quite aside—which might excite that almost frantic rage with which Poe greeted Lever's *Charles O'Malley* and its detestable 'devilled kidneys'. But undoubtedly the book is not a good book, and those 'vital spirits' which we have noted in its author's best work not merely begin to 'fail' here, but, with the exception of a few flashes, fail altogether. Interest of course is not wanting to a particular kind of reader—that rather inhuman kind who may be called the critical student. For him it is worth while to compare the book with *Percival Keene*, also a work of the declining years. For that too goes back to the sea: and on the sea Marryat could never be wholly dead; in *The Poacher* he is almost wholly so. Everybody knows, of course, or should know, that mere improbabilities, nay sheer impossibilities, need matter of themselves little or nothing in a novel. You do not only forgive them but you hardly notice them till you are familiar with the book and have leisure to attend to its minor details. But, in order to make you thus inattentive or thus forgiving at first, there must be the driving power which is only conferred or infused by very interesting incident or very live character. And as in life so in literature, the character need not be, though it may be, intricate and problematical. It must be *live*, according to its own scheme and schedule of liveness. Dukes and cooks, fairies and charwomen, saints and sinners, bookmen and illiterates, they can all be made to live, and they must be so made if the book is to live itself.

Unfortunately Marryat's last sea-book, *The Privateersman*, cannot be so well spoken of, as it was possible, though with qualification, to speak of its last predecessor as such on the great scale. My friend Mr. Hannay may have been stern to Percival: he is simply just to Alexander, the *brevet*-hero of this other book, who commits the almost unmentionable crime of deserting a woman when they are together in flight from pursuing Indians. It makes the matter worse not better, of course, that she has been a sort of Amazonian tyrant to him, although (or rather *and* that) she has at the same time coveted if not loved him. He was apparently impervious to the stings of salvation which Henry Kingsley has indicated in the famous words of his scoundrel Lord Welter, 'There are some things a fellow *can't* do.' And this is not all. Marryat had saddled himself with the too often crushing handicap-weight of autobiography in some of his best books, and had come in a winner. Here it is altogether too much for him. Few things are odder in the differential calculus of novel criticism than the way in which the autobiographical form ceases to be drama and becomes mere *recit.*[1] It has become so here, and though there is adventure, fighting, and so forth all through the book, it communicates no liveness. If it does not displace *The Poacher* from that uncomfortable position of 'last' which racing reports (I never quite knew why: does anybody bet on it?) cruelly and specially publish, it is because it attempts less. Both Mr. Hannay and Mr. Courtney have allowed it a slight recommendation to mercy as a document of its title-subject, but I do not find that much of a one.

As for *The Pirate and the Three Cutters* little more than mention is required. It has no great positive faults like the two just noticed, but its melodrama in the *Pirate* is a sort of enlarged replica of the pirate episode in *Percival Keene* and its farce in the *Cutters* is mainly Marryat's second or third best fun. I would rather read it again, though I have just done so, than either the *Poacher* or the *Privateersman*, but that is about all I can say.

To some readers (or skippers) it may seem that this examination of Marryat's actual work has been somewhat too extensive. But long and wide practice of my own in criticism, and rather exceptional acquaintance with the work of other critics both past and present, has convinced me that such examination is absolutely necessary in order to attain a really satisfactory result. It may be said, 'Yes: it should be made, but only the results should be published.' That is perhaps the natural sentiment of a tabloid age, but it is a very unsound one. Superficial generalisations are perhaps not the least tempting things in criticism, but, like other tempting things, they are not the safest. And I think this examination may have shown that Marryat was something more than a mere retailer of naval yarns, though his sea stories are far above all his others and at the very top of their own kind.[2] The adventures of Peter and O'Brien in their escape have long been traced to actual records; and just recently

[1] It suggests in an odd manner more unsuccessful imitation of the most unsuccessful work of Defoe.

[2] This is no challenge to partisans of Clark Russell or of the late Mr. Conrad. Their kinds are different. I certainly prefer Marryat to Fenimore Cooper.

the very interesting experiences of a contemporary midshipman (published first in *Blackwood*) have been said to be origins likewise. I am not quite sure about this, for there must have been hundreds if not thousands of Peters and Jacks, not to say Franks and Percivals, about between 1790 and 1815. But every artist is entitled to his material: he need only contribute the skill in working it up.

Now the Navy richly deserved its artist and had hitherto lacked him. If Chaucer had given us a 'Shipman's Tale' of the *métier* it would have been worth having, though from a certain famous line in the Prologue it might have resembled unpleasantly in some parts the blacker incidents in Marryat's piratical melodramas. There is splendid stuff in the great Elizabethan time, and for my part I decline to agree with those naval expert friends of mine who tell me that the loss of the *Revenge* deserved a court-martial and (had he survived) the dismissal of Sir Richard from the service. But though people were beginning to write history in English they had not begun to write novels proper. Towards the end of the seventeenth and the beginning of the eighteenth centuries, Congreve and still more Charles Shadwell introduced sailors to dramas, but the stock sailor was rather like the stage Irishman. Defoe, contemporary with both, seems in his usual uncanny fashion to do more than he really does. There is a lot about ships in *Robinson Crusoe*, some in *Captain Singleton*, and a whole 'Voyage Round the World' in the book of that name with 'New' before it in the title. But it does not come to very much on the whole; and it has nothing or next to nothing to do with the Navy proper. Smollett, of course, almost opens the ball on that subject, if to rather jazz music. Fanny Burney's Captain Mirvan is not far from deserving some of the lashes which he had no doubt distributed liberally among his crews: while, on the other hand, Miss Austen's sailors, though or because she was so closely connected with them, are the most sentimental, and to some out-and-out 'Janeites' the least attractive of her characters. Scott hardly touches the sea, though Nanty Ewart has considerable possibilities, and Lieut. Taffril is a good super. So Marryat had a pretty clear field as far as literature went: and such a collection of material as perhaps, fresh but not too fresh, subject for subject, nobody has ever had before and perhaps nobody will ever have again. The Navy had to a great extent worn off the squalor and the brutality which had clung to it so long: though no doubt cases like that of the *Hermione* were still possible. The system of 'press', which Marryat disliked and William IV disliked him for disliking, was not on the whole a pretty one;

but one rather fails to understand, on its own showing, why the men made it necessary. There was a great demand for novels; there were ample and profitable ways and means of disposing of them; the hour was there, and had only to find the man with powers to suit. It got him.

These powers were of course powers of no exceptionally 'high-brow' cast; but they partook, as I have endeavoured to show in gross and in detail, of what is the central driving force of the novelist: and though this force was probably more or less exhausted at his death and had undoubtedly flagged some time before his death, this failing or flagging has no retrospective effect. You see the force in *Frank Mildmay* not yet in hand, and in *The King's Own* getting into hand rather imperfectly; in *Newton Forster* working more evenly but rather less effectually and then sharing the fate of other kinds of life as they flourish and fade. I think I have seen the word 'autobiographic' applied, with or without a suspicion of depreciation not merely to *Frank Mildmay*, where it is certainly nearly unavoidable, but to the histories of Jack and Peter which though as certainly not without auto-biographic touches, are different in substance. Now, of course, actual experience will help a novelist mightily; and is almost of necessity found in the best novelists; while want of it, as in the case of Richard-son, will probably account to no small extent for shortcomings. We find it in Fielding and very specially in Smollett; in Dickens and again very specially in Thackeray. But it is not the mere repro-duction of autobiographic experience; it is the working upon and of it that is needed: and that is what we find in Marryat's two best books as they have been ranked here, and in all the best parts of his books everywhere.

Of plot he was no master: and oddly enough from one point of view, less so from another, there is more of it in his worst book, *The Poacher*, than anywhere else. The beginning and the end are here really, or at least might be, connected. But the middle is mere packing, not weaving. It is at the best strung by the chase after Joey, whose successive adventures might have happened to half a dozen different persons. His characters, too, are almost entirely external—sometimes actually labelled or ticketed by catch-words. The one most curious exception to this has been touched on more than once: but not the least part of its curiosity has yet to be noticed—that it is a sort of anticipation in reverse, failure, refusal, or whatever you like to call it, of one of the most modern of novel personages. Eugenia in *Frank Mildmay*, Aramathea Judd (in a slightly different order), the two

Nancys in *Snarley-yow* and *The Poacher*, are all no better than they should be, though Aramathea, as far as we are allowed to know, was spiritually rather than bodily improper. The other three are more elaborate, but the dealings with them are uncertain and insufficient. If Marryat had been a modern novelist he would have combined them all, added to the combination a good deal of what he has actually given Mary in *Jacob*, but also added a great deal else. Whether it would have been a success in the hands of a modern novelist one cannot say, and it is not necessary to guess; that it would certainly not have been a success in any such hands as Marryat has shown is certain, and so he was no doubt wise not to try. What he could do with those hands he has also shown us: and 'while it was day', to borrow not the least great of phrases, he succeeded.

The character was, as admitted, always what is called external character and what has just been said practically implies that: but it was external character that was wanted. So in the third great novel-requisite of description the picturesque, if not out of place, would have been superfluous—a distinction by no means without a difference. Marryat has done some fair description of the regulation sort in his two diaries, and there are some striking bits elsewhere—especially that of the death trap in the desolate island in *Frank Mildmay* where the dog saves its master at the price of its own life, and at the same time shows the cause of former fatalities by mistaking the wet moss overhanging a cliff-edge for solid turf. But of that very different kind of description which deals with action he is a wonderful master. It is not merely experts who admire the club-hauling of the *Diomède*, though it be more technical than fighting; and as for the fighting itself one could almost sit through a Pacifist lecture if one concentrated one's remembrance in abstraction over the battle of the *Aurore* and the Russian frigate in *Mr. Midshipman Easy*, the unlucky but this time really historical and autobiographical mistake over the Maltese privateer in *Frank Mildmay,* Willy Seymour's chucking of his hat in the French Captain's face in *The King's Own*, and even the quieter but still not unlively escape of the *Calliope* from the line-of-battleships, with the pretty boat fighting for sauce, in *Percival Keene*.

So again of the fourth dimension—dialogue. Marryat here as elsewhere is not what the Greeks called a pancratiast. His funny talk is too often merely punny: and though puns are much better things than it is the fashion to think now, and has been the fashion to think before, you can have too much of them, and they do vary in merit. Nor is his 'society' talk very good; nor some other kinds. But when he has got, as remarked before, his hand in, he 'can do it'. And this brings us naturally to the last, but far from the least interesting, division of the matter—the general question of Marryat's style. Criticism of it may be comfortably divided into the sacred three parts. There is the view expressed in its extremest form by Poe, in the review above referred to, that it is a bad style or no style at all. This shades down into a milder judgment that you wouldn't expect any style here, and it doesn't matter if there's none. And this again colours up into more of an approval, sometimes into frank declaration that at least at its best it is the very style for the purpose, the very spirit of the man; and that so it hits both wings of the best definition of style itself. And as far as this last the present writer would certainly go.

If my memory does not deceive me, the light-of-love hero in the *Astrée*, reproached for adding a new lady to his list of beloveds, retorts that a particular place or niche was vacant in his heart and that this lady exactly fitted it. Now it seems to me that a hundred years ago a particular place was vacant in the hearts or heads of good novel-lovers and that Marryat just fitted it.

That should be enough to say.

1928.

THE COLLOQUIES OF ERASMUS

BY one of the coincidences which amuse the wise but are overvalued by one and contemned by another kind of the unwise, the name of Erasmus cropped up in those rather embittered controversies which have recently been, if they are not still, disturbing the Church of England, *after* this little paper had suggested itself to its writer. Not that there was anything new in the connection of Erasmus and controversy. He was what vulgar moderns call 'in hot water' all his life: indeed he may be said to have lived in a world of hot water. But some time after his death, his reputation settled itself into a quieter kind of European notoriety. During the late sixteenth century, the seventeenth, and even the eighteenth, people read Erasmus when they were at school, and read him afterwards, for different reasons. But this reading for a long time again has, as anything general, ceased: though he has for a good many years now been the subject of invaluable editing by the present President of Corpus Christi College, Oxford,[1] and though Dr. Mangan's book[2] has just dealt with him at large in America and England both. But Dr. Allen's work is intended mainly for scholars: and Dr. Mangan does not like the Colloquies, which are meant to be the exclusive subject of this article.

There are no doubt reasons of various kinds which unfit this book now for the school-book it once was: but as there is no intention here of recommending the resumption of it as such, that does not matter. What does matter is that it is a very curious and interesting piece of literature. Indeed it may be questioned whether Erasmus ought not to be honoured and kept in reading more as one of the first modern men of letters than as anything else. His scholarship is, as scholarship is fated to be, rather *hesterna rosa;* his theology was of that kind, perhaps the most dangerous of all kinds in all subjects, which never can make up its mind on which side of the hedge or wall it is coming down. But he was a man of letters in his heart; a

[1] *Opus Epistolarum Des. Erasmi Roterodami,* edited by Percy Stafford Allen (volumes I-VI, 8vo). *Selections from Erasmus,* edited by Percy Stafford Allen (illustrated, 12mo). *The Age of Erasmus,* by Percy Stafford Allen (8vo). *Erasmus' Service to Learning,* by Percy Stafford Allen (brochure, 8vo). Oxford University Press.

[2] *Life, Character and Influence of Desiderius Erasmus of Rotterdam, Derived from a Study of his Works and Correspondence,* by John Joseph Mangan. Illustrated. Two volumes. 8vo. Macmillan.

man of letters once is a man of letters for ever; and the Colloquies are at once a proof of this as concerns himself, and a pattern for others. You may almost call Erasmus, long before Montaigne, the first essayist: only the intense *Drang nach* drama in his time induced him to give his things a more or less dramatic form. Sometimes, indeed, as for instance in the Convivium Poeticum where Housekeeper Margaret and the footboy diversify the talk of the bards, bring in beet-root instead of lettuce, et cetera (and when Margaret finally declines to give them anything to eat or drink except mustard), the thing could be made to act with hardly any difficulty at all.

Of the vividness and vigour of his presentations of life and society there can never have been much doubt or question among competent readers: and this quality must have been recognised in itself, though not as his, by hundreds and thousands of persons who never opened the Colloquies themselves. The description of the inn in *Anne of Geierstein*, one of the liveliest of Scott's later passages, is almost a literal translation, eked with action, from Erasmus: and it would be not quite uninteresting to know how many passages describing escape from wrecks owe royalty in part or in whole, directly or indirectly, to the Naufragium. His account of the experiences of a pilgrim at the shrine of Our Lady of Walsingham might never have been written except for the rather ill-natured ecclesiastical satire which it displays: but it is again vivacious enough, and capable of being made trustworthy by an intelligent reader. The piece which shocks Dr. Mangan and in which a damsel in distinct need of reformation receives it from an old gallant of hers who is himself reformed, is only a transfer into colloquy of one of the liveliest farce-moralities of that most agreeable Dark Age Prioress Hroswitha; but it is at once moral enough and lively enough. This may also be said of the somewhat similar batch dealing with maidens who shrink from or quarrel with marriage. But in all these cases the author is more or less indebted, for better for worse, to his subject.

Now perhaps the great charm of the Colloquies to a real lover of letters is the way in which their writer shows himself able to write engagingly and interestingly about anything from broom-sticks to Grammar. The book begins with several scores of pages—something like a hundred and fifty in the pocket Tauchnitz edition—of intentionally school-book character, even descending to what in mid-nineteenth century English we used to call 'Ollendorffian' forms of address at meeting people, sketches of probable subjects for conversation; titles of dignity; games; professional manner of things, ending with two long Convivia—one Profanum, one Religiosum—in which things in general that come under the two heads are discussed. And in all this there is nothing silly or caricaturable as there was in the excellent Ollendorff. You can get—if you keep your intelligence awake and have a little precedent knowledge to help you—a much more intimate acquaintance with that all-important time than you are likely to have had before. And if you are shameless enough not to care about learning or profiting by anything, there is plenty merely to delight and amuse you. Sometimes, indeed, he seems to be anticipating a sort of 'Young Novelist's and Dramatist's Guide' as in his lists of possible speeches and replies between Master and Servant and the like.

If, as has perhaps been the case, rather disproportionate attention has been paid, especially in ordinary books of reference, to the religious element in the Life and Works of Erasmus, there is of course considerable excuse for this. The quarrels in which he took part half against his will, were quarrels than which it would be difficult to find any of more importance in the history of the modern world: and they are not 'sopited'—put to sleep with a fair chance of not waking—even yet. Moreover, though this other fact is rather curious, there is hardly any aspect of a literary man upon which it is so difficult to concentrate public attention as his literature. Take the rather interesting colloquy, Abbatis et Eurditae, in which two persons answering to these descriptions and, further, as at that time they were almost certain to be, 'persons of quality', figure. The abbot is shocked at what he finds in the lady's room. 'Why?' she says, 'Isn't the furniture elegant?' But the offending articles are not exactly furniture but books. 'Why,' she asks again, 'mayn't a *heroina* [the word appears to be used almost in the sense of "*Grande Dame*", if not even of "lady" in our best or implicit meaning] have books?' Perhaps, if they are French, but not if they're Greek and Latin as these are. Doesn't he himself read? 'French, but not Greek and Latin', and so on. Now it is of course possible to take this as merely an excursion or skirmish in the continual battle against monkery and nunnery: and no doubt also it is this to some extent, perhaps mainly, in original intention. But it has far more interesting possibilities than this. It advises us of what is not the least interesting feature of the Renaissance at large, the prominence of the 'learned lady' who was not a mere schoolmarm or bluestocking but 'lady' as much as 'learned'. Perhaps the best thing in it comes from the mouth of the unblushingly illiterate and good-for-nothing abbot when he says, 'With immense labour learning is obtained: and then you have to die', which is better still in its native Latin, '*Immensis laboribus comparatur eruditio: ac post moriendum est*', and which, if not original, remains consummate and unanswerable. But the lady scores fairly often: and the whole thing is alive. Moreover the combination of life and literature is seldom lacking for long in this miniature and colloquial encyclopaedia. Alchemy comes in: they say modern atomic theories may bring that back: and it is only to be hoped—though one fears that there is not much chance of it—that the new Alchemy will be as fortunate in English literature as the old was from Chaucer onwards. Although the queerly titled dialogue, Ichthyophagia or Fish-Eating, between a butcher and a saltfish-monger is obviously ecclesiastical in main tenor, all manner of oddments are brought in: and though the stranger Funus (an elaborate account of death-beds and so forth—which follows) might incur charges on the score both of taste and sentiment (Erasmus is vulnerable on both grounds), it has other attractions. He is indeed never exactly kindly—kindliness was not the characteristic of the Renaissance either in the queer fashion which accompanied the occasional savagery of the Middle Ages, or in the homely one which at least our and the German eighteenth century provided.

But, here as elsewhere, he shows that he had many of the gifts which make a first-rate novelist. The famous Inn passage which has been already spoken of and other things of which Charles Reade made use in *The Cloister and the Hearth* show this sufficiently in one sense but quite inadequately in another. The half-hatched novelist, the essayist almost or quite out of the novitiate, appear constantly; and perhaps something else at one time regarded as even less dignified than either—the miscellaneous journalist. Fleet Street when it saw him, which it had plenty of opportunities to do, and which then had or had not for its chief literary association Chaucer's beating or not beating (the beating would have pleased Erasmus much) the Franciscan friar, must have yearned for him with precocious instinct. His interest in things general; his gift of treating them; his almost entire freedom from 'pontifying'—a proceeding sometimes indulged in by journalists and occasionally successful but never so for long—all called him there. Some pontifying itself and other weaknesses of the journalist may be found by the malicious:

as for instance in the curious Coronis[1] Apologetica which was written in the month of September of the year 1524. But this only makes him more natural both as an individual and as a forerunner. He maintains the *persona* with his own personality throughout.

And in all this stuff there is, despite its deliberate and formal imitation of the ancients now and then, the distinctly modern 'man of letters' tone. That there are approaches to this in the ancients themselves is of course true. There are passages in Plato and Xenophon which any intelligent editor of a monthly magazine or weekly review would be extremely glad to have to-day. Some people have regarded Cicero as (outside the orations) sometimes at least a model 'contributor' and the Rhetoricians, both Greek and Latin, are even better as such on occasion. But still there is the 'unplumbed, estranging' difference between ancient and modern in all, and Erasmus (though he edited half their extant library and knew the rest) is on our not their side of it. The change in religion is only the most obvious and perhaps the largest constituent of the attraction: many others would take a good deal of trouble and more space than we can afford to single out and characterise. But a good example of the result is the Colloquium Senile—not in itself one of the most interesting perhaps, but really a specimen. Four old men meet like Oldbuck and Lovel in the beginning of *The Antiquary*, at the starting place of a coach, in this case destined for Antwerp. They turn out to be old friends who have seen little or nothing of each other since their student days in Paris. They agree to engage the whole of the vehicle that they may talk freely: and quite eighteenth or early nineteenth century details are given—such as that if you want a driver who isn't drunk you had better come early to the stand. They take their seats and talk. The first subject is naturally their respective looks: and the widely different ways in which the forty-two years of post-collegiate life have treated them. Then they tell these lives. The first man had taken to business on leaving college; had married a wife with whom he lived happily for years till her death; had accepted public office of some but no great distinction and profit; and in his later years had contented himself with 'retired leisure'. They all agree that it is no wonder he looks young. Next comes Polygamus who looks extraordinarily old, and who for any person acquainted with the Greek language has explained the cause of his

[1] It is perhaps just desirable to remind readers that Coronis, like Colophon and sometimes its own kinsword, Coryphe, was used for the flourish at the end of a book.

senescence already, to at least some extent. *He* had never given up wine, play, et cetera: and though very sorry when any of his numerous wives died, he put things right again by never remaining more than ten days a widower.[1] The third who looks older still, has in part an unhappier lot to tell. He started excellently, furnished by his father with plenty of capital for foreign trade, and engaged to a beautiful girl with a big dowry, but a shipwreck deprives him of all his wealth: and as he is now a beggar the girl's parents break off the match. After debating whether he shall hang himself or join a religious order he decides on the latter course and tries several. As any one who knows anything about Erasmus will expect, the accounts of his experience are not rosy. But at last his father dies; he goes back to trade, marries, and seems fairly satisfied. There remains only Eusebius whose name again tells stories. *He* accepted a prebend early, studied medicine as well as theology that he might better discharge his duties as a secular cleric, and passed a quiet and happy life in doing his duty. The piece ends with a little bit of farce between the drivers.

The thing as was said above is not exceptionally interesting or amazingly clever: but it shows the emergence of literature from certain more or less definite forms with again more or less definite subjects into a stage where the world is all before it to choose what it likes, treat this as it likes, and call itself what it likes. The drama had had this outgate and outlook from fairly early times; the Greek epigram had shared the privilege to some extent in verse and the Rhetoricians had availed themselves of it in prose. In the Dark and Middle Ages the spirit was making way for itself in odd burrowings and short flights such as those of which an admirable account at last exists in Miss Helen Waddell's *Wandering Scholars*. The opening wide of the gate and the multiplication of excursions from it was sure to be one of the chief points of the Renaissance: and the Chief Porter for opening and not barring the gate, the Chief Director not of residence but of excursions, was Erasmus.

The Dial, April, 1928.

[1] I have sometimes wondered whether that odd person, Amory, took Mr. John Buncle's combination of deep grief and rapid consolation from this pattern.

XENOPHON

WHETHER 'tis nobler in the soul to take opportunity or to make it, who shall decide? According to the motto which the heralds gave to Mr. Gilbert Glossin, temporarily of Ellangowan, 'He who takes it makes it', so there is no difference: but this motto was not held up for admiration. On the other hand in the special case of opportunity, I think there is something to be said in favour of taking. Your opportunity-*maker* is occasionally a criminal, and very frequently a nuisance. And it so happens that, in the present instance, an opportunity has been offered to me of doing something which I have long wished to do without any but a partial chance of doing it—that is to say of writing a few words about the elder of those two Xenophons, one of whom was certainly *our* first, if not *the* first historical novelist, while the other, after a long interval of time, has been thought to be our oldest existing novelist in prose of a type not in the least historical. The opportunity itself I owe to an amiable editorial utilisation of the Loeb translation of the lesser writings of the author of the Anabasis.[1]

I believe that, since the days when I myself learnt and taught the classics, there has been a good deal written about Xenophon in the usual way of text-recension, discussion of authenticity, et cetera. I cannot pretend to full acquaintance with this; but as I have pointed out, more than once, and sometimes but not always to the horror of my fellows, this does not incapacitate me at all for the business that I myself undertake. That business now is the consideration of the literary value of a certain body of literary work—generally if not universally attributed to a person called Xenophon—an Athenian, as it would seem, of the last half of the fifth and the first half of the fourth century before Christ; a friend and disciple of that other most interesting person (or myth if you like) called Socrates: and one who left (or is said to have left) a rather unusually various body of writings—the military-travel-book already mentioned as the Anabasis; the historical or political novel called the Cyropædia; the contemporary history called the Hellenica; the curious collection generally entitled Memorabilia (which is not exactly 'Memoirs') of Socrates; and a still more curious collection *as* a collection, though

[1] *The Loeb Classical Library. Xenophon. Memorabilia and Oeconomicus.* With an English translation by E. C. Marchant. 16mo. 532 pages. *Scripta Minora.* With an English translation by E. C. Marchant. 16mo. 464 pages. London: Heinemann.

no one of the single sections may be as important, of 'Minor' works including a little treatise on House- and Farm-management; an account of a Symposium or banquet (Socratic again) at Athens; a dialogue between the not wholly tyrannic 'tyrant' Hiero of Syracuse and the poet Simonides on the comparative advantages of sovereignty and private citizenship; an enthusiastic biography of King Agesilaus II of Sparta, Xenophon's personal friend; three equally spirited and practical tractates on Cavalry-training, Horses as horses, and Hunting; with one or two directly political and economical pamphlets. With all of these in Greek I am acquainted, as well as with some of them in English. I need not say that the Loeb Library most properly provides its stuff in both.

One of the chief things which have made me wish to testify about Xenophon is the old, but I think by no means obsolete, habit of talking of him in a patronising manner and indulging in that most uncritical of critical or uncritical tricks—depreciating comparison with others. The Anabasis, says one, is all very well but it has no 'fire', no 'energy' about it. The Cyropædia, says another, is sadly unhistorical. The Hellenica, says a third, 'follows' no doubt Thucydides in one sense, but what a long way off it follows him in another! How commonplace is the Socrates of the Memorabilia and the Minors when you compare him with Plato's! Sometimes they go further: 'Isn't it rather shocking that we find him so often on the side of his country's enemies?' 'Isn't it more shocking still when he simply raids the unfortunate Persian at the end of the Anabasis to fill his own and his men's pockets?' 'Isn't he almost Victorian in his constant talk about *kalokagathia* "gentlemanliness"?' And, worst of all, doesn't he make Ischomachus lecture his wife about housekeeping and the beauty of boots in tidy rows, and even the use of *blanc-de-perle* and its opposites. Lastly, did not the late Mr. Ruskin admire Xenophon? and is not the late Mr. Ruskin (except with a certain section of politicians) entirely out of fashion?

Well: I never adopted anything that Mr. Ruskin said in my life, though I may have been frequently charmed by the way in which he said it; and as a matter of fact I liked Xenophon long before I knew, or could have known, what Mr. Ruskin thought of him. But let us very briefly examine the above depreciations in themselves. Most of them, as will have been seen, are merely examples of the Fallacy of Comparison above indicated. Perhaps 'fire' and 'energy' are not exactly Xenophon's strongest points: though the famous 'Thalassa' episode, with the Euxine bursting on the eyes of seafarers by blood and custom after months in the plains of Mesopotamia and the rocks and glens of Kurdistan, can hardly be said to be lacking in either. Perhaps also (as I think is also said) there is not much of technically military tactics or strategy in the book. But why should there be? What business have you to ask it to be anything but what it is? And it 'is' a very pleasant and a by no means unprofitable thing, good and early travel-writing with some fighting; not a little character; excellent description; and (if it be not treason to mention this with praise in America) the first chronicle of Beer!

But the Cyropædia is unhistorical? Now really at this time of day there is no excuse for this sort of folly. Perhaps the ancients, except a very few keen wits like Lucian, did not very clearly distinguish fact from fiction: and it is part of the charm of mediæval writers that they seem frankly incapable of doing anything of the sort. But it is part of the Burden of Modernity—laid upon it or Sinbad-like assumed by it as you like—to know the difference: and if anybody finds it a very severe burden to know the difference between the Cyropædia and history, he must be an exceedingly weakminded person. Then the Hellenica is not so good as Thucydides. What is? Let idle paradoxers gainsay as they may, Thucydides is one of the greatest of all historians, and probably *the* greatest of all historians of things contemporary. It is no disgrace to be beaten even in a canter by him. In the Socrates matter at least the wisest judges have generally admitted that, if Xenophon's man has not, as he probably has, more of the real original in him than Plato's, he is at any rate an invaluable complement or supplement. If it wrings any one's withers to hear about somebody else being a gentleman, there is nothing to be said except that there are many writers with whom he will not be troubled in this way. And as to the advantages and beauties of a row of boots in good condition and well cleaned it surely is not necessary to urge that! But perhaps it is. Far too few people seem to know that seven pairs of boots wear much longer than seven times as long as a single pair; afford much more comfort in proportion; and look much better than a succession of single pairs worn in all weathers without time to recover themselves.

But enough, or almost enough, of mere defence. No doubt, in point of depth of thought and height of style Xenophon could no more have written the close of the Platonic Apology than Addison could have written the close of the Hydriotaphia. No doubt he cannot tell an anecdote as Herodotus or Izaak Walton can. But why not have them all for what they *can* do instead of rejecting, or at any rate grumbling at, some of them on account of what they *can't?* Now Xenophon can do a rather unusual number of things, and can do most of these things rather unusually well. So useful is his 'middle style' (to glance at Addison once more) that it has received, unless I mistake, the rather doubtful compliment of being taken as the model of the artificial language called literary modern Greek. Real—that is to say ancient—Greek prose is always pleasant to read. It has at once more form than English and more substance than French: less stiffness than classical Latin and less want of backbone than modern Italian. As for German, in *prose*, comparison would be absurd. But for what we may call a certain average of its good qualities you cannot go to any one more safely than to Xenophon. And he always applies his style to his matter competently: while it cannot be too often repeated that, for variety as well as competence, he, perhaps partly by favour of fortune and survival, is rather exceptional. The merits of the Anabasis have been already dealt with—indeed it is difficult to think that they could ever have been questioned if the book had not had the worst of all books' fates—that of being made a school-book, and one usually read at a time when purely literary enjoyment is very rare indeed. To the dull the Cyropædia may be dull: certainly not to those who can by a surely pardonable act of literary squinting, keep one mind's eye on it and the other on *Waverley* and the *Trois Mousquetaires* and *Esmond!* To another or the same partner in the creation of dulness the Hellenica may assist in providing it. But the truth is that, after the great tragedy which appropriately reached all but the fall of the curtain at the Goat's River, Greek history *is* rather dull till the meteoric rise of Macedon. And Xenophon at least provides you with no little puff or burst of amusing partisanship when he talks of 'the fire-breathers'—those Boeotian *parvenus* who had the impudence to get the better for a little of Athens and Sparta—meeting with a check.

Next we come to the 'common-place' dealings with Socrates and lo! there are many agreeable finds. To think of its having been Socrates who originated the excellent modern contention that men should use no perfume but *eau de Cologne!* Not indeed that he specifically mentions the product of those manufacturies of Farina and others which very likely were not at the moment working. Even Julian who knew the Rhine and whom *eau de Cologne* would have much benefited, says nothing about them centuries—some three parts of a millennium—later. But Socrates argues elaborately and convincingly at the beginning of the Symposium that men's perfumes and women's perfumes ought to be different. From this the application to the doctrine about *eau de Cologne* is sufficiently obvious. But it is curious that Xenophon, like others of us gentlemen of the literary kind who write about various subjects, goes near to contradicting himself elsewhere. For when that wife-lecturing Ischomachus rebukes his spouse for employing—let us say Rachel and other coloured powder on different parts of her face, he asks her what she would think of *him*, if he adopted these means of making himself beautiful? To which of course, if she had read the Symposium she could only have had to answer 'Yes: but you yourself have laid it down that men's and women's cosmetics *are* different.'

To speak more seriously, the point which has always made me like Xenophon so much—it is a point which, I am glad to see Mr. Marchant has by no means neglected—is the extent (though 'point' and 'extent' do not, at least Euclidically, go well together) to which our author shows us the mind and character of a Greek of average qualities, but possessing more than average powers of expression in literature. To look for any such showing in the great epic or tragic writers would of course be absurd: and our earlier lyric remnants are too fragmentary and not sufficiently miscellaneous, while the bulk of the Anthology (or Anthologies) is too late and too literary—epithets which fit, still more tightly, the Romances. The historians and the pure philosophers have their own business to attend to. There are touches in the orators but only touches. Aristotle is too encyclopædic. Theocritus and Menander are in different ways rather 'made up': and Lucian, besides being 'late and literary' is a cosmopolitan rather than a pure Greek.

There remains of course Aristophanes, Xenophon's own contemporary, a Greek of the Greeks, as great a realist as he is a great idealist, and a far greater man and writer than our good colonel of cavalry and gentleman-farmer by any scale of computation or valuation. But that is just it; he is *too* great. Aristophanes—like Shakespeare if within a smaller range—is constantly getting beyond the national, beyond even the cosmopolitan, into the pure human. In his naughtiest and his most trivial as well as in his most political and most poetical passages he is largely if not wholly of, and for, all time as well as all place. Now you can't say this of Xenophon.

On the contrary *he* is eminently, if not wholly, of his time and his place: and accordingly he tells you curious things about them. Take for instance that at first sight odd piece of information given in the Agesilaus and possessing a sort of unintended comment or explanation in the Hiero that the Spartan King would not himself keep or run horses for the chariot-race, but quite approved of his sister Cynisca doing this. Incidentally, this is interesting at the present moment when there are probably—in England at least—more ladies keeping racing stables than there were in the whole course of the nineteenth century put together. But its original and lasting interest is much less limited than that: and it is only one of numerous things that you must go to Xenophon to find out about. That is to say you must if you really want to understand some of the most interesting people in the world's history—not least interesting because their wisdom is so essentially like our wisdom, when we have any, and their foolishness, when they have any, so apparently different from the foolishness of which we have so much.

The Dial, June, 1926.

A RECONSIDERATION OF SWINBURNE

IF there is anything (I do not think there *is*) for which I would give up the privilege of having read *Atalanta in Calydon* and *Poems and Ballads* when they came out, it would be the opportunity of beginning their author's poems at the recent end and reading them backwards, without knowledge of what was to come. What would be the result must of course be guess-work. The vulgar opinion—I do not use the word 'vulgar' offensively—no doubt would augur some disappointment at first, removed more and more decidedly as one came to the original masterpieces. I am not so sure of this.

For Mr. Swinburne came to his own pretty early, and he never lost it; and it was his own and nobody else's, though he had of course inherited much of it. If it did not show decisively and triumphantly in *The Queen Mother* and *Rosamund*, that was because these attempts were made in a division which was not their author's, and with little or no excursion into his great province of lyric. *Atalanta in Calydon* did not so much change this as supplement, enlarge, improve it immensely. The famous chorus of the 'making of man' is no mere purple patch on the garment—it is only the central device and crowning craftsman's-piece of a coherent and artistically designed web of verse. *Chastelard* followed, with blank verse less deliberately archaised either in early Renaissance or Classical fashion than that of the two preceding volumes and with *short* lyrics—real songs—in it. And then came *Poems and Ballads.*

But let us return to our fancied view-point of reversed approach. One curious thing about Mr. Swinburne is that, intense as his mannerism may appear, it has not coloured subsequent poetry very much. There was of course a period of mere pastiche and mimicry, which was ludicrous enough. But the special quality of Swinburnian verse—like that of much but not all of the greatest—is parodiable but not assimilable. And it is very questionable whether this special quality, brought into contact with a sensitive nature which had not as yet experienced it, would not produce nearly as much effect if got from *The Duke of Gandia* as from *Chastelard*, from any of the late lyrics at their best as from the *Atalanta* choruses and the constituents of *Poems and Ballads* throughout. Now what *is* this special quality?

It is allowed on all hands to be closely connected with metrical mastery—and some seem (mistakenly) to think this mastery a quite new thing, while others appear (as mistakenly) to consider that the appellation 'metre-master' settles and exhausts the matter. It can be easily shown that Mr. Swinburne only developed, to the utmost limit yet reached, franchises and potentialities which had been sometimes in abeyance, but always in existence, for centuries past in English prosody: and the veriest highflier as to the Divine right of metre must acknowledge, as I do, that it will scarcely account for the whole of his charm.

The fact is that there is hardly any poet, in any language, whose power of treating any subject *poeticamente*, 'in a poetical way' (to use the two epoch-making phrases of Patrizzi in the sixteenth century and Hazlitt in the nineteenth), is more instantly and unmistakably obvious than Mr. Swinburne's. One is driven, not in the least Pharisaically, but as a result of much not cheerful observation, to surmise that the complementary faculty of recognising this power is not itself universally possessed by mankind. They must 'take an interest in the thing represented before they can take pleasure in the representation', or they must be more or less elaborately brought to take pleasure in it by this or that other means. Now Mr. Swinburne was not eminently successful in teaching people how to love him, or in attracting them by baits of subject; so that it is truly said that he was never a popular poet. I think it would be found not uncommonly—I know it would be found in some cases—that the most enthusiastic admirers of his poetry were the most uncompromising disagreers with most of his non-literary, and some of his literary opinions. But to those who could feel 'the poetical way', his 'way with them' was, from the first, absolutely irresistible; and it remained so, more or less, till the last. It was certainly at its most irresistible in 1878, with the second *Poems and Ballads*, when the poet was past that 'Age of Wisdom' which has not infrequently proved itself the limit of a poet's summer; nor did it ever really wane.

This 'way' consisted in throwing, over whatever subject the poet treated, an atmosphere of poetic glamour—a word for which, much as it has been abused, there is no synonym and no substitute. The subject does not exactly disappear; but it ceases to be more than a sort of accompaniment to the treatment. Even then, and when the accompaniment itself is most prominent, it is *universalised* to an extent which might delight the most Aristotelian of critics if he would take it in the right way. I read the other day that somebody was 'the *heroine* of "Dolores"' (the good man probably meant

'At a Month's End', but it does not matter much). 'The *heroine* of "Dolores" '! The heroine of 'Dolores', it need hardly be said, is every woman of the enchantress-kind from Lilith to whatsoever name or person the reader pleases in the twentieth century—and she is none of them. So everywhere. Individuality, character, the untranslatable *dianoia*—these things should not be looked for, or at any rate looked for first, in Mr. Swinburne. He got nearest to character in *Chastelard*; less near in *Bothwell*; he was farther off still in *Tristram*. His personages, as personages, might almost be those of the Period of Allegory: and if you cannot be happy without personal company, if you want what you are pleased to call 'ideas' to supply your own deficiency in them; if you must have the opinion you agree with, the discussion which you think 'does you good', local habitations as well as names for your places, specified circumstances of action, machinery, what not—then Mr. Swinburne's poetry is not the poetry for you.

But if you want *poetry*, no matter on what subject, if you can bring the true *silex scintillans* of heart and brain, to have the sparks struck out of it by the true steel of the poet's art, then it *is* what you want, and the sparks will become continuous and grow into a cataract of fire. There may be bad judgement, bad taste, bad several other things in this poet's work, but there is never bad poetry, though at some times it may be better than at others. Such slight things (I suppose some people would call them so) as 'Stage Love' in the first *Poems and Ballads* or as 'Pastiche' in the second are crucial examples. Both are short; there is nothing ostentatiously novel in either, and in fact there is an almost ostentatious disclaimer of novelty in the very title of the second. But both have that very and peculiar atmosphere of poetry which has been referred to—the *aura* of inspiration in the writer and intoxication in the reader—the gathering magic of colour and sound, of metre and phrase, of expression and suggestion. It is impossible, with any critical justification, to dismiss the imagery as separable ornament, to characterise the versification as merely a very pleasant tune to which nothing particular is set, even (as is commonly done) to stigmatise the voluminous diction as mere verbosity. All these things are indissolubly and naturally connected: they form the *body* of the poetry itself. And once more, it is a question whether that body faded or decayed, whether it lost its beauty of form and colour much, from its first full growth to its closing scene.

But Mr. Swinburne's poetry had another attraction less genuinely poetical, not more popular, but very seductive to some tastes. He was notoriously one of the most scholarly poets of a literature which can boast of Milton and Gray, of Coleridge and Landor: and his knowledge of English poetry was unique, or only matched, with time-allowance, by Southey's. It was scarcely possible to catch him in ignorance of a noteworthy poet, not easy to catch him in ignorance of a noteworthy passage, from the Elizabethan period onwards: and though even the half-absurd and half-ignoble plagiarism-finders could hardly have accused him in their way of business, his marvellous metrical proficiency was undoubtedly due in part to his knowledge; and the whole of his work was saturated, so to speak, with its own ancestry. It was never obtrusively learned: but it had a quality which is vaguely troublesome to those who have no learning. It smelt not of the lamp but of 'honey and the sea', like its own laurustinus. Yet the honey was the honey of Hybla: and the sea had washed the shores, and had caught and returned the melodies, of England and of France, of Provence and of Italy.

In such a poet the critical impulse which the foolisher sort have thought so alien from poetry, and the wiser have recognised as almost inseparable from it, but not always consciously developed, could not but seek expression. Now Mr. Swinburne's prose was not wholly criticism; but it was almost wholly this. No one, himself speaking critically, could say that as a whole this prose is equal to the verse. It has, *as* prose, many admirable passages: the *William Blake* especially contains dozens of them. It includes, as appreciation, some of the finest and justest estimates of English literature of which that literature itself can boast. But prose is not like poetry, a steed whose wings its heavy rider *cannot* keep down. You may fear God and honour the King without missing anything of the beauty of the 'Hymn to Proserpine' and the 'Song in Time of Revolution'. Mr. Swinburne's longest verse lines are not too long to be lovely, but some of his prose sentences are; his fiercest flings in verse are not offensive, but some of those in prose are certainly ungainly. The subject recovers its supremacy and abuses it. In particular, it is unfortunately true that as an unfavourable critic he was, with the rarest exceptions, almost negligible. His praise was frequently excessive; but his blame was almost always haphazard. Yet I do not know any writer who more imperatively demands *excerption* in this respect. From the volumes of his prose, beginning with the *Blake* a selection of 'views and reviews' could be made which would be inferior to hardly anything else of the kind that could possibly be constructed, for beauty of mere writing, for illuminativeness of criticism, and for the exhibition of that heart-felt delight in great work which is itself so delightful—and which unluckily is by no means too common in criticism of poetry by poets. Of poetical jealousy I do not remember the very slightest exhibition on his part—a thing almost as unusual and quite as worthy of remark as the drinking of five pints of port per man at Mr. John Thorpe's last wine-party.

But if the prose—to retain, or indeed to obtain, any wide reading—demands the sieve, there are some people at any rate who would refuse to apply that implement to the poetry—who indeed are freer from doubt on this subject than they were years ago. For the Swinburnian verse-quality is everywhere in the Swinburnian verse, and that quality is, as has been said, the quality of pure poetry. Miss anything, and you miss something of the quantity of that quality; miss many things, and you will lose in each something of the phases of the quality itself. You cannot evolve the humming-bird lightness and flash of 'Rococo' or 'Anima Anceps' from the tumultuous rush of the 'Proserpine' Hymn or the 'Song in Time of Revolution'; you cannot divine either of these from the melancholy gliding pageant of the 'Triumph of Time' or the stately sadness of 'Ilicet'. 'Between the Sundown and the Sea' gives no specimen of 'In the Bay' or 'Evening on the Broads'. It is the glory of this kind of poetry that it never 'speaks by its foreman', that you can never, as you can in some other kinds even of very great verse, judge of what will be by what has been. Every line must be read; for every fresh line, even if it have connection of word or image with another passage, has its chance of beginning or completing for the reader the new caress of:

> With stars and seawinds in her raiment
> Night sinks on the sea,

the new shudder of:

> Until God loosen over sea and land
> The thunder of the trumpets of the night.

The Bookman, June, 1909.

THE POETRY OF ROSSETTI

'JOHN DRYDEN enemies had three', runs a good old epigram, and it proceeds to state that though he got rid of one the other two rather stuck to him. I should say that the reputation of Rossetti had three enemies likewise—Belatedness, Detraction, and a Legend. The second he did to some extent get rid of, though the Blatant Beast is hard to choke off entirely, and I have heard echoes of the 'Fleshly School' calumnies and stupidities from persons who were neither exactly fogies nor exactly Philistines, within, I think, the twentieth century. Still, on the whole, the dull Ishmaelitism of the famous pseudonym—rather appropriately assumed in its way, for it was Ishmael masquerading as Philistia—probably does not influence many readers now. But the other two, even thirty years after the poet's death, still do some harm to him. Quite recently Mr. W. M. Rossetti has had to arise once more and spread the fraternal shield (long may he be preserved to repeat the pious office!) over his dead brother. Indeed, when a man has the singular ill fortune to attract industrious parasites of the *gens de lettres* kind early, his Legend is never destroyed. It can always be neglected by the wise, but the wise are not generally in the majority. Of these things no more; but I ought, no doubt, to explain what I mean by 'Belatedness'.

Very seldom has an artist, either in line and colour or in words, come so tardily before anything that can be called the world as Rossetti. He was, in reality, extremely and wonderfully precocious, both as poet and as painter; a man who can write 'The Blessed Damozel' at nineteen in the year 1849, and paint 'The Girlhood of Mary Virgin' at twenty-one, in 1851, might almost frighten anyone who knows what usually comes of and to youthful prodigies. But Fortune, to use the words of the curiously different poet whose name opened this paper,

> took care to lay him softly by,
> And kept his fate among her precious things—

a seclusion to which, it is only fair to say, his own idiosyncrasies vigorously contributed. It is curious to remember how difficult it was for anybody not in his circle, not assisted by chance, and not gifted with that instinct of 'pushing' which has been referred to, to obtain any fair notion of Rossetti's powers for the twenty years between 1850 and 1870. His poems were unpublished, or as bad as unpublished; his pictures were mostly unexhibited, and lurked in private galleries. I give my own experience, not because it is mine, but because I think it fairly typical. It never happened to me as a boy to come across the *Germ*, and though I had the good fortune to discover the *Oxford and Cambridge Magazine*, it was not a complete copy, and neither 'The Blessed Damozel' nor either of her companions in that 'gazophile' met my eyes. I think the first thing I ever saw about Rossetti was George Alfred Lawrence's reference, in the latest 'fifties, to 'the sad Guinevere' who was already peeling herself off the walls of the Union at Oxford—though whether this came to me before or after the dedication of 'The Defence of Guinevere' herself I do not know. Then one began to hear more and more about him; but anything save hearsay was unattainable—at least unattained. While Morris himself, and Mr. Swinburne, were taking us youth by storm in print, and when one could go up from Oxford and find Burne-Joneses on the walls of the 'Old Society', and perorate about them with stealthy dons giggling behind, Rossetti was still a Great Unknown, except (as far as drawing went) by the Tennyson illustrations and (as far as verse went) by somebody or other's MS. copies of 'The Blessed Damozel'. The first time, I think, that I saw anything from his own hand was in the early spring of 1868, when I went from Oxford to take a mastership at the Manchester Grammar School. Manchester is nothing if not hospitable, and before long I found myself at a homely two o'clock Sunday dinner, in a very beautifully equipped house. As I was going to my seat, I saw a picture on the wall, and said to my host, 'I beg your pardon, but don't I know that?' So he said, 'Well, if you go to picture-exhibitions or care for engravings, you probably do,' and I found that the dining-room was panelled with Turners and Coxes, and the like. When the meal was finished, my host said, 'If you like pictures, perhaps I can show you something that you *haven't* seen,' and taking me into another room, he showed me, among others, Rossetti's 'Hesterna Rosa'—the water-colour, not the earlier pen-and-ink sketch. The picture is small and it has not the splendour of the later Rossettian colour. But it took me off my legs at once; and when, many years afterwards—after its author's death and after that of its owner—I saw it in the fascinating but rather ghastly 'intermediate state' of Christie's Museum of Proserpine —I found that it had not lost its power. And I never lost a chance afterwards of repeating the enchantment.

For the poetry, however, one had still to wait, how and why

everybody knows, and it was two years more before the expected and long-ordered volume of 1870 came to me in the Channel Islands, where I was then living. It was curious to think that one was already familiar with Swinburne and Morris and Rossetti's own sister—that an actual school was coming up round them, for O'Shaughnessy made his appearance this very same year—and that he, the master and prior of them all, he who 'fished the murex up', was still unknown except in a few live magazine specimens (the *Fortnightly* had given a foretaste of sixteen sonnets the year before) or in the inaccessible depths of dead ones.

When the book actually came there could hardly be much mistake about it, except in the case of persons congenitally incapacitated for appreciation of poetry as such, or of those who were prejudiced by arbitrary and limited conceptions of what poetry ought to be. It is true that, except as regarded Blake and the almost unknown Flatman (who was not such a bad poet after all), there had never been a case, in English, of a person uniting, by temperament, gift, and profession, *pictura* with *poesis*. But this union happened now to coincide with a general drift of poetic spirit and form which rendered the mixture especially valuable. The enormous increase in visual appeal which dated from Coleridge and Scott has perhaps, by strenuous effort, been at last made something like an established dogma in books, but it may be questioned whether it is even yet thoroughly understood. And besides standing in this general relation to the group from Coleridge to Keats, Rossetti stood in a more special one to their great *diadochi*—Tennyson and Browning. It was not merely accident or commission, it was Fate and metaphysical aid that made Rossetti illustrate 'The Lady of Shalott', and 'Mariana in the South', and 'Sir Galahad', and that marvellous series of 'Stanzas for Pictures', as he might himself have termed them, which forms the central appeal of 'The Palace of Art'.

But Rossetti had carried the marriage of the two arts, and the concurrent deepening and varying of the appeal to word-music, further still. If the volume of 1870 was to a slight extent—through that belatedness which has been noted—robbed of its due freshness of attack by things like Morris's 'Golden Wings' and 'Praise of My Lady', like Swinburne's 'Ballads of Life and Death' and 'Madonna Mia', there was no possibility of mistaking the independence and originality of the general tone. This was partly given, beyond doubt, by the poet's practice in translation from the early poets of his ancestral country. But Rossetti, though only an Englishman of the quarter blood, was extremely English by acquired *ethos*, and if he had imitated one of his uncles (who changed 'Polidori' to 'Polydore') and had called himself 'Rossiter' there would have been good warrant for it. There is nothing in the least exotic or affected about 'Jenny' or (to anyone at all lettered) in 'The Burden of Nineveh', while what may seem to half-read critics the most extravagant preciousnesses can be more than paralleled from Shakespeare.

Indeed, as for the hundredth, or in the Latin sense '*six*-hundredth', time I turn over the volume (on the dainty end-papers of which the Guernsey bookseller was kind enough to impress his respectable name and place of business) I feel once more, as I have often felt, its remarkable freshness and variety. People used to be, and to some extent still are, fond of speaking of Rossetti as if his atmosphere were like that depicted in the one healthy and amusing novel that Ernest Feydeau by some miracle succeeded in writing—that of a heavy-curtained studio full of bric-à-brac and perfumed with incense, where you were expected to smoke nothing but hashish and eat nothing but preserved ginger. 'Lord, what fools *such* mortals be!' Of course it was trying the average reader high to begin with 'The Blessed Damozel'—one of the sublimest things in poetry; but what reader, unless he was 'only an excellent person' or only a Philistine dunce, could miss something of its sublimity, its passion, its music, and that sense of vastness which many poets have tried to give but which hardly anybody but Milton and Dante (for even Hugo is more terrestrial and oceanic, less of the universal) has achieved? And then came the contrast of 'Love's Nocturn' with Time and Space exchanged for its own 'murmuring courts' of dream, and its first example of the complicated but never-entangled metres (the 'Damozel' at least *looks* simple) in which the poet was to be almost supreme. 'Troy Town', 'Eden Bower' and others might be more questionable—not that they are not beautiful in themselves, but that this refrain-ballad trick, unless most carefully managed, is apt to irritate some even of the very elect. But 'The Burden of Nineveh' comes to console these very persons. At first the poem was perhaps, if anything, over-praised; it has since, I believe, been a mark of one kind of superiority to dismiss it as slightly 'Victorian'—word of as fatal effect as 'Potztausend!' in 'Up the Rhine'. It is certainly a very great thing. 'The Staff and Scrip' and 'A Last Confession' (clearly Browningesque) and 'Dante at Verona' may be passed by—with no disrespect—to come once more to 'Jenny'. I do not think that I quite did this justice when it first appeared; after forty more years' reading of poetry I think of it very highly indeed. It is practically unique, though it makes a good pendant to the 'Burden'; I do not know how anything like it could be produced except by taking Musset at his very best in two different moods, beating up with a little good Baudelaire, and straining repeatedly through an English sieve of our finest texture in *genre* poetry. But, alas! this detailed comment takes too much room. How the peculiar Rossettian conception of the Ballad triumphs to the utmost of its actual form in 'Sister Helen' (to be afterwards purged of all apparent trick and perfected miraculously in 'Rose Mary'); and the sleepy exquisiteness of 'The Stream's Secret'; the anticipation of the 'In Memoriam' revival in 'My Sister's Sleep', and the great Emblem-poem of 'The Card-Dealer', and the translations—all must go. But the sonnets of the 'House of Life', of the 'Pictures' series, and the others cannot be passed so lightly.

It shocks some good folk very much if you call Dante and Christina Rossetti the greatest sonnet writers in English next to Shakespeare. Indeed the tongue that so speaks is apt to invite the incidence, upon the skull that covers its audacities, of shillelaghs many and violent from quite different quarters. Without any cudgel-play let it be said that the preference is based on a sense that form and matter are better married in Shakespeare and in the brother and sister (different as their form itself is) than in any others. This opinion extends hardly less to the 'Songs'. In these latter especially—for the sonnet insists on more uniformity of atmosphere, though the objects presented may be different—that variety which has been asserted above for Rossetti, and which has been so seldom granted him, appears. 'Love-Lily', that marvellous thing 'The Wood-spurge', and 'The Sea's Limits' are all perfect, but they might almost have been written by three different poets; and 'The Sea's Limits' at least is worthy of any poet that any language can show.

I once knew a most reprehensible taker of licences with the English language who used to talk of the 'Paradisaical scrunch' of the Poetic Moment. He had probably been reading Whitman. But I know what he meant; and I am happy to say that I have felt it thousands of times and hope to feel it hundreds more. Considering the small bulk of the work, even with translations and the gleaned odds and ends that have been added to the two original volumes (the second of which largely repeated the first) there are very few poets indeed who are so liberal of these delectable pangs as Rossetti. In 'Sibylla Palmifera', for instance, there is one in almost every line.

You may—to use its own phrase—'draw in as simply as your breath' the majestic picture that is constructed for you—or rather that rises like an emanation—as the verses accrue; you may hear, soothingly enough, the music of the rhythm and word-sound; you may understand without effort or difficulty the atmosphere of attraction which is added. But all the while, and in addition likewise, the bright and poignant shafts of phrase pierce to the joints and marrow of the soul, healing and charming as they pierce, but piercing all the same.

> Under the arch of Life, where Love and Death,
> Terror and mystery, guard her shrine, I saw
> Beauty enthroned.

In old time persons—probably not nearly such fools as many of us to-day—used to write, or at least were accused of writing, folios on a single text. I think one might write at least a considerable quarto on this one sonnet—even on this opening clause. And even then it would be impossible to expound the 'passionate and irretrievable' beauty of it—to use its own characteristic words. Irretrievable, but not irrenewable: for if all passion, as Bossuet says, has *quelque chose d'infini* in it, the infinite may defy exact recovery of moments but is at any rate incapable of exhaustion.

Poetry of this kind is as various as its subjects and practically itself defies—as poetry always should—too general analysis. It can make whatever it touches poetry; and that is the test. But it may be once more permitted to point out how completely erroneous is the notion that Rossetti's only singing garments are copes of stiff brocade and mitres of mystical design.

> You know not what a book you seem,
> Half-read by lightning in a dream,

if it has the imagination of Coleridge in the thought, has the directness of Dryden in the expression. In all the myriad attempts at word-description of physical beauty, where will you find a simpler phrasing of combined technical knowledge and sensuous appreciation than:

> The shadows where the cheeks are thin,
> And pure wide curve from cheek to chin?

And these things are not in the least inconsistent with the Donne-like 'metaphysicality' of some of the sonnets and the Keatsian iridescence of others. Nay, the *other* profession—the pure painting—

never interferes with this poetry. It is Ancilla Domini, not a meddlesome mistress nor a termagant wife.

King David knew something about poetry, and though when he spoke to Ahimelech he was not thinking of it, the words of his speech suit the poetry of all the greater poets as few others do: 'There is none like that: Give it me.' Every wise lover of poetry may apply them to Rossetti. And if the neophyte wants guidance to a single poem combining a certain bulk with poignancy of interest, splendour of colour, power and variety of metre, passion, pathos, intoxicating quality, grip of individual phrase—if he wants something as unique as 'The Ancient Mariner' itself, let him say, 'Give me "Rose Mary".'

The Bookman, June, 1911.

ANDREW LANG IN THE 'SEVENTIES—AND AFTER[1]

EVEN before 1870 the Press had quite got rid of most if not all the disadvantages which in earlier years had hung about it, and which had deterred men of some social and undoubted intellectual rank from doing it service. No more had not merely the neophyte but the journalist of some experience outside as well as inside journalism to think himself lucky if he could clear ten shillings by a full morning's work: only in the remotest country villages did old ladies deplore the fate of their nieces who married contributors to penny papers. The lift which had been given, in respect of more or less known contributorship, by the *Edinburgh* and the *Quarterly*, by Blackwood and Fraser, had, with less or more of the element of 'knownness' extended its influence to daily and weekly prints; and men leaving Oxford and Cambridge had for a full generation, though perhaps as a rule under some pretence of by-work on their way to Bench of this or that kind, taken the Press's sovereigns.

Anybody of tolerable intelligence could of course see that this new Island which had risen from the waves, though providing comfortable colony-places and wholesome food for respectable people in a very satisfactory manner, was in a way a sort of Island of the Sirens—of the Sirens in their proper vocation, which it must be remembered, though it often is not, was not so much to gobble sailors up or drown them as to keep them from their business and prevent their reaching nobler goals than it could itself provide. I believe there are some people who regard or affect to regard my friend of nearly forty years, the late Mr. Andrew Lang, as having been to some extent a Victim of this Sirenity of the Press and it may be worth while to consider this, with some other points about him.

I did not know Lang in his very earliest literary days, for though he was a fellow of my own College, Merton, his fellowship only began some months after my Postmastership ended; and though it actually followed from this that we had been for some years undergraduates together, it happened that I was very little in his college, Balliol. He had come up rather late, having passed through two Scottish Universities, St. Andrews and Glasgow, but I doubt whether anybody ever spent, either in northern or southern Academies, days more preparative for a literary life, than he had when

[1] An address prepared for the Royal Society of Literature 'and read to that body by Sir John Squire, deputising for the aged absent lecturer.'

he first listened to the Siren's voice. Indeed my doubt would be audacious enough to extend itself further, and question whether anybody, undergraduate or don, Oxonian or Cantab, about the year 1869 possessed knowledge of ancient and modern literature as literature, coupled with power to make use of that knowledge in a literary way, to a greater extent than Lang.

At the same time nobody was ever less of the typical imaginary pedant or merely bookish person than he was. Some physical defects —at the very time when he had just published his first book in 1872 considerable doubt was entertained by the faculty whether he was not hopelessly consumptive—prevented him from being a great practical sportsman. But he used to inform his friends, with just pride but perfect consciousness of the double edgedness of the classification, that authorities in cricket had ranked him as 'a change bowler' and he never lost interest in the game or (though to a somewhat less extent) in several others, during the whole of his life. In what used to be, and perhaps always should be the greatest of all Press subjects whether on the more abstract or still more on the party side, he could with difficulty be got to show any interest. I used to say of him that he couldn't be a Liberal and wouldn't be a Tory. He did not with any willingness treat religious subjects, while Science in the more limited sense but with the largest capital, was not his business, yet the *Encyclopædia* held few other subjects on which he could not write something worth reading.

I do not know in what paper Lang made the first of his many thousand appearances in periodicals. He had, I think, family connections with the *Saturday Review*, which had already for some years exemplified and harboured the great though rather indefinable change in English journalism. New papers, which did not always live to be old, were constantly starting in the late 'sixties and early 'seventies: and to one of them at least—most virtuous and hospitable but ill by any profit rewarded, though it kept itself alive and contributed to the alive-keeping of its contributors for a considerable period—to the *Academy*, he was, I think, a supporter from the beginning. But the fact was that no editor who had the very slightest fitness for his business could hesitate about annexing anything of Lang's that was offered to him and promptly demanding more. I have had myself no short or small experience of editing or assisting to edit; a very large experience in contributing; and, until quite recently, what it is not, I think, extravagant to call an immense experience in reading this division of literature. I do not hesitate to say that, allowing for his not taking service in the political, the religious and some technical departments, Lang was quite the king of all the contributors to 'the papers' that I have known. His vessel did not carry—thanks to the limitations just mentioned it did not require—such heavy metal as H. D. Traill's; I fancy that it may itself have been of slightly too heavy a draught in respect of knowledge on the part of the reader to be able to skim the waves of universal popularity as did, especially latterly, the craft of our common friend Sir Edmund Gosse. But for a compound of scholarship and lighthandedness, of multilegence and complete freedom from pedantry, of what may be called literary good manners, infinite wit and a peculiar humour he had, I think, in his own generation no equal—certainly no superior.

And wherever it was first shown there I am sure appeared, though it could hardly be separately recognised till it was followed by something else, a peculiarity which has not yet been mentioned but which depended without doubt on things that have been. And this was Lang's extraordinary individuality. You could not, after you had seen a little of his writing, mistake it for any one else's or any one else's for his. Nor did this individuality depend upon any tricks of style in the lower sense like the snipsnap of Macaulay; the chaotic riches of Carlyle; the repetitions and word-groupings of Arnold; the infused blank verse (in their so different kinds) of Ruskin and Dickens; the elaborate rhythm and colouring of Pater. It was most commonly said to be like Thackeray's, and no doubt there was a strong resemblance of spirit; but I really doubt whether the greatest similarity between their manners was not the fact that neither had *any* manner easy to analyse or capable of being pinned out and down. Only great incompetence or great prejudice—for choice perhaps a skilful combination of the two—could fail to recognise this idiosyncrasy. I remember talking about him, not long after his death, with a person by no means incompetent but the contrary, a scholar, a man familiar with society, an expert in various kinds of press-work, but one, I think, who did not like Lang either personally or critically as much as I did. He had been indulging in some little drawbacks and *distinguos* to some of my commendatory remarks; but when I came to this point of absolute individuality he boggled no more. He fully admitted that what Lang could give you nobody else could; that he copied nobody and that nobody had ever succeeded in copying him. I have indeed been told that some wicked men in clubs have ticketed others as 'Sham Langs' but the resemblance was merely caricatural in personal ways and simply non-existent in literary form.

Curiously, but rather conveniently and almost immediately after writing the preceding paragraph, I saw in print a description of Lang's style as 'a waggish drawl'. The context, unless it was ironical, seemed to show no hostile intention in this; but hostile or friendly, serious or ironical, it was extremely, though no doubt not quite unintentionally, illuminative. As adequate, or even as partially correct, one could not accept it for a moment. Lang's speech might from anybody who did not intend to be specially complimentary be called a drawl; I have been told that his consciousness of it was one of the reasons for his refusing professorships though he did sometimes lecture. But how his printed matter could produce on any one the effect of drawling is a mystery to me—the drawl must have lain in the mind's ear that read not in the mind's mouth or pen that wrote. And this explanation, so frequently applicable in changed applications to mis-estimates and misunderstandings is even more valuable as regards the 'waggish'. Of course if anybody takes this word to be a synonym for 'humorous' we begin to see a great light—for humorous 'in a quiet way' (as a good-for-nothing satirist-contemporary of those days observed of something else) Lang always was, except perhaps sometimes, though rarely, when humour was doubtfully in place. But 'waggish' he was never—or very seldom, on a few occasions when I think he did it on purpose by way of throwing more contempt on his subject. Yet the description is, as was said, valuable. It explains his immense popularity, especially in the number of miscellaneous and non-political matters that he wrote about for so many years in the *Daily News*, because it is quite possible that a certain proportion of the *vulgus* did take this quiet humour for a variety of the drawn-out joking they admire on the stage. And it is possible that others may have disliked and may now dislike it because they took it at the same 'angle of the moral oxygen' and did not like that angle, not being able to see round it.

It was not till just this side of the middle of the 'seventies that I actually met Lang; for during their earlier years I had been living first in Guernsey and then in the north of Scotland. But I had, of course, seen a good deal of his work in different places and it so happened that his first book *Ballads and Lyrics of Old France* dealt with a subject which (partly I suppose owing to my residence in the Channel Islands with Hugo for neighbour though not acquaintance) I had myself taken up some years earlier. The title, however, which has just been given was not the whole one; for 'and other poems' was added and these other poems supply a considerable part of the matter. To begin with a book of verse has always been or more less the proper thing—in fact I believe it is not improper even now. But it was not the proper thing as yet, though it came to be so before very long, to begin with a book of prose compacted of short newspaper articles. I have sometimes been sorry that the double entry did not then prevail: for the contrast-combination in Lang's case would have been very remarkable, and might have 'set' the idiosyncrasy of the writer with a useful decision at an early period, before the reading world. As it was, the world read the articles with eagerness as they appeared and then forgot all about them individually while rather neglecting the verse, which is certainly not negligible. Probably few people have had a better right to claim, as (though in different words) he did claim, the benefit of Anne Evans's great definition of humour 'thinking in jest but feeling in earnest' than Lang: but the 'feeling' never got proper recognition. Its verse expression was somewhat unlucky in point of time. There is not very much in this particular book, though some of the translations necessarily employ it, of the formal French versification which a little later became so common from his and other hands: but the whole is more or less of that pre-Raphaelite colour which was having its day if it had not fully had it, and much more than less of that great school of nineteenth-century poetry which after starting under Keats and Shelley, and restarting after a short interval under Tennyson and Browning had with no interval at all, taken the pre-Raphaelite turn.

Now fashion (which if not exactly a synonym for 'day' is closely connected with it) though not necessarily either a bad or a good thing, is well known to have perhaps more bad than good effects and consequences. However good it is in itself it can be exaggerated or caricatured and by unskilful imitation turned to bad. If it is bad in itself, why, it *is* bad, and there's no more to be said. Whatever its intrinsic quality, people are apt to get tired of it to its own unfair disadvantage; or to make mistakes about other things which are not the fashion or, worst of all, to take more fancy to these *because* they are not the fashion. Comparatively few are those—and profoundly grateful to Providence or the Muses should those few be—who can appreciate all poetry which is poetry whether it be Job's or the present Poet Laureate's, Donne's or Dryden's, Sappho's or Christina Rossetti's, Cowper's or Mr. Swinburne's. To these fortunate ones—perhaps there is no one who possesses this best of good fortunes entirely and absolutely—date and subject, form and language, are of comparative unimportance: many instances have been given, some certainly not merely jocular, of recognition of the poetry without understanding of the language.

Their critical appreciation has something in it of water-divining or reaction to atmosphere—the rather hackneyed but beautiful word *aura* would be better still. I do not think many people who possess this sense—for one can give it place in the rather numerously occupied room of the sixth senses—have refused its satisfactory exercise to Lang's verse work—though some of them may not think that he had the faculty in its highest degree. Much is translation, and translation of famous things in pure lyric, where, it has sometimes been said, you must, to succeed, be as good a poet as your original was, and even then you will give another good thing not the same.

Therefore when you find the poetical atmosphere or *aura* in a translation the translator must be entitled to the credit of some of it: and I think it is to be found in the book I am speaking of as well as in the more definitely and temporarily fashionable *Ballades* of some years later. And a very uncommon talent, not easily distinguishable from genius, was displayed in the prose translation of the *Odyssey* which he did in collaboration with another dead friend, and for some of the latter years of his life a colleague of mine, S. H. Butcher. I think I have heard this book described by a person professionally connected with bookselling as one of the most popular translations from the classics he has himself known. That it was at the same time one of the most scholarly might be put down, not merely by Lang's enemies but by a not ill-natured reader, to the fact of Butcher's participation, but that his attribution would be insufficient ought to be seen by any one scholar enough himself to appreciate not merely the singly turned out Theocritus, but almost every part of Lang's work. That he was not, in certain restricted senses of 'scholarship', a great master of it, may be true enough. But he was penetrated in a way which was getting rarer in his own time and has been increasing in rarity ever since, with a sense of Greek and Roman literature which, when it was more common, was frequently disjoined from any extensive knowledge of English, and was very seldom conjoined with any knowledge of other modernity except perhaps French which itself did not ascend beyond the *grand siècle* with Montaigne or Rabelais or both. There was, of course, in a few cases and at one time a certain acquaintance with Italian, the coming in and the going out of which have always both been rather mysteries to me. Every girl from Scott's heroines to my own sisters seems to have been taught Dante and Petrarch and Tasso and even Ariosto as a matter of course. Have these been changed for civism and genetics?

Now how many modern languages Lang knew, in a fashion capable of satisfying the examiners, I do *not* know. But I do know that all his work was, as I have said, saturated with knowledge of literature ancient and modern.

Of course some one may say: 'As far as the printed Lang of the 'seventies is concerned, we can form our own opinions: we only need you for your accidental and illegitimate advantage of having known him personally.' There may be something in this, but not much. In the first place, by far the larger part of the printed 'Lang of the 'seventies' never got *re*printed at all, and though the extraordinary 'kenspeckleness' of his manner might enable a tolerably keen-sighted person to follow him all through the files of the *Daily News* and the volumes of the *Saturday* as well as in the signed matter of the *Academy* and elsewhere—that is not exactly everybody's job. There is, however, something more to be said of the work before one turns to the man. I have seen this very 'dispersedness' (as Shakespeare or Shakespeare's stage-direction-maker might call it) brought as a sort of charge from quite early dates to almost or quite this day against him. There is no doubt that the public does like to have something definite by which—if we are amiable we say 'to remember', if not quite so 'to call' a man. It is not mere nastiness to say that Gray owes more than half his fame to the less intrinsic advantage of being 'the author of the *Elegy*'. There is particular luck in this because a whole department of poetry and of literature is thus conveniently pinned to a man's coat or vice versa: 'Gray? Oh yes! he wrote the *Elegy*'. '*Elegy?* Oh yes, that's the thing that Gray wrote.' And so with many others. Now in all the small and closely spaced type of the columns that stand under Lang's name in the catalogue of the London Library you cannot, I fear, pick out a single entry with which Lang can be thus differentially and monopolisingly ticketed. There are or were people who would tell you that he intended *Helen of Troy* to be such a ticket and that it is only a failure of one. I venture to differ with the first half of this: but there is a certain amount of truth about the second, though I think the book deserved more success than it obtained. What was said above as to ill luck of times and seasons comes in here with quiet force. But if anybody desires to test Lang's poetic value in the first instance, at less expense of effort, let him read the 'Ballade of his Choice of a Sepulchre' and the Burnaby sonnet. At the worst he will not have wasted his time: for a result of dissatisfaction will show that he does not himself know poetry when he sees it and had better let it alone. Some people not so hopeless prefer, I believe, one or other of the Gordon epicedes to the Burnaby one: but that is only an instance of the common error of judging by subject not treatment.

The mention of the Sepulchre piece—one of the most charming things of the kind that, in a tolerably wide familiarity with verse, I know—will lead with peculiar propriety to what may be called the specially epitaphic part of this paper. Dismissing for a moment Lang the architect, and artist, what was Lang the man? There has been some talk about this lately: and as only a comparatively small minority of the hearers, that is to say, readers, of this talk can be supposed to be in a position to check it by extensive personal experience, it is perhaps just as well that those who *are* in such a position should put in their evidence. I may have said it before in print—but what I say twice is not necessarily untrue—that I do not think anybody outside his own family knew Lang by frequent companionship and conversation much better than I did. For not a few years we walked together—people walked then and consequently talked—for about three parts of the length of more specially habitable London, two or three times a week. And if any one should say, 'Ah! he couldn't get rid of you!', this is futile; for he could easily have done so. Being a faster though not a much more legible writer than myself, he had always done his leader ten minutes or a quarter of an hour before me, and needed no other excuse, if any at all had been wanted, to go.

This frequentation continued on the scale mentioned from nearly the middle of the 'seventies to not far from that of the 'eighties and on a somewhat reduced scale (I had given up contributing to one of the papers concerned) for another ten, with all sorts of miscellaneous companionships. When I moved to Scotland in 1895 our meetings were necessarily fewer and farther between: but I don't think he often missed coming to see me in Edinburgh on his annual way to St. Andrews. Now I cannot say as Rupert, Lord Derby, said on being sarcastically asked as to the qualities of a member of his cabinet that he 'had heard no complaints'. At no time in his life I should think, and at none of the greater part of that life which I knew, was he universally popular. I have always thought more or less, and since the complaints have multiplied and became acrimonious I have thought still more of two incidents, one in literature, and one in life, which bear upon the matter. The first is the case of the immortal Scrub, who was sure that people in the company were talking of him because they laughed consumedly. It was not Lang's habit to laugh consumedly; but he sometimes had an air of not being violently interested in things and persons, which people who were not oversure of themselves might mistake. It is curious that in such a case it should not occur to anybody that perfect immunity from discomfort is provided by simply not troubling yourself whether the other person is interested in you or not: but unfortunately it seldom does occur. The other story, which in fact had nothing to do personally with Lang, is still perhaps illuminative. A thousand years ago, or perhaps a little less, there happened in a country drawing-room, about afternoon calling-time, to be present a sufficiently ordinary company—say, one married couple, one at least temporarily single man and four or five ladies, married and unmarried. The coupled male having some appointment or other left his wife and went forth, bestowing a quite amiable, but not theatrically enthusiastic nod-bow on the other man, whom he did not know very intimately. When he met his wife at home later she said (I fear, laughing), 'Ah! *you* don't know what a state of mind you put Mr. Dash in this afternoon. As soon as you had shut the door he got up and began to walk furiously up and down saying, "Why won't that fellow shake hands with me?"' Now it happened that 'that fellow' had very recently left Oxford where, a thousand years ago or a little less, handshaking was, whatever may be the case now, quite out of fashion. With men of your own College you hardly did it at all. With outcollege men, as a civility, you probably did it if you met them at the end of term just before they were going down, and perhaps at the beginning of it when you met them for the first time. At casual meetings, unless there were formal introductions, never.

Now this not quite unamusing story came to my knowledge before I ever knew Lang: and as I have already said he had nothing personally to do with it. But not very long after I did know him I began to think of him in connection with it, and recent things have brought the remembrance and resemblance freshly home. Several people seem to have interpreted Lang's manner as that of one not thinking them worth shaking hands with, when as a matter of fact he was probably not thinking about them at all except as coincidences of existence. I suppose he could not be called invariably affable; but your invariably affable person requires a certain extra touch from Providence to prevent him from being frequently intolerable. Now in all those years, many of them thickly frequented years, of which I have spoken—I never found his company other than agreeable. In the earliest days he did tell somebody—at least the somebody told *me* so—that I laughed like a character in *Les Cloches de Corneville.* But as I didn't know how the person in the *Cloches de Corneville* laughed and he didn't say it to me, I fear that I was not much moved.

As a rule you could not have better company, of your own sex; I have known no better story-teller. To this day, speaking as a critical Literary Epicurean, I do not know for which of two heard story-tellings I ought most to thank my stars—Mr. Anstey Guthrie's *Vice Versa* told on the eve of publication by Lang who knew it in process of manufacture, or one of Mr. Kipling's, recounted by its author before he had actually put it to press. But the first experience was, of course, an exception: and Lang was quite as good at ordinary conversation on a great number of subjects: politics and religion, as above, being almost the only ones excluded. Providence had further been kind in pre-arranging that though I was utterly unfitted for either of his two favourite sports, cricket and angling, I have never been tired of reading reports of cricket and possessed a brother-in-law who was sometimes allowed (except by the others) to be the best fisherman in Hampshire—so that I was not a philistine or an ignoramus on either subject. And as for books, one more thing at least is specially worth saying on that head. I do not think I ever met a man so utterly free—I am sure I never met one more so—from one of the commonest and most contemptible of the plagues that beset the 'littery gent' be he poet or proseman or both—jealousy of others who write about the subjects which he himself, more or less, specially prefers. 'That's *my* thunder' is the motto of the Dennises all over literary history. I have known lifelong hatreds spring from no apparent cause but this. But I never saw a touch of it in Lang after I knew him: and I am entitled to speak on the matter because, as I have mentioned already, he and I both began with the same subject—Old French—and I was, before very long, luckier in getting hold of creditable and profitable employment on this subject than he was. And he actually introduced me, if not directly to these, to others which were likely to lead to them. But it was quite impossible for him to do anything ungenerous, even as it was impossible for him to do anything unliterary. And this last word may give us a keynote to a brief conclusion or summing up of the whole matter of Andrew Lang both in the 'seventies and as long as I knew him. I have said and now repeat that with him literary did not mean pedantic. I don't think I ever knew anyone whom it would be more absurd to call a pedant: it was not much more adequately synonymed by 'bookish', for that word generally implies limitation to books. The Muses have, with the vulgar, a bad reputation for neglecting the garments, the manners, the age, and other trimmings (as one may call them) of their lovers; they did not do so with Lang. And the quality of his literariness itself was, if not as unique as his delivery of it, very unusual. It was pervasive but not obtrusive; varied but not superficial; facile to a wonderful degree, but never trivial or trumpery. It may be that in one way it did not concentrate itself enough—did not leave two or three big books instead of forty or thirty little ones; and in another concentrated itself too much by writing not very small books on subjects which might have been adequately treated in not very long essays. So also in his behaviour there may sometimes have been a little too much abstraction, and too much indifference to the existence of those agreeable folk who always put the worst construction on everything. I once heard him abused for affectation because he had lunched off two oysters and a pancake. What use to suggest to this kind of abuser or accuser that he probably confined himself to the two because he did not want a third and to the one because he did not want a second? Yet I venture to imagine that explanations of this kind lodged with the recording Angel would not be rejected, though that weary official might perhaps suggest that they were quite unnecessary. Meanwhile if Lang is (more's the pity!) gone, and some of his work gone with him or recoverable only with infinite labour and pains, there is a great body of it accessible; and the old 'Take it and Read it' may be said with unusual confidence to anybody hesitating about the matter. 'Selections', of course, suggest themselves and have been suggested. It is possible to conceive not merely one but more than one which would supply reading of the most refreshing kind. But it would be an extraordinarily difficult job; and while selections often fail to satisfy their readers this selection would be so unlikely to satisfy the selector that he would probably never get it finished. So the *Tolle, lege*, had better be completed with the most elegant Latin available for whatever of Lang's you come across. It is ten to one you will not go wrong.

1929.

BATH IN LITERATURE

BATH in Literature starts for me, and has long started, with a passage in our oldest letters; doubtfully certain in its application perhaps, but far too good to be given up without the positive reasons which do not yet exist, or at least are not known. This is the so-called 'Ruin', the finest to some tastes of our very oldest Old English or Anglo-Saxon poems. It is not merely a fragment, but what one may call an internally dilapidated fragment; and no names are mentioned in it. But with the undoubted facts—that Bath was a Roman station; that all Roman stations were ruined more or less by the time this piece could have been written; and that the hot springs mentioned in it exist in Bath to this day, and do not exist in any other suitable locality—the identification of poem and place is scarcely rash. Indeed, as such identifications go, it is almost what classical scholars are wont to describe as 'certissima'. And with at least an equal amount of certainty, it 'starts' Bath in Literature on a much more exalted plane than any legends about Bladud or any discussions about Sul. For the poem, doubly a ruin as it is in subject and form, is not merely a good one, but has elements at least of greatness.

One had thought, or at least hoped, that the largely increased study in English Universities, and even schools, of older English literature, had as a consequence increased the knowledge of things like this, but its latest editor, Miss Kershaw, seems to be doubtful. The 'Ruin', unfortunately, is a ruin in two senses as just said, for though the 'mickle English book of various things wrought lay-wise', which Bishop Leofric gave to Exeter Cathedral nearly nine hundred years ago, is still as a whole quite safe there, somebody at some time amused himself by dropping hot ashes (not even tobacco ashes) upon two parts of it, with ghastly results of defacement. To make things worse in one way, but better in another, it has some unique words in it; and wholly for the better, it shows what is rare in Old English poems of anything like its age, attempts or chance-medleys at the greatest grace of accomplished English verse—rhyme. Worked out word by word it is rather a puzzle, though ingenious folk have even succeeded in identifying the red tiles and plaster, as well as other features of the existing Roman Baths. But the best thing about the piece is the general impression which its dilapidated details cannot hide, and which I may, I hope, be allowed to represent in words of my own, written some thirty years ago in *A Short History of English Literature*. 'Perhaps the deepest and noblest of all emotions, not merely personal and sensual—the feeling for the things that are long enough ago—finds expression, and worthy expression, as the poet looks on the masonry shattered by fate, the crumbling mortar gemmed by hoarfrost;[1] as he imagines the once stately heights reduced to ruinous heaps, the warriors who sat there, the hot baths boiling in their lakelike cistern, the busy market-place silent, the merry meadhalls overwhelmed by the fiat of destiny.'

I have always thought since (some time even before I wrote what has just been quoted) I read this first, that we have here what may, in more than the slang sense, be called the bones of a great poem, and even some of the flesh of one. But with its greatness there is undoubtedly mixed (as happens very often with great poems) sadness. There is no sadness except for very punctilious or very sensitive folk, in the next great appearance [2] of Bath in literature—next with the trifling interval of at least some half millennium in writing and probably nearer a whole millennium in subject. The punctilious may object to Chaucer's immortal Wife of Bath that her morality was, despite her own ingenious defences of it, very dubious; and the sensitive may add that by her own confession she was a fearful plague to most of her numerous husbands. But let us hope (with some dubitation) that her pilgrimage made up for her earlier peccadilloes; and if we may believe her (which it would be rude not to do), all her husbands admitted considerable easements to her tyranny. Speaking with that exactness which is incumbent on the scholar, one is bound to warn readers that, though in titles and citation she is always called the Wife '*of* Bath', the poet in his text only says that she was 'of *Beside* Bath', purposely, I think, if wickedly (and Chaucer was nothing if not wicked in the milder sense) leaving to his commentators the business of deciding where this 'beside' was. Depend upon it, he knew the way of commentators well enough. I believe some—relying on the 'cloth-making' of which she had such mastery, and of which she wore from coverchief to hose such beautiful specimens—have pitched upon Bradford-on-Avon. But never mind that, 'Wife *of* Bath' she is till the day when

[1] Miss Kershaw would translate 'lichen', but details of this sort, of which there are many, do not matter here.

[2] There are appearances between, for instance in Geoffrey of Monmouth, but they are hardly 'great'.

there shall be no more books, and no more memory in those who have read them.

And perhaps, though there may be more poetical passages in the 'Canterbury Tales' than those which deal with her, there are none which exhibit better that wonderful 'comprehensiveness' in a certain way, which Dryden rightly attributes to Chaucer in what is itself for its age a wonderfully comprehensive criticism of him, prefacing his own paraphrase of the 'Wife's Tale'. The notice of her in the general Prologue, with a few hints of something further, is almost purely pictorial; nowhere is that extraordinary skill in word-painting, which has tempted so many actual painters, better shown—indeed hardly anywhere does it make actual illustration more superfluous. Then there is the very long, very naughty, and immensely amusing particular Prologue to her own Tale. It is so long that her companions remark on its continuance; and so naughty that Dryden himself, who was certainly not squeamish, didn't dare to paraphrase it; though its intensely natural and dramatic properties make it hardly offensive at all—certainly far less offensive than many things much less 'improper' in substance and elaborately decent in language. And there is the Tale itself, which, if not absolutely constructed with a view to Mrs. Grundy's approval, has nothing that need offend anyone else, and though satirical in a pretty high degree, is almost 'pretty' in another sense.

Now for a time everybody who could read in England (certainly not quite the majority) read Chaucer himself. Then after a brief period of obscuration, everybody who read English poetry read Dryden's version of this particular Tale, and Dryden's popularity had hardly entered upon its own period of obscuration when a return was made to Chaucer himself. Since that, more and more people have become acquainted with him every decade and almost every year. And so there have been only two, and those short, gaps since 1400, during which any English reader with the slightest taste for literature could fail to connect the name of Bath at least with the name of a great poet, and with some more or less accurate idea of one of not the least characteristic of his works.

As almost everybody who wrote or read English literature during the fifteenth and early sixteenth centuries knew Chaucer, this excellent dame (one cannot exactly call her a 'lady', but 'dame' was the style in which she was actually addressed) may be said to have kept Bath in literature as well as in memory, during all that time. But the actual time did not contribute much to the keeping.

Indeed, it did not contribute very much to literature itself. Neither does Bath figure at all largely in the great Elizabethan library, whether that be limited strictly to the Queen's reign or extended as usual later. It was bad luck, doubtless, that Shakespeare, though he had a great deal to do with the northern end of Gloucestershire, seems never to have come to the southern.

Drayton was essentially a Warwickshire man, and notice or no notice of any place in such an *omnium gatherum* as the 'Polyolbion' would hardly require insertion or comment in such a composition as this which I am now endeavouring to put together; nor could Spenser's 'Wondrous Bath', mentioned currently in the 'Pageant of the Rivers', receive more notice. He was a northerner in one sense, a Londoner in another. In fact, London began to be too much of a magnet for everybody, wherever they were born; and though the mild genius of Samuel Daniel allowed itself to be born and also to die at Beckington, which is not so very far away, I cannot remember that he ever mentions our city. In the troubles of the mid-seventeenth, the Pyrrhic victory of Lansdown may have attracted threnodies on the relatively numerous and disastrous deaths of some of the very best of the King's younger champions; and the medicinal virtues of the place were beginning to be scientifically (more or less) celebrated. But of anything in serious literature like the 'Ruin'—of anything in comic, satiric, and miscellaneous literature like the three memorials of the 'Wife of Bath'—if anything at all survives, it does not at the moment survive in my memory.

One has made what one could of a trifling thousand years or so. But it was not till England settled down at the Restoration that Bath really came into its own as regards literature, and literature found its own in Bath. Only eight years afterwards, in June 1668, Mr. Pepys took that merry journey—with his wife, and poor 'Deb' Willet (soon to be the occasion of terrible things) and the ever present Will Hewer and the mysterious Betty Turner—which led them by the rather roundabout way of Huntingdon, Bedford, Oxford ('a very sweet place'), Hungerford, Salisbury, and it would seem Warminister,[1] to Bath; going no further than to Bristol and staying a short time at Bath on the way back to judgment and Mrs. Pepys's red-hot tongs. She and Deb 'mightily joyed' at coming into Somersetshire, for they were both Somerset girls; and Samuel himself found the Baths, though not so large as he expected,

[1] The name is not given, but the route seems to identify 'a town' with Warminster.

'pleasant' when he went out that evening, tired as he was, with his landlord to inspect them. They all went to the Cross Bath next morning at four o'clock, that they might bathe before 'company' came. But company, much company, 'very fine ladies', did come, and it was all 'pretty enough', though finical Mr. Pepys doubted whether it was 'clean to go into the water, so many bodies together.' Apparently the wicked practice of the Bath chairmen, in extorting extra hire before they would carry you home, did not trouble him; and after two hours in the water (which the doctors would hardly allow now) he went home and to bed in the correct way, and 'sweated' another hour. After which the indefatigable creatures, at eleven, went to Bristol and saw Deb's family (who would hardly have been so kind to Mr. Pepys if they had known everything) and drank Bristol Milk (which is *not* Punch, as certain Pelagians do vainly talk, but glorified sherry) and came back to Bath at ten o'clock and spent the whole of the next day there. It was Sunday, and one deeply regrets to hear that 'in the great church a vain pragmatical fellow preached a ridiculous affected sermon.'

Perhaps these trifles may seem to occupy disproportionate space in a small room, but it is always difficult to tear oneself away from Pepys when one gets to him, and he dispenses one from troubling about his contemporaries. His usual companion, Evelyn (who would not exactly have liked to be called his companion) did, I believe, go to Bath, but I have not got him at hand now. Dryden himself probably knew it; for he certainly made one long stay, and perhaps some shorter ones, at his father-in-law, Lord Suffolk and Berkshire's place, Charlton Park, not many miles off. But I do not think he ever mentions it, except in connection with Chaucer. His enemy, Shadwell, who, badly as he wrote, and 'dull' as he certainly was, was no mean copyist of manners, was pre-engaged with eastern watering-places, Epsom and Bury St. Edmunds. And besides, one must hurry to the eighteenth century.

If a century and a city could be regarded as regiments—and much more difficult presentments have been effected by ingenious logicians —there can be little doubt that Bath might take the title of 'The Eighteenth Century's Own', and the eighteenth century, or a very large part of it, as far as its literature is concerned, that of 'Bath's Own'. The union was not at first so close as it was later; we do not think of the strictly Queen Anne men, Swift, Addison, and Steele, even of Gay and Pope, as much connected with Bath, though Gay's beloved and Swift's epistolarily flirted-with Duchess of Queensberry

—Prior's 'Kitty'—was one of the persons who, rebel to all others, submitted to Nash's benevolent tyranny. It is in the days of the Georges, especially the Second and Third, that 'The Marriage of Literature and Bath', as the Middle Ages would have put it, becomes closest; and it is a fact of curious and perhaps occult significance, that the last and brightest of the children of that marriage—the work of Miss Austen—was produced wholly before the death of George the Third himself, the extension of the fecundity into the nineteenth century balancing its less prolific and intimate character in the two first decades of the eighteenth.

'The Shapes' of this alliance, to use a striking phrase of Walt Whitman's, 'arise' in almost bewildering multitude and vividness. With Richardson, indeed, Bath did not agree—I agree with my regretted friend Mr. Austin Dobson, that it was much too lively for him. But his great enemy—or rather the infinitely greater novelist whom he thought his enemy, but who was much too generous to be so—Fielding, was almost a Bathonian—by no means merely in consequence of his friendship with Ralph Allen. Horace Walpole did not like Bath, and was not much in it; but I have always been pretty sure that this was a result of one of those quaint and rather affected filial pieties of his, because two of Bath's very greatest patrons, Pulteney and Chesterfield, had been his father's enemies. But Pulteney and Chesterfield themselves make a host between them; though the speeches of the one are not extant and the letters and 'characters' of the other have long been most unjustly undervalued. And though I do not know that the delightful verses that they jointly wrote on the more delightful Miss Lepel were written at Bath, they ought to have been, for they breathe at least one lighter part of the very spirit of the place in humour and rhythm:

Had I Hanover, Bremen and Verden,
  And likewise the Duchy of Zell,
I would part with them all for a farthing,
  To have my dear Molly Lepel.

I have already elsewhere requested the reader to remember: (1) that a great stir was being made about 'Bremen and Verden' at the time; (2) that Verden is to be pronounced like Cherwell and Derby; (3) that 'farden' was then not in the least a vulgarism, but the correct sound of the coin. These things observed, the little thing makes a *carillon* of the most delectable. And they always rang the bells at Bath when distinguished visitors came in those days.

I cannot remember, or even imagine, that Gray had much if anything to do with Bath, though Miss Speed might have attracted him if she had been there; and though Goldsmith wrote a Life of Nash, his own life was too much occupied with drudgery and wasting the hire thereof beforehand in London. But Smollett, whether he did or did not (I believe there is some dispute about this) regularly but unsuccessfully practise here in his earlier days, gave, in his latest and in *Humphrey Clinker* one of the liveliest, if not the most favourable (for though not quite so much here as elsewhere he was always a grumbler) of the contemporary sketches of its heyday in prose. For verse one must of course go chiefly to the once famous, and still in a fashion remembered, if not read, 'New Bath Guide'. It is still worth reading, and will amuse its readers, though the amusement is sometimes rather *broader* than it need be. But if Anstey sinned somewhat in this way, did not Polly Lawrence, the 'Pump Room Naiad', draw other verses, decidedly elegant and perfectly clean, from such an otherwise far from clean and very inelegantly 'crazy' personage as John Hall Stevenson? To readers of Boswell, Johnson's visit in 1776 with the Thrales (a visit which, through an audacious 'fish' for an invitation, Bozzy shared, paying for the hospitality by recording an unfavourable remark of the Doctor's on his hostess) is familiar. But the most noteworthy thing in it does not directly concern Bath itself, being the excursion to Bristol to inquire about Chatterton, with Johnson's characteristically rough but as characteristically generous and sound judgment of the unlucky 'whelp' of genius who had foolishly insulted him. The connections, however, with Bath of Mrs. Thrale herself, *Thralia dulcis*, the 'bright' (or is it 'light') 'papilionaceous creature' as Carlyle so happily calls her, were very much more frequent, and lasted very much longer, sometimes bringing with them those of Fanny Burney. Meanwhile one of its very greatest glories had been conferred on it, independently of other relations of his with it, by Sheridan in *The Rivals*. I unblushingly prefer this delightful thing not merely to Sheridan's other plays, but to everything else in eighteenth-century drama, except *She Stoops to Conquer*. For *The School for Scandal* is after all of the School of Congreve; and it is at least doubtful whether *The Critic* would have been written but for the *The Rehearsal*. *The Rivals* is *The Rivals* and suggests nothing else. Even Falkland and Julia are true to their time and place.

(I must beg pardon for this explosion, but one must explode occasionally.)

The brightest days of Bath were by no means closed at 1800, and what I have called 'Literature in Bath'—that is to say its connection as a place of visit or residence with literary persons—went on almost indefinitely. But as an actual scene of a contribution to great literature itself it figured almost finally (for the famous episode in *Pickwick* is after all an episode merely), though with extraordinary brightness, in *Northanger Abbey* at the beginning, and *Persuasion* towards the end, of the too brief career of their other 'inimitable' author. To say anything critical about these would be as perilous as it would be unnecessary. But it is safe as well as relevant to dwell a little on the 'extraordinary' way in which the locale is in a fashion *incorporated* with the story. By some curious fate, while I know England at large and the West in particular—at least as well as most people—I was never in Bath till I was nearly sixty, though I had been a devotee of 'Jane' before I was sixteen. But I have somehow always *seen* the place as the background of the two novels or the greater parts of them, and the first time that, just twenty years ago, I stood on Beechen Cliff, I was tempted, useless as I knew it to be, to look each side of me for 'those two *very* nice young ladies', Miss Catherine Morland and Miss Eleanor Tilney.

A slight return to the history of the visit of the Four Friends—though, as the Moses Pickwick who first excited Sam's wrath and then his alarm about the state of his master's spirits, was actually a Bathonian, the whole book in a way belongs to Bath—and we must, as they say, draw to a close. Exactly how Mr. Winkle managed to execute his remarkable feat of agility in running *round* the Crescent, I have never been able to understand. He could no doubt have done it in the Circus. But anyone who makes oversights of this sort a cause of serious quarrels with Dickens, deserves to have a new verse of the 'Three Jolly Postboys' extemporised for his benefit. And in other respects there is hardly a better part of that unique book, of which some free-thinking devotees have said that if everything else of its author, except *David Copperfield* and *Great Expectations*, were unknown, he would stand even higher than he does now.

It will probably be best, after the good old pantomime manner, to finish here with this blaze of fireworks. Almost exactly when Mr. Pickwick went, Landor came, or rather came back, and his coming occasioned the bodily presence of Dickens himself and not a few other *sommités* of nineteenth-century literature. Indeed, in the middle twenty years or thereabouts of the century, he, as he had done earlier, produced here some of his own great works, and committed some of his worst, or at least most foolish acts. For Landor was never really bad; even when he threw the cook out of the window at Florence, where that fortunate menial found something more spoilable than Bath stone, but much softer. And one might add many other things and persons newer and older, for scarcely a year passes without something being added to the literary history of Bath, and in the very last twelve months the pleasant 'Woodforde Diary' gave us fresh associations.

But I should not like to conclude without at least a mention of the latest possession, if he be also the latest loss, of Bath in the department of literature, my late friend, Mr. Frederic Harrison. One can go farther even than Landor, at whose death Mr. Harrison was almost entering middle age, to connect him chronologically with our succession. For if not in Bath, Mr. Harrison was, as Queen Berengaria says, 'somewhere else', a doubtless sturdy little boy of seven or eight, when Mr. Pickwick's disgraceful conduct at whist sent Miss Bolo home 'in a flood of tears and a sedan chair', one of the finest rhetorical double duties ever put on a preposition. And when he died, he was unquestionably the *doyen* of English literature, though not in the least a 'Ruin'. But all things and persons, whether already 'Ruins' or not, must come to an end, as well as make a beginning, and so must this article.

1925.

SOME THINGS PAST

I NEVER knew Miss Florence M. Gladstone, whose death was reported not long ago in the newspapers. But it so happened that I had not very long before put on paper some notes on a book of hers (*Notting Hill in Bygone Days*, Fisher Unwin, n.d.) dealing with a part—if only an outlying part—of Kensington my knowledge of which happened to be even older than hers, but of which very little book-notice had been taken till her own attempt. Court sojourn and the concomitants thereof saved Kensington proper from the very time at which it began to be known. But its northern neighbours were less lucky. A tempting rhyme—

Pitt is to Addington
As London is to Paddington

disposed of the easternmost of these at—or before—the very birth of the nineteenth century, though it lived to receive, also in a way to outgrow, the additional stab of 'Tyburnia'. Bayswater and Notting Hill, the not very easily separable midmost or westernmost, hardly came into existence as 'residential districts' till towards the middle of that century, but from early days they suffered to some extent, whether from the pollution of Paddington or (as I rather believe) from the subdolous arrogance of the pure Kensingtonians, or from both, I know not. The disuse of the picturesque name 'Kensington *Gravel-pits*', which might fairly have been extended from the Edgware Road to Shepherd's Bush, was a misfortune. As for '*North* Kensington', which gradually came in and is now recognised, it was a dreadful blunder, at once suggesting 'cotton velvet', 'German silver', and other combinations where the adjective admits limitative degradation of the noun. But even the older and proper names acquired a certain not wholly complimentary atmosphere, early or fairly early. It so happened, too, that in the 'sixties the region began to seem to the Jews desirable and to the Greeks a refuge. Now, though we English are hospitable on the large scale to an almost extravagant extent, we do not like particular regions to be too abundantly colonised by some of our guests. Miss Gladstone touched, I think, gently on this. I am not reviewing her book here, only recalling, partly by its aid, memories of my own many of which extended to Kensington itself. Of some little importance to the world at large is her misdating of the filling up of the last of the actual 'Gravel-pits', that which existed *inside* Kensington Gardens, between Uxbridge Road and the great Conservatory, as 1830. My parents returned to London and brought me with them only in 1850, and for years after that I saw and played in the said pit, its sandy, gravelly sides and floor remaining roughened by tools and weather; its edges fringed with small but beautiful and quite untrimmed yew-trees; and its whole a joy. Possibly it began to be regarded as a danger, and the absurd 'shepherding' of the present time as regards children was coming on then. Perhaps indeed the yews only shared the fate of over-tidying which befel many trees in that part of the gardens—the magnificent Scotch firs celebrated by Matthew Arnold; the finest guardians of the Broad Walk; the avenue to the right thereof below the Palace, which as children we called 'the Cathedral'; and most constituents of that beautiful piece of tree-planting which used to make the woods round the Round Pond a complete amphitheatre—the sections being taken for seats and the rides for the staircase ways. But at any rate the yews disappeared when the pit was filled in, and they made a formal children's playground of it. As if any such playground could be one-tenth as good as the playground you make for yourself! This, however, is a digression, allowable because it illustrates the earliness of the present commentator's familiarity with the region concerned. In 1850 that region, though after the breaking up of the 'Hippodrome' which Miss Gladstone describes, it had already been largely built over, was nothing like 'filled up'. The financial misfortunes or mismanagement of the principal landowner, Mr. Ladbroke, and others, probably (I was too young to know) having something to do with delays. St. John's Church had topped the actual hill for some years already and St. Peter's at its north-east-by-eastern foot had not yet been begun; but further north those most dismal things, rows of half-built houses, existed and before long a monumental sight, the finely begun but unfinished church of All Saints remained shut up for years. This district, from Portobello *Lane* (as we called it then) to the Grand Junction Canal and Great Western Railway was all rather dismal fields with at their end huge mounds of 'dust' preparing those familiar with them for the same in Dickens's *Our Mutual Friend.* Westbourne Grove itself was, *aedite posteri*, a rather agreeable place, a little resembling the High Street of a small but lively country town, as did the actual High Street of Notting Hill. But 'The Grove' lived up to its title by being the more truly rural of the two, though it had not the advantage of '*The* Gardens'. There were shops—and quite good ones—not 'multiple wens', but individual butchers, bakers and candlestick-makers, who understood, stuck to, and took an interest in their individual businesses and customers. Even these shops had in some cases been simply 'fronted' on 'villa' houses, while some of the actual villas, and their gardens, moreover, remained. The shops had not extended to the western buildings, then called Norfolk Terrace, but now I believe whelmed in Westbourne Grove itself, while the last structure on the east was a *çi-devant* and not much *çi-devant* farmhouse, with stables and farm-buildings appurtenant, which had been converted into a school, one of the succursal but proprietary and preparatory schools of King's College, London, of which there were then some half dozen scattered about, on what exact terms of relationship I am not sure. At any rate they had the privilege of putting the arms and motto on prize-books, some of which, if I am not mistaken, the institution itself gave. I was there for two or three years, as I had been for two or three years earlier at a dame-school in Norfolk Terrace, at the other end, as noticed, of Westbourne Grove. So that I was a Finch of that Grove at both ends of it. My first school was frequented by a dozen or so of small boys, say, from eight to eleven, and one very pretty small girl of the same age, the youngest sister of the Dame who kept it.

Midway between Westbourne Grove and Notting Hill Gate lay one of the new, but not newest, patches of houses, called Pembridge Villas. We lived, on coming from Southampton, first on the eastern or London side of this, and then, after an intervening sojourn in the neighbouring Chepstow Place, on the Western or Notting Hill side, where my father first lived and then bought a house. After 1863, when I went to Oxford I was only there for half—and that a much-broken-into half—of each year; and after 1868, when I married, I was there only on short and far-between visits till my mother's death in 1877, since when I have never entered a house in the neighbourhood, and scarcely a dozen times experienced the well-known and weird sensation of walking through streets in which you have lived, suffered, and enjoyed of old, and where now you know no one, and no one knows you. So though I had a sort of headquarters latterly and at least reversionary property—much lessened, alas! by anticipation—in the Notting Hill district for nearly thirty years, it is only from 1850 to 1863 that I can speak of it in an intimate and—as it were—citizen-like manner.

To say that this appears to me to have been by far its best time may raise a laugh in those readers who are not too much bored even to laugh. But I think there is some justification for the saying quite outside the admitted (in the double sense) 'fondness of eld'. The place still had a sort of rurality about it, and had certainly not yet acquired that peculiarly deadly aspect of the more modern 'Suburbia', which makes its streets look like London streets in some indefinable manner vulgarised. The rather-too-celebrated Potteries existed—my sisters, I think, 'district-visited' there—but they were not town-slums, The actual Park of Holland House ran down to the Uxbridge Road, and what is now called 'Holland Walk' enjoyed the thoroughly English title of 'Dead Man's Lane'. St. John's Church was looked on as a sort of chapel-of-ease to St. Mary Abbotts and the connection with Kensington was generally close. (It may have been specially close in our case, for my parents before moving to Southampton had lived for some time in Kensington Square, and we still had many friends there; but I think it was fairly general). One tobogganed down the back of Notting Hill itself, and picnicked in Kensington Gardens. The Hebraic-Hellenist invasion had hardly begun; and the good folk who journeyed up every morning in omnibuses with coachmen of almost Wellerian type on the box, to offices or chambers in the City were almost pure English or Scotch. I remember the—in both senses—mighty shipowner, Duncan Dunbar, among the latter. We had 'architects, artists and men' of other sorts quite unlike Mr. Pecksniff—and I don't feel in the least ashamed of having been, if not by birth, at least by early and fairly long sojourn a 'Man of the Hill of Notting'.

Kensington News, 1928.

SPECIALISATION[1]

IN the forty years which have passed since Peacock wrote a certain famous and fatal sentence about the ratio between the amount of nonsense talked on Education, and that talked on any other subject, the tide of such talk, whether charged with sense or loaded with nonsense, has assuredly never yet ebbed; but the current of it has set in different directions. And none of these directions, for some—indeed for many—years past, has been more noticeable than that of Specialisation. The word has indeed already become one of those 'blessed words' to which some of not the foolishest of men have been disposed to assign an influence the reverse of blessed. 'Impossible as it is for anyone now to take all knowledge for his province'; 'The necessity of substituting for windy generalities exact and scholarly research into particular subjects'—we know these tags, we know the sentences and the paragraphs to which they lead up, we could write them in our sleep or dictating twenty screeds at once to twenty different amanuenses, or in any other fashion and circumstances the most opposed to thought.

Of this kind of commonplace, or platitude, or truism, or 'falsism', there is of course a vast and various stock among the floating rubbish of the world. And not all of it does positive mischief—for the simple reason that a great deal of it never gets translated or transformed into action at all. There have been times when the educational division of the kind was in this case; but these times are hardly ours. The decree that all the world can be educated, must be educated, and shall be educated, has gone forth in a very practical sense for a long time past: and it is impossible that its administration should not be affected by the sets and currents of opinion just referred to. That the holiness, the value, the duty of Specialisation is preached we all know; and there cannot, I think, be very much difference of opinion on the point that the preaching (as preaching does not always) has to no small extent passed into practice. Of the propriety of this in one large, pushing, and popular branch of Education—that which is commonly called Science—I give no opinion: because no opinion that I could give would be worth anything. I dare say it may be very proper there: and may lead to solid and valuable results. But these matters are not my trade: let those whose trade they are see to them.

[1] Written in the year 1900.

Fruantur alii ; non moror, non sum invidus

as the poet observes. It is in the department of Arts, not in that of Science, that I question the desirableness of Specialisation, except at a very late period: and it is in this department that it is now being most strongly urged. In Literature, in History, in Philosophy, the word not merely to the graduate but to the undergraduate is 'Specialise'; and there are by no means wanting those who would even extend it to the Schoolboy by at once complicating his curriculum and encouraging him to direct particular attention to parts of it.

No elaborate demonstration of the fact can possibly be needed; there are hardly likely to be many, if any, denials. Almost everywhere the tendency shows itself. For instance, thirty years ago or thereabouts, it used to be the custom, in Scholarship or Honours Papers at Oxford, to set a dozen or more questions, of which it was generally understood that eight or nine should be answered in a three hours' examination. The object of course was to give the candidate an opportunity of showing a fairly wide acquaintance with the subject, whatever it was; and it was supposed that twenty minutes or so would enable him to do this in regard to any particular point. For showing, on the other hand, general knowledge and reading as well as (if he happened to possess it) original thought of any kind, he had a choice of Essay subjects with the whole three hours to bestow on one. Now, I am told, it is considered proper so to reduce the number of questions that forty of fifty minutes may be devoted to any point or points on which the candidate 'may have specialised'.

Again, when just fifteen years ago the Modern and Mediæval Languages Tripos was founded at Cambridge, those who arranged it (among whom I had the honour to be the least) endeavoured to plan the examination so as to secure a fair comparative acquaintance with large breadths of the subject. But before many years had passed this offended the specialisers and I understand the subject has since been boxed off into divisions, and 'parts', and 'periods', and subkinds to their hearts' content. Yet again, a generation ago at Oxford most tutors in at least the better colleges, and not a few Professors, lectured on the general subjects with less or more inspiration, satisfied that the reading of the books prescribed for Honours would give sufficient ballast and direction to the subjects of Roman History, of Greek Philosophy, of mediæval affairs, or whatsoever it might be. Now, I understand, there may be fifteen or twenty lecturers at different colleges taking different subperiods of Roman History alone so as to enable men to 'specialise' in them. I have for some time past been expecting with interest to hear of a course on 'The Relations of Caesar and Servilia' treated *à la* Feuilleton or *à la* Zola as the case may be; or of one on 'The Clubmen in the Civil War—their tactics, strategics, equipment, and uniform'; or on 'The points of contrast and likeness between Dorsetshire and Dewetsdorp as theatres for guerrilla'.

The great attention which the English universities, especially Oxford, have for many years given to History; and the small attention which, until very recently, either has given to Literature other than ancient, have made this tendency more prominent in regard to the former subject than in regard to the latter; but I think it has shown itself in both with regard to Philosophy. In Literature, however, all the Universities, English and Scottish alike (my knowledge of Irish University affairs is too small to allow me to speak of them) have gone *remis atque velis* into consortship with Specialisation by the adoption of the so called Higher Degrees; Oxford, the last to resist, having succumbed at last. The regulations for the attainment of these new doctorates vary, of course, in different places: but in most cases they are avowedly, and in all really, baits and inducements to Specialisation. For a certain number of years, or terms, or what not the aspirant is invited to study such and such a special subject, and then to send in a monograph about it, on the basis of which, supplemented or not by examination, the degree is to be awarded or refused him. He is to begin this special study the very moment that he has obtained the normal ordinary degree—B.A. or M.A. as the case may be—of his University. The more ardent specialisers would even recommend him to select this subject considerably earlier: and would arrange (in some cases, I believe, they have actually arranged) the Honours subjects of that Degree examination so as to favour this direction or deflection of study.

And with regard to the general economy and organisation of the Universities themselves, the cry is all in the same tune. 'Let us have more Professors and Lecturers: smaller and more specialised subjects; wider option of sub-divisions: more complex and harlequin Honour schemes.' The famous boast of M. Duruy, at which Mr. Arnold used, with such sweet sadness, to tell us all that we ought *not* to laugh, has certainly received a most delightful topsyturvification in the dreams of most of our University reformers at the moment. They would like to be able to boast that in every University of Great

Britain there were twenty or fifty Professors or Lecturers teaching at any given moment each a different branch of the same general subject to a different student: that of each dozen Honours candidates no two were taking up the same combination. Let theses and 'programs' lie in the quads as thick as pear blossom in a West Midland orchard in latter spring. Let the student of sixteen begin to turn his thoughts towards the dialect of South Eastern Hallamshire in the sixteenth century: or the probability of there being more than sixteen authors of the Fairfax MS. of the *Cursor Mundi:* or the strong reasons for believing that Heraclitus was really *Jean-qui-rit* and Democritus *Jean-qui-pleure*: or those which determined no matter what leader in the Barons' Wars to march through the parish of Chipping Clodbury and not through that of Steeple Chumpstead. 'Specialise; specialise early; specialise always; whether you be teacher or learner, historian or man of letters'. Let us have no more books like Gibbon's or like Hallam's: but either enormous expatiations on small periods in the manner of Macaulay or of Freeman or else strapped bundles of monographs, after the fashion dearer to this very latest day.

Now all this seems to me utterly wrong; if not quite utterly bad. I am not now directly occupied with the amount of useless literature which it helps to inflict upon the world. The major part of writing no doubt has been and always will be rubbish: and the particular form in which each generation chooses to shoot its quota is not a matter of very great importance. The historical monograph in which every point is treated very much as a leading article writer treats the daily dreadful telegram or speech which is his text—the literary monograph in which (with diagrams of the affiliation of MSS. which look like a cross between a daddy-long-legs and a figure in Euclid) it is triumphantly demonstrated that nobody who has ever been heard of wrote anything that was ever assigned to him, and that everything that exists was written by somebody else—have merely taken the place of their congeners of old time. They are hailed by appreciative reviewers as 'a new instance of the application to literature (or what not) of that great process which has achieved such marvellous results' etc.; they are sent as gifts to those *du métier*; they find their way to their own place on the shelf where they are chiefly disturbed by other specialists who wish to show that everything in them is wrong. The whole thing renews itself as doth the moon (though it is not nearly so pretty) and there is no need to say more about it.

It is in connection with its effect as an educating process that I think it worth while to make a protest. Once more, I do not pretend to give any opinion as to this effect in Science; probably it is harmless there, or even beneficial, because the wall of hard and impregnable fact is there to keep the enquirer from straying. But in all the domain of Arts I think young men as unfit to specialise as Aristotle (according to the remarkably early testimony of Hector as well as his own) thought them unfit 'to hear moral philosophy'. And I am quite sure that specialisation and subdivision in teaching is as bad as premature specialisation in less or more independent study. The simple fact is that the young man—the student of undergraduate or very early graduate age—has neither the knowledge nor the judgement required: and that the training (such as it is) which Specialisation will give to his faculties is not the training they need. It may be the case that, as I have granted, Specialisation in Science only brings the mind into closer and directer grapple with fact, with the actual Laws of the Universe, with the things that you can't alter, that you can't 'fudge', that, if you ignore them, will simply trip you up and make an obvious fool of you. In all Arts subjects except Grammar and the more formal parts of Rhetoric and Logic (I am not of course speaking of the Practical Arts where the same saving check exists as in Science) exactly the contrary is the case. In History and Literature especially (in Philosophy less so—because the *intellectus* must always sooner or later be *sibi permissus* there and will find itself describing much the same gyres as others have described) the nearer you come to the particular, the more bewilderment, uncertainty, opportunity of eccentricity and delusion there is. The *dolus* here is not in the generals: but in the particulars.

The general characteristics, for instance, of Greek or of English Literature and the way in which they are illustrated by the chief writers, the main transactions of Roman and of English History, are matters upon which only crotcheteers will seriously differ. This Professor may expound and that student may apprehend them with greater or less grasp, accuracy, vividness of give or take than another: but the things as wholes have at least an approach to the certainty and solidity of physical facts. They may be made more or less clear and attractive as such facts are themselves made by atmosphere, eyesight, optical instruments and the like: but they are not *mana*. When you come to particulars all is changed. They are enormously and sometimes bewilderingly numerous; they are very often narrated in an irreconcilable fashion by authorities not readily to be distinguished in point of value; they constantly require, in order to their understanding, knowledge of further and yet further facts quite out of the immediate subject; and worst of all, even taking the facts, their interpretation and construction admits of being conducted to absolutely contradictory results. There are probably no two better types of the partisan *plaidoyer* which, partisan as it is, never neglects the document and never merely generalises, and of the summing-up that avoids partisanship as much as possible while still garnering every fact and document and concluding in the most judicial manner possible to the writer, than Grote's and Mr. Gardiner's Histories. And I need not say that for any trained dialectician it is the easiest thing in the world to sum up from Grote's documents dead in the teeth of his conclusions in almost every point and to draw from Mr. Gardiner's conclusions very different from his in a very large majority of points. The multiplication of the document actually opens the door to inference and opinion instead of shutting it.

Now this kind of dialectic may be amusing: it may be to a certain extent worth doing; it may be (I think it is) a valuable intellectual exercise at some times and periods of life. But those times and periods are not those of youth or very early manhood. In the first place the process requires the very training in surer, narrower, more formal studies which it is now proposed to oust in order to put this in its place. In the second it requires the accumulation of an amount of information which it is physically impossible for the undergraduate to have acquired—which it is the business of the graduate still to acquire. The very same persons who would give the schoolboy a smattering of a score of subjects instead of a sound training in three or four would encourage him when he has hardly ceased to be a schoolboy, when he has yet had thorough discipline in no one single art or subject, to take some such art or subject, not in its rudiments or general principles but in a special application or division of it, and to avail himself of his general ignorance in order to master this particular knowledge. He has no really extensive knowledge of English Literature; let him specialise on Icelandic or Moeso-Gothic, on Layamon or on Langland. He has not mastered those elementary and universal lessons of political and social history which are found in the stories of Greece and Rome; let him attack Machiavelli and the Italian tyrannies. And let him if possible (fortunately it is as yet possible hardly anywhere in this country) be encouraged to do this by the sight and hearing round him of a Babel of Professors and Lecturers teaching little snippets of big subjects, and not only not 'boasting to find the whole' but shutting ears and eyes to it, abhorring and evading anything like large treatment, dissuading from general reading and miscellaneous acquisition of literature, coaxing the flock into special cells and pens the walls of which may be very safely trusted to keep the inmates ignorant of almost everything outside whether they do or do not witness much of that which is within.

It should hardly be necessary to say—except that when such things are not said misunderstanding generally follows—that the ideal of the specialists is not the only wrong ideal and that some things with which they wish to do away are not ideal things at all. It certainly was the case, and it may be the case still, that some English Professors did and do much less than they should; and it certainly is the case that some Scottish Professors are supposed to do much more than they can. I never in my life heard nor can I conceive more inestimable lectures than those of Dean Mansel on Philosophy; but then they used to be delivered at the interesting but erratic recurrences of the κυανομηνία or blue moon. On the other hand (putting Honours work out of the question) to give a hundred and seven lectures in English Literature to an 'Ordinary' class of a hundred and seventy persons in twenty-two weeks—to be expected to get some view of the whole of this English Literature into these lectures and to know that all but some five or ten per cent. of the class at the outside will pass beyond the range of our instruction at the end of that time, is not a thing which any but a very light hearted person can take easily, or which will leave him even a very great deal of time for sitting down to eat and drink, not to speak of rising up to play. But these things and many other things are beside the present question and I only wish to have no inferences drawn, one way or the other, from silence about them.

Multiply teaching by all means: in such sense and to such degree as may make it thorough. If it be possible in any way to combine the professorial and tutorial methods in Universities generally, increasing the Professorial element in England and the tutorial in Scotland, let this also be done by all means—always remembering (what I think is not always remembered) that the best Oxford tutors have never so much guided as helped the undergraduates who went to them, that a tutor is not either a schoolmaster or a 'coach' and had much better be neither. But all these things and others do not necessarily imply specialisation at all. It is quite as easy to have half a dozen or a dozen people teaching subjects of really *educating* size and scope as the same number teaching snippets, and encouraging the production and reading of monographs. 'If I were dictator', and if it were my lot to start that all pervading system of State Education in Humaner Letters for which Mr. Arnold sighed (I do not say that I think it would be a good thing) I am at least, after more than thirty years practice as schoolmaster, as journalist doubled with examiner, and as professor, quite certain what the general lines of my scheme would be. I should have a school curriculum, from whatever beginning age might be chosen to eighteen or so, in a few obligatory subjects—the classical languages, elementary mathematics, history and geography taught in the older fashion, and modern languages within reason—but all thoroughly drummed and rubbed in from the formal point of view. I should have a University course from eighteen to twenty-two or three for Honours men, with for its base an extension of the school curriculum adding philosophy and more history and literature but carefully abstaining from specialisation of any kind and not giving much option. From twenty-three to thirty I would have a man *read*: read *à bride abattue*, follow out his undergraduate readings in every direction, work up the modern literatures, read if he had a profession in the line of that chiefly but not solely; read, read, read, always and ever, till he had mastered (as he might without difficulty) the best things in literature, the general range and stretch of history, the facts of politics and philosophy—in short the greater drifts of the past course of the world in fact, in thought, in art. During these seven years, or such part of them as he could afford to give, the library should be his university, his college, his school, his professor, his tutor, his 'period', his 'subject'.

And then—but not till then—he might begin to specialise with some chance of doing so to his own advantage if not to that of others. According to ancient tradition a man should not be made a bishop till he is thirty; and the specialist also is a kind of *episcopus*.

University of Edinburgh Journal, Autumn, 1949.

ANCIENT AND MODERN LANGUAGES[1]

IT is one of the most hackneyed of banalities—I saw a fresh instance of it in a literary journal just before beginning to write this paper, and there hardly passes a week in which it does not find utterance somewhere in discussions on education—that early forced acquaintance with classics, old and new, disgusts and sickens those who are forced so to acquaint themselves; and that it is only by good luck, and rather exceptional good luck, that they ever manage to disentangle themselves from this prejudice. Gentlemen, I will borrow from Thackeray (one of the most illustrious persons who have allowed themselves to endorse this notion) a phrase which, with all respect to him, seems to me the only one for it—'Bah! it is bosh'. If it is in any case not bosh, then there must either be some unfortunate indisposition on the part of the pupil (and undoubtedly all boys have not a disposition towards literature), or some even more unfortunate awkwardness on the side of the teaching.

For my own part, I confess the utmost indebtedness in this respect to my own school—King's College School, London—and I believe that if I have made any contribution, however small and however flawed, to the study of literature itself, it is in no small part due to the training which we received there. Our headmaster, Dr. Major, was, in my time, an old man, and he was a more than competent scholar in pure scholarship of the older school—Latin and Greek, and even Hebrew, for which he had a particular affection, and which he still taught as it was taught, I think, in no other school of my day except Merchant Taylors. There was already a Modern Department, into which the unfortunate creatures who were doomed to a commercial education were drafted; and the teaching in the main school, while admitting plenty of history, geography, etc., as well as French and German, was frankly classical and mathematical. But Dr. Major's devotion to the older literatures did not in the least prevent him from being devoted to English also. He had edited Milton; he had arranged a very good book of selections for Latin prose-making from Addison and Chesterfield, and I may say that his whole teaching of the sixth form (which he took entirely himself, and in which I passed the greater part of my five years at the school) was thoroughly literary. We had no definite hours of 'English' instruction, and (perhaps for that reason) I own that I am

[1] An Address delivered to the Classical Association of Scotland.

still a heretic as to such instruction in schools after quite elementary stages; but the whole of the teaching of Greek and Latin was soaked in the literary spirit, and we had frequent English essays, and a good sixth form library of English poems and novels and *belles-lettres* generally, to complete the process.

One of the points in the system which even then distinguished us from most sixth form boys, I think, was a thing which became utterly unpopular and out of fashion almost everywhere a few years later; I do not know how the case stands with it now. This was extremely copious learning by heart of Greek and Latin poetry. I do not remember that this was much done in the lower forms, where in most schools it was then more common, and I can see now, though I don't know that I ever troubled myself about it then, the rationale of the difference. We did not waste much time in actual repetition, and so far as I remember, anyone was at liberty to keep his seat when his turn came, and signify ignorance, without special rebuke. But in the monthly class examinations, those who had learnt could show their knowledge by the not cumbrous but infallible method of setting down the first and last words of the lines, and this counted very largely for general position. (A wiseacre once asked me how boys were prevented from learning the first and last words *only*, and I requested him to try the process. I don't know whether he did.) By this means I think I learned, in between three and four years, the first three books of the Aeneid and the Odes of Horace, some Homer, and most of the iambic part, with some of the choruses, of two or three Greek plays. And I venture to think that the common denunciation of such learning as rote-work, mechanical, unintelligent and the rest, is itself about as unintelligent as anything can be. It is, to begin with, infinitely better that if a man wants a quantity or a construction, a vocable or a phrase, he should be furnished with it by Virgil or by Aeschylus in the chamber of his own memory, than that he should have to hunt it up in grammars and dictionaries. But this is not so much to my present purpose as is the advantage obtained by having, in the same memory, the permanent possession of large patterns and examples of the most perfect literary form that the world has produced. I do not believe much in *memoriter* teaching of a boy's own language. He has not to expend sufficient brain work on that, he gabbles the matter too easily, and it does probably get soiled and rumpled in the process. But in the classics (and, if I may venture to say so, in the foreign modern languages also) I believe it to be not only a great help to exact scholarship, but one of the very best possible *adminicula* to the teaching and learning of literature.

Another feature, still more peculiar to the school, and to many persons I know likely to be still more questionable, was the licence we had, in the same monthly examinations, of translating verse into verse. I am well aware of two objections to this which, long before I have got these words out, will have probably occurred to many here, that by allowing it you provide for lax and inaccurate translation of the original, and that you almost supply an incentive to slovenly diction and versification in English. No doubt you do, if the system is badly worked. But this may be said of most things; and I am sure none of us here present, if he found a boy frequently erring in this way, would hesitate in his case to recall the privilege. On the other hand, the process is certain, in anyone of the age of sixteen or thereabouts who has any literary faculties at all, to arouse them. You get rid at once of the mere 'construe'—that abomination, at least after the merest rudiments are passed, not merely I suppose to gods, but I am sure to men, and I should think to fiends. You must have *some* grasp, however faint and erroneous, of the literary value of a passage of Lucretius or a passage of Aeschylus before you can even attempt to English it in verse; while you may ram your way 'at great blows of dictionary' (as the French say) through either in prose, without feeling what distinguishes the former from Erasmus Darwin and the latter from Sheridan Knowles.

But one of the most powerful and obvious engines for combining the literary and linguistic teaching of ancient and modern languages, and insuring that it *shall* be literary, is in connection with composition in Greek and Latin. Of course, in the earlier stages of the teaching of this, the pupil must necessarily be *in statu pupillari*, that is to say, in leading strings; you must pick and choose and, perhaps, even frame his originals for him very carefully, and guide his hand in the making of his copy pretty frequently and pretty closely. But when a certain degree of expertness has been attained, the reins can be loosened, and the field of exploration and expatiation opened more and more widely. I confess once more, frankly, that for the beginnings and direction of my own interest in English literature, I know no book of literary history, no book of literary essays, no anthology, nothing of the kind, to which I owe half the debt that I owe to those two admirable handbooks of the late 'fifties and early 'sixties, Holden's 'Foliorum Silvula' and his 'Foliorum Centuriae'. In the former (it was, let it be remembered, before the author of *Men and Women* had been generally 'discovered'), I first read Browning; in the latter, I made first acquaintance, if I do not mistake, with that magnificent passage of Mr. Froude's on the close of the middle ages, which hardly falls short of Sir Thomas Browne himself. It was a custom of the school that the head boys of the sixth form themselves chose the passages for the week's compositions, which were submitted to, but almost as a matter of course approved by, the headmaster. And the comparison and discussion of these passages furnish me with one of my earliest memories of practical literary criticism. In fact, if I were myself arranging books of the kind today for the highest forms of first-class secondary schools, and for university use, I think I should extend the field of comparison and literary suggestion by including a certain number of passages from the best writers in French and German for translation into Greek and Latin. It is astonishing to what an extent this process of 'shifting the grip', as I may call it, of exerting the literary muscles first to get hold of the meaning and shades of the original, and then to reproduce them in another language, stimulates and develops those muscles themselves. And this is why I have never much liked, except in the very earliest stages, a process which has high and ancient authority, the process of retranslation. For here, the most important part of the intellectual exercise is done beforehand for the worker, the food of the eater is given him half-digested already. You may get a more correct result, but not half so valuable a process.

But it may be said that all this time I have merely been dealing with indirect and side-long methods of literary teaching, that I ought to grapple more straightforwardly with that teaching as such. I am by no means certain that the challenge is wholly a wise one, or that the direct and *separate* teaching of literature as literature is any part of the business, at least of schools. It is their business to prepare for it—to make its ways smooth in the future, rather than to engage in it for the present. Whether we shall ever get the public back to the understanding of the fact that it is the business of education, especially of school education, to teach a few things well rather than many things badly, that it even is its business rather to produce a habit of mind that can learn anything than to teach any particular thing at all, is more than I can undertake to say—it is certainly not a thing about which I am at all sanguine. At any rate, though I have, perhaps, written as many literary histories as most people here present, I am by no means inclined to recommend the study of literary history too early. And I know nothing more likely to suggest false knowledge and encourage real ignorance than the kind of literary history which alternates scraps of mostly second or third-hand criticism with snippets of inadequate extract, and presents the conglomerate as pabulum to the unpractised digestion of the novice. A really good primer, to give a sort of outline sketch-map of the subject, is of course not a bad, and may be a very good, thing; but to what extent it is likely to be assimilated and remembered, otherwise than as a kind of soul-killing store of second-hand dicta, I am again not so sure.

One thing, however, I am pretty sure of, and that is, that you can hardly begin too early (though in the lower forms, it must, of course, be done with strict consideration of the faculty of the recipients) the practice of giving a really literary account of the authors who are linguistically read. Here you have your real body to dissect, and to illustrate your observations by, not merely a few dead diagrams and dry bones to hold up as instances. It is, perhaps, rather unfortunate that considerations of so-called 'easiness' and 'difficulty' so much determine the stage at which authors are read; but, even so, a good deal more might probably be done than is sometimes done with them in the purely literary way. You can hardly expect a boy, at the age at which boys ought to, and sometimes I hope still do, begin the 'Anabasis' to recognise the brilliancy of Mérimée's comparison of Xenophon to Froissart. But you may lead him some way towards it by bringing out the resemblances of Xenophon to Scott or Kingsley, and showing him how the Retreat, if not the Advance, has all the colour, the scenery, and the dramatic arrangement, if not the character, of a great historical novel. And as you go on you can do more. Any book of Homer or of Virgil will give you opportunity to drive the nail as, and where, it will go, as to the difference of epic and romance, as to the comparison with Milton and with Spenser. Any play will suffice to lay the foundations of some knowledge of the history of dramatic criticism; any ode of Horace to perform the same office in regard to artificial lyric; any oration of Cicero or book of Caesar or Sallust, to begin tracing the outlines of the nature of prose style. But above all, no author, as it seems to me, should be read without at least some attempt being made to 'place' him in regard to the history of his own literature, and that of his own kind or subject. No matter that for a long time the knowledge so gained will have frontiers of ignorance and darkness: it will serve all the more as a starting point, and a temptation to explore farther and drive them back. On many members of an average class the details given will fall, of course, as seed on barren ground, but that is inevitable, and will do them no harm. On some they will pretty surely serve as seed on good ground, with the true evangelic result.

But I would by no means have this literary treatment confined to a prologue, or an episode, or an appendix of the teaching, which can be taken or left like the corresponding parts of a book. Even in the lower forms to some extent, and in the upper with increasing frequency, there are constant opportunities of throwing in literary approximations, illustrations, germinal hints. For instance you are reading Od. I. 23, and you come to *veris adventus* with the suggestion to substitute for it *vepris ad ventum*. You may, if you like, treat this from the bare point of view of textual criticism with reference to authorities. You may go a step farther in the purely literary direction, and say which seems to you the more Horatian or the more poetical. But if you have the teaching of literature really at heart, you will be able to draw the attention of those in your class who are fit for such things, to the curious fact, that in these two readings there are contained, certainly not of malice prepense, two great theories or systems of poetical appeal—that mainly to the intellect, and that mainly to the senses—on the one hand the 'approach of spring' with its vague and various suggestions, and on the other the shiver of the bramble in the wind with its shadow against a possible wall, and its nodding and crossing with the background and foreground of other plants. Nay, it would be worth while, for the potluck of the future, to point out further that Shelley would almost certainly have written *veris adventus*, and Keats most probably *vepris ad ventum*.

Or you are reading the *Agamemnon*, and you come to ὀμμάτων δ'ἐν ἀχηνίαις, Ἔρρει πᾶσ' Ἀφροδίτα. You will not, of course, miss at least the two possible renderings which locate the ἀχηνία respectively in the eyes of the statues and in the eyes of the beholder: but you may or may not proceed to draw attention to the wide literary and poetical difference between these renderings, and you may or may not 'improve' the passage as affecting the charge, sometimes brought against classical poetry, of being barren in 'sentimental' or 'subjective' tendency. If you do, you will be making the teaching *pro tanto* literary: if not, not.

You will observe, of course, that the few observations I have thrown out are not in the nature of a formal programme. They do not threaten any oppression or over-pressure to that Little Mary of the educational system—the timetable: they do not demand that room shall be made for fresh specialisation or fresh smattering. Their suggestion is one itself of suggestion chiefly; it looks to the inculcation of a literary *habit*, to the suffusion of a literary *colour* in the teaching of all languages, ancient and modern, foreign and vernacular, rather than to the fencing off of certain hours and certain courses for something ticketed and stamped as 'literature'. It proposes far less the imposition of a new burden than the lightening of the old by suggesting a new interest to, at least, some students. I say at least some, because I quite recognise that the purely literary interest is not universally even dormant, and that in some cases you cannot awake it. But I believe that in many you can, and that more often than is sometimes thought. I can say this—not in the least with the intention of putting a feather in my own cap but as a matter of pure experience—that though the teaching in my own class is almost purely literary and even neglects some aspects of the matter that commonly go by that name, I have never in one single year failed to receive from students, more or fewer, who had got their certificates, who were not going to read for Honours, who did not want testimonials, and had no other reason for ingratiating themselves—assurances that they *had* 'learnt to read' and to enjoy reading for reading's sake. That seems to me the object and the test of what I have here meant by literary teaching: and I believe it to be possible, and am convinced that it is desirable, to begin such teaching quite early—perhaps earlier than it is generally begun; and to extend it very widely, perhaps more widely than it is generally extended. Only, of course, in order to do this the teacher must himself not merely have some knowledge of literature but must feel some interest in it as such. If he has not got at hand the parallel instances, the mediate and higher generalisations and inferences, the grasp of differences and agreements, the classification of documents and kinds, he cannot bring them in: and if he regards them merely as so much additional top-hamper, he either will not bring them in at all or will not bring them in interestingly. Much, again, though not everything, will depend upon his material. I suppose everyone who has any business to be a teacher, after a little experience of his scholars or students, gets to feel their mouths, as a rider feels the mouth of his horse, and knows what can be done with them and what cannot. With a class containing a few very promising or many tolerably promising persons, more of this literary application may, of course, be given than in one of unmixed dullards; but I should doubt whether any large class ever consisted wholly of these. At any rate the opportunity may always be given, the bait now and then, in any case, cast.

I have purposely made this paper short because of the suspicion to which I have already referred that somebody may ask, in the words of one of the most precious and venerable characters of English fiction, 'Who deniges of it?' a question which is always intended to put, and sometimes succeeds in putting, the questioned person in a very unenviable position. But if I have been preaching to the converted, I trust to their agreement to excuse me; and if I have been preaching to any unconverted, I am very particularly glad to have had the opportunity of the preachment.

1905.

DULLNESS

THE curious 'passivity' of the modern mind—the expectation that everything shall be done for it; that at every moment there shall be some external machinery, apparatus, conspiracy of other folk to occupy, amuse, caress, cajole it—has been justly complained of by serious shepherds of the people in matters of religion, politics, education on the one side, of amusement and common domesticalities on the other. But perhaps it nowhere shows itself more than in certain respects of æsthetic; and hardly anywhere more than in this malady which makes the soul carry about with itself, and transfer to other things and persons, an atmosphere—a sort of cloak—of 'dullness'.

To some extent, of course, this, like other maladies and cachexies, is a case of being 'born so'. Everybody must have noticed, if they have taken any notice of children at all, that among the class-distinctions of these engaging incumbrances besides Liberal and Conservative, Platonist and Aristotelian, and others, there is this of self-amusing and not self-amusing. There is one kind of child which (perhaps not invariably without calling Satan to its aid) always finds something for its idle hands to do, is always more or less 'interested'. There is another, which unless it is constantly talked to, played with, 'taken' somewhere, given money to spend, provided with new toys, etc., is miserable, comes to its (unfortunate but perhaps not guiltless) mother, whining 'It's so *dull!*' and (too probably this time) does not receive the invigorating, disabusing 'spank' which is its due. For it must be admitted that whether these two races represent an exact original division of mankind or not, education and breeding seem to tend more and more to the multiplication of the second division and the discouragement of the first. And, what is worse, this discouragement, which maternal affection and nutricial want of other things to do, *plus* rather mistaken amiability and sense of duty, have always made common in the case of children, has of late been carried much farther in the case of adults. To do our mentors of the pulpit some justice, they do take some note of this—especially in regard to that specially soul-destroying invention the cinema, and the habit of attending professional football matches. (Putting the professionalism aside I should myself from personal experience say that football was one of the most interesting games to play and one of the most uninteresting to look at, while to read about it beats

Guicciardini). But nobody pays any attention to these matters: and more and more the demand for something to be done to, for, with, before—any preposition except *by*—you, seems to be a condition precedent if you are to escape dullness.

Now, most literature—most even of the greatest literature and certainly most of that which, though not exactly great, is not to be despised—requires this small thing to be done *by* the reader. All without exception save the lowest class of mere dime novels and the police and other reports—stuff approaching nearest the cinema itself—is greatly improved, at any rate taken out of the possible vein of dullness, by activity instead of passivity on the reader's part. It is said that there is or was a hymn of some sect, Anabaptist, Solifidian, or the like, which had for refrain, or at least for last lines:

> Down with deadly Doing!
> Never—never—*do!*

This, in more ways than one—some of them too political for present handling—must be taken as a motto of modernism: but it is particularly applicable to the kind of reader who finds things dull. He has not got in his possession, and he will not take the trouble to provide himself with, the necessary box to make the match strike, and he finds fault with the match. He has not the wedding garment of 'interestableness', and is not merely shut out from the supper but abuses it for a bad supper—as very likely the interloper of the parable did, although it is not recorded of him.

On the other hand, the reader who deserves to read not only carries with him a receiver which at once admits all that is intrinsically non-dull in his author, but a transmuter which converts many things dull in themselves into what is interesting by suggestion and association. Take an extreme instance. You have to read, as a work of necessity and mercy, a novel in which somebody (*not* as somebody to be laughed at or with) speaks of the 'Emperor Augus*tine*'. And if Fortune has been moderately kind to you, and you have improved her gifts with moderate assiduity and success, this addition to the ancient *Almanach de Gotha* drives dullness away for an indefinite period. You compare Augustus and Augustine; and imagine what an emperor the Saint might have made, finding it rather more difficult to make a saint out of the Emperor. Naturally in trying to assemble favourable views of Augustus (the gorgeous vesture of *Antony and Cleopatra* becomes a leaden cope crushing him down for

Englishmen), 'Prends un siège, Cinna!' comes into your mind, and you giggle as that parallel passage of Crabbe's:

> We saw my Lord, and Lady Jane was there,
> And said to Johnson, 'Johnson, take a chair!'

follows Corneille's in your memory. Whence by natural opposition the said mind reverts to that excessively improper but decidedly witty epigram on Fulvia which Martial attributes to the Emperor, and rebounds therefrom to the marvellous fragments of the same language, purified in meaning by Christian philosophy and having lost nothing in beauty by the blending of technically classical purity in language with the stronger and stranger virtues of non-Roman race, in passages which star the *Confessions* and the *City of God.*

Of course, anyone may say with a certain amount or at least a certain appearance of truth, 'But this is a sort of revoke, if not even worse: you are playing cards previously up your own sleeve, not those dealt to you.' But after all, do not all save the very best—perhaps even the very best—'hands' that literature has to offer require supplementing and completing from the factories or stores of the reader's mind? I have known elaborate attempts made to prove that the *Dies Iræ* is a composition of a very inferior order—attempts of course which only proved that the attempter's mind was entirely unprovided with the necessary tally, wrench, key, spanner—any mechanical parallel you like—to enable him to fit, turn on, open what was presented to him. The great Mr. Addison saw in Chaucer nothing but an obsolete and ineffectual buffoon: he evidently thought him—I am not sure that he did not use the word—'dull'; and I am afraid, though I do not agree with them, that a very large number of people, increasing constantly for the last hundred years or so, have transferred the compliment to the great Mr. Addison himself, though they would not think him a buffoon. I have seen the word applied, more than once or twice, to Gibbon—whom even Mr. Boffin enjoyed for many nights, despite or because of his amazement at the shocking character of some of the 'Declinings and Fallings'; and whom I, impervious to such illegitimate allurements, should call about as good an author to take down for half an hour's diversion as any but the very best. Irony is dull to a very large majority of women, and, I suspect, to a by no means small minority of men; and I very much doubt whether more than a very small proportion of either sex really appreciates beauty of style.

Of course there is no intention of denying that there is such a thing as Dullness positive, intrinsic; Dullness which offers no such fantastic escapes or relief as 'the Emperor Augustine'. Dullness accurate in and to fact, proffering nothing that, exposing its carbonated alkali to some more potent acid, will evoke a burst or even a fizzle of laughter; Dullness plain and plane, impregnable and invincible. But this is more common in life than in literature—I suppose for the very simple reason that the stupidest people rarely—they do sometimes—write books. Silly ones down to the silliest not infrequently do; but then in silliness, if you have not too much to do with it and it does not concern practical affairs, there is often if not always something amusing. 'Lord! what fools these mortals be!' may not be an utterance expressing the most wholesome frame of mind in any mortal, but it generally expresses a kind of enjoyment. There can be no enjoyment in face of real Dullness, really felt.

But there is, as has been partly pointed out already, no lack of means whereby to reduce the stock of this bane of life and literature alike to its lowest terms. Indeed, it must be said with a great deal more truth than exists in some other descriptions of the objects of Education, that one of the chief of those objects is to exercise and supply the pupil in the methods and with the means of fighting and minimising Dullness. There must, to begin with, be Faculty of doing and Will to do this—the fact that we presume in everybody Faculties and Wills that only exist in some is the main source of the very costly and rather ghastly blunder called Education in modern times.

But supposing the faculty and the will to exist, in whatever degree, they can be *educated*—that is to say, 'brought out' not 'stuffed in'. This is not a treatise on Education—heaven forbid! It is enough to say that any *real* process of it is a safeguard against finding things dull. For real education means first of all gymnastics of the mind which enable it to wrestle with things, to shape them in other forms; to extract from them whatever virtue they have; and, secondly, feeding the mind with 'provisions'—in every sense of that much-misused and stunted term. The most universal genius we know of obviously found nothing dull; Goodman Dull himself was a joy to him in the contemplation no less than in the creation. And I should warrant pretty constant freedom from dullness even to the man who, like the Socratic philosopher of old and His Majesty's horses for the last racing season or two, was '*second* best in everything'.

The Criterion, October, 1922.

MONTAIGNE AND FLORIO

IF the question were asked what translated books have exercised most influence on the English mind (the authorised version of the Bible and other religious books being ruled out of the competition) I do not think that any third could enter, with any chance of success, for the first prize against North's *Plutarch* and Florio's *Montaigne*. These two books represented influences parallel and even to a certain extent identical; for we know from Montaigne himself how great was the action upon him of Plutarch in substance and of Amyot's *Plutarch* (which North's directly represents) in style. They were both favourite reading with the English people for something like a century in their original forms, and remained popular in revised and slightly altered versions for much longer. Both—the one indisputably, the other to an extent not much affected by the dispute whether a particular copy of Florio was or was not Shakespeare's—influenced the author who, more than any other, has himself influenced Englishmen. The famous passage of the *Tempest* in which Gonsalo sketches his 'plantation of this isle' is almost unmistakable in its closeness to a passage occurring at p. 102 of Florio's 1st ed., and though other parallels are more dubious, they might perhaps be supported. Lastly, both, though in different ways, owed not a little of the influence they possessed to a very curious coincidence of what may be called their temperament (for a book has a temperament as well as a man), with the temperament of the English people at the particular time. I have nothing to do here with the Plutarchian part of this thesis; and it is Florio's *Montaigne*, not Montaigne by himself with whom or which I have to do. But the sympathy between the book and its readers, and the quality in the one which made it react so powerfully on the other, are matters very germane indeed to the subject, and not to be neglected in any fit discussion of it.

Almost everybody knows that Montaigne was long held, and indeed no doubt held himself, to have been of English extraction. The notion has been vigorously impugned by recent patriotic scholarship in France, and is now generally given up; though I confess that, having myself examined the evidence very carefully, I do not think it so conclusive as it appears to others. It is, however, a matter of little moment: the point of real importance being, that whether Montaigne had English blood in him or not, he had distinct and, for a Frenchman, unusual affinities to the English character, and especially to English character in a phase which it was just entering in his time, and was to pass through for something like a century afterwards. As there is generally a glimmering of some mistaken truth at the back of the most ludicrous and glaring falsehood, this resemblance probably lies somewhere at the bottom of that Montaigne-Bacon craze, which, though even more demonstrably preposterous than the Shaconian mania, has been held by some. And it is to be noted, for the better correction of national pride, that the points of contact between Montaigne and Bacon personally, and between the spirit of Montaigne and that of Englishmen generally, in the very late sixteenth and almost the entire seventeenth century, are by no means exclusively or mainly points to be admired. Some of them are very nearly, if not entirely, the same as the points which Macaulay has brought out, with much of his usual exaggeration, but with all his usual vigour, in his portrait of seventeenth-century, and especially post-Restoration, statesmen in England. They may be also found, in a different order of thought and observation, by comparing the work, at the completion of the period, of three men so different in origin, education, and station as Pepys, Roger North, and Defoe, and noting the veins of similarity which run through them. When, not to multiply illustrations, the excellent Roger expatiates on his brother's good stars which forced him to London during his wife's last illness because, 'when she must expire, and probably in his arms, he might have received great damage in his health', he writes in exactly the same spirit with reference to another as that which made Montaigne, in a famous letter, point out to the jurats of Bordeaux that for him, their mayor, to go to them in their trouble with the plague would do them no good and expose his worshipful self to danger. A hundred more or less similar instances of meanness, selfishness, candid cynicism, materialist resignation to the comfortable which meet and startle us side by side with the almost fantastic chivalry and idealism otherwise distinguishing the seventeenth century, receive parallel comment and illustration in Montaigne and in Englishmen of the age succeeding his. And the causes were no doubt the same in both cases, though they affected England later than France, and therefore showed their effects later. They were the revulsion and reaction from the early Renaissance enthusiasm for learning, from the vast impulse of discovery which followed Colombus like a secular wave, the bitter satire of the religious wars, the sense of change affecting civil politics, the feeling of personal insecurity, the far-reaching shadow of philosophic doubt. Of the mood or temperament likely to be produced by such causes, Montaigne is almost the Bible, though he is a Bible containing better and nobler things no doubt, and by virtue of his admirable literary quality furnishing much antidote to his own bane. But that much of his popularity when he was presented to Englishmen was due to the diversion, not accomplished but begun, of the national character into a somewhat lower channel than that in which it had run for centuries, I have very little doubt; and that it had (in the infinitesimal way in which such things can have) something to do with increasing the change I do not think impossible. It is time, however, to come to the actual consideration of the book itself, not as Montaigne's, or at any rate not as Montaigne's only, but as Florio's, and as presented by him to an audience of Englishmen in the reign of Queen Elizabeth and on the eve of the accession of James.

The author of this notable English book, whose birth by calculating backward from a date on his portrait is set at 1553, was no doubt an Englishman by place of nativity. He was the son of a Protestant minister of Florentine extraction, who had fled to England, was pastor of an Italian congregation in London, at exactly the middle of the sixteenth century, was under the protection of Cranmer and Sir William Cecil, and was domiciled with the latter till imputations were made on his morals. He was also, it would seem, a teacher of Italian and an author. His son John is said to have been educated first abroad, the Marian Persecution having driven his father from England. Then he went to Oxford, training others before, at the mature age of twenty-eight, he himself matriculated in 1581, at Magdalen College. Before this he had published *First-Fruits* (English and Italian dialogues), 1578, dedicated to Leicester, and a translation of Ramuzio's *Navigations* in 1580. After Leicester's death Southampton and Pembroke became Florio's patrons, and he appears to have been able to live in London and haunt the society of literary men and literary ladies. The *Montaigne* was licensed in 1599, but not issued till four years later. The reign of James brought him promotion: he was made at once Reader to Queen Anne in Italian, and a year later Gentleman Extraordinary and Groom of the Privy Chamber to the King. Latterly he lived at Fulham, and died there some time in the autumn of 1625. His wife was named Rose, and he had a daughter Aurelia. His books, including manuscript works, he left to the Earl of Pembroke, to be placed either at Wilton or in London, but they are not known to be at the former place. During his lifetime, besides the works noticed above, he published a *Giardino di Recreazione*, 1591 (a collection of Italian proverbs); *Second Fruits*, a continuation of the *First Fruits* with the Garden annexed; *A World of Words* (an Italian-English dictionary), frequently reprinted, and after his death enlarged by an English-Italian part said to be from his MSS. This *World of Words*, indeed, is one of the most delightful, of a delightful but too much neglected, class of books—the older dictionaries which supply English at its best, and illustrate it at its quaintest. Something, but not much, is known about him personally, and as with all persons who had the fortune or misfortune to be in any way connected with Shakespeare, more guessed. Sir William Cornwallis informed a world greedy of personal details that Florio was 'less beholding to nature for his fortunes than wit; yet lesser for his face than his fortune'; adding that he looked 'more like a good fellow than a wise man'; but yet was 'wise beyond both his fortune and education'. Daniel, the poet, called him his friend and brother. Florio himself describes himself as 'Resolute John Florio', and the Shakespearian commentator, improving on all this, after his kind, must needs add to it that Florio was the original of Holofernes in *Love's Labour's Lost*.

That Florio must have had an abundant vein of that coxcombry which distinguishes most of the lesser and some of the greater men of the Elizabethan time, a very slight examination of his work will show. The 'Address to the Reader' of the second edition is nearly as good in its substance as in its signature, 'Still Resolute John Florio'. 'Enough,' quoth the Still Resolute One, 'if not too much, hath been said of this translation,' and he proceeds to observe that, 'if the printer' [of course only the printer, and Resolute John being careless of the matter], 'hath corrected the faults as he was directed, it is much amended, if not, know that through mine attendance on Her Majesty I [Resolute John] could not intend [superintend] it.' No sycophancy to readers, gentle or other, here, it will be seen: no sinking of Resolute John's important court employments. As for 'the printer', there may be two opinions. There are of course errata, which are errata merely; but a careful study even of the first few essays will show any reader that, despite the general excellence of the translation, the resolution of John sometimes exceeded his carefulness or his knowledge. In the famous exordium, 'a well-meaning book' is certainly not happy for *un livre de bonne foy*. At the end of the first essay, *sang espandable* is very feebly rendered 'remaining blood', and two essays later, 'to carry the keys of the castle upon the deceased of the captain' is marvellous ungainly for *porter les clefs de la place sur le corps du trespassé.* A great number of these little slips are noticeable, and, as it is pretty certain from the general tenor of the translation that they did not come from ignorance, it stands to reason that they can only have come from a certain amount of haste in the original composition supplemented by the intense devotion of Resolute John to his duties as Gentleman of Her Majesty Anne of Denmark's Chamber.

The translation, as a whole, cannot be called unfaithful, despite the liberties and the occasional downright mistakes. But, except from the merely pedagogic-pedantic point of view, such a plea is hardly needed. Save for the purposes of a 'crib', or of a pure exercise in scholarship, intended to benefit rather the writer than the reader, it is of infinitely less importance that a translation should be done on the *verbum verbo* principle than that it should, as far as is possible, produce on its reader the effect which the original produces on the reader of that original. And, that it may do this, the certain vital qualities which it must possess consist much more in the spirit and vigour of the phrase, in the gust and character of the version, than in bare faithfulness to the thing translated. In these qualities few translators have surpassed Resolute John when he is at his best. Take, for instance, the short and admirable essay on Fear, the seventeenth of the first book. Here your pedant will boggle at 'I know not well' for *ne scais gueres* in the first line. But would the pedant have thought of anything so good as 'well I wot it is a strange passion' for *tant y a que?* Would the pedant have given us a sentence like this: 'At what time the Duke of Bourbon took Rome, an Ancient that kept sentinell *in the borough Saint Peter* was at the first alarm surprised with such terror that, with his colours in his hand, he suddenly threw himself thorow the hole of a breach out of the citie?' I protest that 'in the borough Saint Peter' affects me as '*his* noun' and '*his* verb' did Lamb. And here again: 'the like happened but not so successfully unto Captaine Julius his ensigne bearer at what time Saint Paul was taken from us by the Earl of Bures.' And here: 'at which siege likewise that horror and feare is very memorable which did choake, seize upon, and freeze the heart of a gentleman that having received no hurt at all he fell down starke dead upon the ground before the breach.' And yet again: 'The poor, the banished, and seely servants, live often as pleasantly and as carelessly as the other.' What a relish is there in writing of this sort! What a curious sense of life and art as contradistinguished from vegetation and drudgery!

Florio gives himself the licence (which could hardly be refused him by any but a very ferocious purist) of transferring bodily to English those Latin-French words of which Montaigne is so full, in regard to which, as students of the original know, he is responsible for the introduction and naturalisation of more than perhaps any other great French writer, and for which he was much grumbled at by sticklers for authority in his own day. Resolute John boldly writes 'suffragant and subsidiary' for *suffragante et subsidiarie*. For my part, whether he had English examples or not before him, I say, 'What for no?' Provided that a word is properly formed in the language from which it comes, and observes the rules of analogy in transferring itself to the language into which it goes, I have never myself been able to conceive any reason of sound scholarship or good economy which can be alleged against its introduction. Even if it duplicates one already in existence it is sure to be useful: and as a rule it does not duplicate, but supplies a new shade of meaning.

Montaigne's great peculiarity is range over the widest variety of subject combined with the presence of a constant and unvarying attitude of mind. On the first point there is no dispute. Except art—for which, save as regards literature, he seems to have felt an interest rather curiously small for a man of his age and country—there is hardly anything in life that does not enter into the scope and scheme of Montaigne's observation, and form a subject for one or more of those apparent divagations which are really perambulations and quarterings of his subject—life itself. The exact definition of his attitude has been far more keenly—has, indeed, been almost furiously—contested. There would probably have been less dissension if the disputants had learnt, what seems to be one of the hardest of literary lessons, to confine themselves to what their author says, instead of making it a mere sacred text, to be reverenced and, indeed, praised, but to be practically expounded in accordance with a Gemara and Mishna of things which he does not say, but which they think he would, could, might, or ought to have said. In particular there has been an unauthorised and unhistorical tendency to suppose in him a custom of speaking tongue-in-cheek, after a manner which cannot really be traced higher than Bayle, though from Bayle's time it became almost habitual with a large class of French writers. That pleasant things were unquestionably and indiscriminately good, but to be used with a great deal of questioning and discrimination, seems to me to have been, as far as he had one, Montaigne's definite rule of choice in action. That his *que scais-je?* expresses an equally deliberate opinion that belief is quite possible, but that it can in no case pass into demonstrated or demonstrable knowledge in things intellectual, I am myself most firmly convinced. I am as certain as I can be about any man's thoughts but my own that his epicureanism, as it is commonly called, did not overpass the limits of the first proposition, and that his pyrrhonism did not pass the limits of the second. Nor do I find the least inclination in myself to quarrel with either, though I think the second too wide. Montaigne's fault, as I take it, was a fault of defect, not of error. He had the French lack, on one and the more common side of the French character, of the romantic, the enthusiastic, the transcendental. It is all very well for him to say fine things about poetry in one place and claim to be 'transpierced and transported' by it: the real man peeps out much more clearly in the remark, when he is talking about women, that poetry is 'un art folastre et subtil, desguisé, parlier, tout en plaisir, tout en montre, *comme elles.*' His marvellously abundant fancy scarcely ever passes into imagination: there are no brave translunary things in him. But, except for the purpose of defining, it is always unsatisfactory to me to talk of what a man is not.

What Montaigne is, more than half-a-dozen generations have decided without hesitation and without mistake. In his own range and circle—that of the practical man who is at the same time thoroughly imbued with literature, of the moraliser who never merely pays himself or any one else with words, of the intelligent user of life as he finds it—it may be doubted whether there has ever been a wiser man than he, and held for certain that there has been no more attractive exponent of this particular kind of wisdom. In one special respect Montaigne must always have had a peculiar attraction for Englishmen. It has been an almost invariable characteristic of our race that we have been either slavish adherents of custom and fashion, or eccentric and rather deliberate contemners of them, or (sometimes) both at once. In contradistinction to this, the determined and yet unostentatious way in which Montaigne displays his intention to *vivre à sa guise*, his reduction of things to unconventional standards without any flying in the face of convention for the mere sake of flapping the wings, must have at once struck us. No one applies the merely practical reason so well as he: no one turns on the dry light so steadily and with so little parade. In our altitudes we may and perhaps should despise him a little: for he is something of a Lord Glenvarloch in the game both of thought and of life, and we are as little disposed to call him a 'great gamester' in either as Sir Mungo was to apply the term in the other case. But it is not very easy to carry on life at altitudes: and yet it has to be carried on. So at the beginning of the stormiest century of our annals Englishmen were presented with this curious reducer of all things to a *que scais-je?*, to a common denominator of the practical reason, to a level where if the great things of optimism are not recognised and are even decently pooh-poohed, there is not the slightest affectation of believing that this is the worst of all possible worlds. Some of them rejected the lesson with heat and became Crashaws in literature and Montroses in politics: others took it rather too seriously, and their name when they became eminent was Temple or Godolphin or (for the influence of Montaigne on the *Spectator* has, I think, been generally too much ignored) Addison. Even here one speaks but figuratively: for all these distinguished persons would no doubt have been themselves, even if there had been no Montaigne in the world. In the vast majority of cases, what Florio and his follower Cotton did was doubtless simply to provide fit pasture for fit persons—to supply, as is the common but not ignoble office of literature, somewhat unorganised and unvocal thought with the ready-made expression of its thinking, far better thought than it could have managed for itself. Like every other writer, Montaigne is after all for moods—moods individual and moods national, moods moral and moods literary. The moods for which he is suited are numerous, and his adaptation to them is remarkable. Those who can will of course always read him in the original: for those who cannot there is certainly no English version, despite its occasional inaccuracies, which can be recommended with half the warmth and sincerity which can be lent to the claims of Florio, 'Still Resolute' after nearly three centuries to achieve his task, and provided by nature and chance with an equipment of parallel language which all Wardour Street, even backed up by the profoundest academic knowledge, cannot furnish now.

1892.

BALZAC'S 'ŒUVRES DE JEUNESSE'

TO have done, at last, something that you have been going to do for five and twenty years, carries with it a certain sense of solemnity. It must be at least five and twenty years since I made up my mind to read the ten volumes which (representing, it would seem, even a greater number) survive, in a kind of suspended animation, as examples of the work which Balzac did during his ten years of unsuccessful probation. I have gone out to battle with them more than once or twice; but like the Irish heroes in the celebrated text, 'I always fell'. The falling was rendered easier by the impossibility of discovering that anybody else had ever succeeded. Everybody has friends who *say* that they have read the *Œuvres de Jeunesse.* I have several. But on interrogating them, it always became clear to a moderately skilful faculty of cross-examination, that they had *not* read them. There was one exception, and that exception was—would I could say is!—Mr. Louis Stevenson. It so happened, somewhere about 1879 or 1880, that I had, for no special reason, summoned up my courage once more to attack this Dark Tower. It happened also that Mr. Stevenson and I were dining together. We talked much of Balzac, and I asked him the fatal question. He answered in the affirmative; and applying my usual tests I could discern that he *had* read them. Then I asked him whether on his honour and conscience he could advise me to do the same. He deliberated for some time and answered 'No'. It was in vain that I brought up, with all possible delicacy, the celebrated instance of de Quincey's 'mono-Gebirism'—that belief in his having been the only person to read *Gebir* which caused so much pain to Landor—and bade him reflect whether any petty pride in being the only English reader of the *Œuvres de Jeunesse* in their totality had influenced his advice. He assured me (on a glass of '46 Hermitage which I had the pleasure on that occasion of setting before him) that he had not the slightest idea of the kind, that he had never in his own life gone through so much to gain so little, and that if he had an enemy it would not be 'Guiccardini or the galleys', but the *Œuvres de Jeunesse* or some equivalent that he should prescribe to that enemy. I took his word, and abstained from them for some fifteen years longer until, as it happened, necessity made it necessary and I did it at last—too late alas! and only just too late to let him know the result.

I do not intend here to revenge myself on the readers of the

National Observer by giving them any detailed account of this astonishing section of literature which (I suppose because people buy it in sets) is kept constantly in print and on sale, but which in all the books on Balzac is conscientiously tabooed, and as to which, now that Mr. Stevenson is not here, I feel myself in the most unexpected and only possible way his successor. I have read them; I know what they are all about, with a possible exception in the case of *Dom Gigadas* and *Jean Louis*, in regard to which even the practice acquired in twenty years' novel-reviewing leaves me rather uncertain of a complete comprehension. There are the three wonderful and terrible mediæval or fifteenth-century romances, *L'Israelite*, *L'Excommunié*, and *L'Héritière de Birague*, the most abashing examples anywhere of the efforts of a man who would fain be a Scott, who could not be a Dumas, and who had it in him to be something quite different from either. Not even in those forgotten followings of Mrs. Radcliffe and Monk Lewis, which sometimes emerge from the cellars of country second-hand booksellers, shall any one find anything quite so amazing as *L'Israelite*, where, without the exhibition of the very slightest faculty of story-telling, villains with a turn of the wrist chuck maidens into cauldrons of boiling oil, where they are themselves literally torn to pieces by the unresting and unassisted nails of a virtuous female lunatic, and where, after some sharp turns on the rack, the good people get up apparently undamaged and engage in athletic hand-to-hand conflicts. *L'Excommunié* and *L'Héritière de Birague*, though not much better, are a little less frantically absurd; you can imagine a dull man who has read some clever books, or a clever schoolboy who may do something one of these days achieving something like them. Then there is *Le Centenaire*, which has the illegitimate attraction of showing us how constant was Balzac's interest in alchemical and similar secrets, which tells us how a wicked ancestor continually refreshed his youth by sacrificing damsels, and which utterly ruins the interest with which it begins by representing a valorous republican general and his heroic orderly tamely abandoning the quest after a murderer, who they are quite sure has committed murder, before a score or two of pages are turned. There is *La Dernière Fée*, which is even more disappointing, because the opening, even to those who perceive in it a distinct study after Charles Nodier, is very good, and because this opening goes off into one of the most tiresome things possible, an *ungraspable* muddle between a real fairy-tale and a commonplace story of aristocratic caprice. Then there is the pair or sequence of *Le Vicaire des Ardennes* and *Argow le Pirate* which complete each other, and together tell the history of a ferocious corsair who maroons his commander, defends Charleston against the English, returns and becomes a model country gentleman, and is executed (with awful reprisals from his pirate crew), for the insignificant crime of sticking a poisoned fish-bone into the artery of a bishop's brother. It ought to be said that the opening scenes of *Argow le Pirate* contain one of the very few anticipations of the future master to be found in these wondrous books—a foreshadowing of that *Physiologie de L'Employé* which was to be so often and so masterfully done afterwards. And last of all and most beautifully titled of all, there is *Jane la Pale*, a story of bigamy in which the legitimate wife very liberally suggests a double arrangement cut short by envious death.

I have read many books by many men; but I never remember to have read any books quite so puzzling as these. One reads the *Hours of Idleness* and says that it is not very good, even as a beginning, for Byron; one reads *Zastrozzi* and *St. Irvyne* and says that they are very bad, even for boyish work in alien art, by Shelley. Many people have done many things in their apprenticeship which did not very clearly announce their craftsman's years. But such a mass of such bad work in the very kind in which the craftsman was afterwards to do masterpieces, produced during so long a period (for it must be remembered that Balzac was of age even when he began them and was nearly thirty when he broke free, and even then not completely free, with *Les Chouans*) I never saw anywhere. And I do not believe that anything of the kind anywhere exists. It is not that the mere phrase is dreadful—*il était en proie à des torrents de volupté*, though very nearly as bad as anything can possibly be, is not so shocking from Balzac as it might be from some other people. It is not that several of the books attempt the novel of adventure and history which was pretty certainly not the author's proper line. It is that the whole thing, that the whole set of things is *bad*—bad in scheme, in execution, in writing, in thought, in everything.

And then a year or two at most after he was content to produce these imbecile things he wrote *La Peau de Chagrin* and the *Médecin de Campagne*, and the wonderful tales that illustrate the *Etudes Philosophiques!* It is not, once more, that the faults of the early works do not appear in these later, for they do; it is that the merits of the later works in some incomprehensible manner do not allow themselves even to be indulgently predicted as possible in the earlier. I confess that after reading them I am almost persuaded never to call anybody's novel bad again, and I only rejoice to think that I very seldom have called anybody's novel bad without a proviso. For what could one have said too bad for most of these?

The National Observer, 26 January, 1895.

VOLTAIRE AND ROUSSEAU

IT is easy to laugh at most things: and there is assuredly nothing of special difficulty in the search for points to laugh at in the practice of celebrating anniversaries. Yet the laughers may perhaps be asked to consider whether the search is worth the trouble, slight as that trouble may be. A practice which has been sanctioned by probably every religion in the world, and which, in the case of private friends, is the practice more or less of every man who is not of the shallowest and most selfish, may surely with no great offence be extended to those famous men our fathers who were before us, and to whom our minds, if not our souls or our bodies, owe gratitude for benefits received. Nor is it surprising that death-days rather than days of birth should be selected for the purpose. In a man's lifetime his birthday is, for want of a better, that on which his friends agree chiefly to remember him. But when he has disappeared from among men, the anniversary of his disappearance naturally takes the place of importance. It is death that finishes and sets the seal on the work for which we value him. Shakespeare or Dante in the cradle is but a possibility, in his coffin he is a fact: what he has done or can do for us is then summed up, if scarcely yet actually known and felt, and is the standard by which he will thenceforward be judged.

No man therefore need doubt or question, in general, the propriety of such a celebration as that which France, and with France Europe, makes this year, and in part this month. Seldom, indeed, has any such commemoration occurred, the interest of which was so little local. Voltaire and Rousseau may have been and were eminent exponents of the French mind, but they were also more than this. They have, like other great men of letters, given pleasure and profit of the literary sort to thousands besides their own countrymen, but they have done more than this also. No man who speaks with knowledge can deny that his own life and ways of living, his thoughts and beliefs, have been in great measure, though it may be unconsciously and indirectly, modified by these two men. Their influence has been fiercely discussed, ingeniously quibbled over, made the subject of endless research and endless talk. Well-meaning persons have triumphantly shown that Bolingbroke said this thing before Voltaire, and that Locke said that thing before Rousseau. But it has not been shown, and never, I dare say, can be shown, that the words and the ideas which in their mouths were so powerful, would, had they never existed, have had the same power and force in the mouth of others. It may be a rough, but it is a true saying, that there are three things which chiefly distinguish the England of Victoria from the England of Anne, and that the same is the case with other countries. The first is the greater love felt and shown for nature and for man, existing as this love no doubt still does, side by side with much practical brutality and callousness towards the beauty of the one and the well-being of the other. The second is the wider and more intense spirit of enquiry, the greater unwillingness to accept wrongs and absurdities merely because they exist, the sense that authority is something different from truth, and 'It is written' something different from 'It is'. The third is the cultivation of science, of literature, and of art, not as pursuits ennobling and respectable merely, not as means to ends, not as professional and traditional employments, but for themselves and for their own sake, as things capable of supplying the place of many pursuits, beliefs, and institutions, which have occupied the attention of men in old times. All these great changes have no doubt been brought about by the labour of many men; but of these many men none have done more than the three great Frenchmen—for we may surely count Rousseau as French—whose names are indissolubly linked together. One of these we are not now celebrating, and the sober Briton may perhaps smile to find a French committee gravely lamenting that Diderot did not, like his great allies, symmetrically die in 1778. But it is quite safe to say that if any man nowadays objects to making the lakes of Wordsworth into the wash-pots of Manchester, and if any man strives to raise and assist his poorer fellow-countrymen, it is more owing to Rousseau than to anyone who ever lived and wrote; and that if any man refuses to put up with an abuse or an anomaly, because it is an anomaly or an abuse, be it in matters social, in matters political, or in matters religious, that man, whether he knows it or not, would have had less inclination to make his attempt, and less chance of succeeding, had it not been for Voltaire. It is possible, indeed, that to some people the changes thus effected may seem of dubious value, nor is it necessary for our purpose to profess faith in their unmitigated excellence. But of their magnitude, of their importance in the history of the world, there can be no two opinions. Those to whose influence they can be traced have, by that fact alone, established their claim to be reckoned among the famous men of the world, and their right to the honours and commemoration which such great men should receive.

Voltaire was born, according to his own account, at Châtenay, on the 20th of February, 1694. He could not exactly boast of the unmingled *roture* which at a latter period became the favourite affectation of those who hated the aristocracy, inasmuch as his mother at least was of noble birth, though not, like Madame de Sotenville, of that specially precious variety *où le ventre anoblit.* He was early set to follow his father's profession, that of the law, and early quarrelled with it, as even in his time it had become traditional for youths of genius to do. His friendship with Ninon de l'Enclos, his introduction by her and by others to fashionable and literary society, his banishment to Holland as a room for repentance, and his consequent approach to the Scylla of imprudent marriage instead of the Charybdis of furtive literature, are all sufficiently famous facts. How for a satire which he did not write he was sent when barely of age to the Bastille, how he began or finished there the *Henriade* and *Œdipe*, how he first made a friend and then an enemy of that singular man of letters J. B. Rousseau, and incurred the more dangerous enmity of the Chevalier de Rohan, are things also well known enough. It is not the anecdotes of the life of great men of which people are most ignorant. Being quotable they are quoted, and many persons are in this way informed of the too lively replies to Rousseau and Congreve, the curiously feeble epigram attributed to Young, the unlucky *Trajan est-il content?* and the strangely misinterpreted *Deo erexit Voltaire*, who have probably never opened a single one of the hundred volumes, or at most that which contains *Candide* or some of its fellows. Literature, however, is indebted to the Chevalier de Rohan. He sent Voltaire to the Bastille, and the Bastille sent him to England, where he laid the foundation of his future edifice of thought, and of the fortune which enabled him to work out that thought in literature without the harassing pressure of daily wants, or the almost equally harassing pressure of hack work to supply them. If it be true that he returned to Paris with eight thousand pounds as the result of the *Henriade*, he had already as much as would have amply sufficed for a bachelor in those nominally luxurious, but not extravagant days. Thenceforward his life lasted exactly fifty years, during which his fame and his fortune never ceased to increase. Some fifteen of these were passed with Madame du Châtelet at Cirey or elsewhere, ten at Paris, five in wanderings or at Berlin, and the last twenty at Ferney, the place with which Voltaire is for all time associated. The too famous visit to Berlin succeeded with little interval the death of the divine Émilie; the sojourn at Ferney was closed by the triumphant but fatal return to Paris. But this triumph was only a concentration and an epitome of the whole half-century. Never, save for the annoyances with which the Berlin sojourn closed, and the less inevitable battles with criticasters and poetasters in which he of his own accord indulged, did his luck desert him.

Very different was the companion life whose close we now commemorate. Eighteen years after the birth of Voltaire, Rousseau, who, it is sometimes forgotten, was of undoubted French origin, was born at Geneva. In the same year as Voltaire, he died at Ermenonville in a manner which is still a mystery. During by far the greater portion of this space of sixty-six years, his own autobiography is the sole authority for our knowledge of his life; and of the latter period, to which his writings exclusively belong, the information which enables us to check or supplement his own statements is always meagre and often doubtful. Hence the life of Rousseau has always been a temptation to the speculative; and some persons have even gone so far as to set down as the fictions of his own brain, many of the events recorded in the *Confessions*. Certain it is that the chronology of the book is often bewildering, and sometimes impossible, yet as a book composed long after the events to which it refers, it does not perhaps lose its authority as a whole from this peculiarity. Two things at least are indisputable, that the life which it records, more or less faithfully, was a life always of difficulty, sometimes of actual want, of sordid employments and advantages denied, of a fame too late and too chequered to be enjoyed, and above all of a series of broken friendships, the breaking of which, to whatever fault it was due, unquestionably caused the bitterest anguish on one side, if not on both. It would be out of place to discuss any of these incidents here. But the impression of pain, as the characteristic of the life of Rousseau, must be the one left uppermost on every mind. Never was there, perhaps, a more unhappy life, whether we regard its troubles as home-brewed, or as resulting from the unkindness of fortune and the perfidy of friends. Never was literary eminence associated in so strange a way with insult and persecution, disappointment and chagrin. At Geneva, at Turin, at Chambéry, at Lyons, at Venice, at Paris, at the Hermitage, at the Isle of St. Pierre, at Wootton, Rousseau appears to us as an incomplete and one-sided Ishmael, with every man's hand in reality or in fancy against him, and without the vigour or the insensibility which would have enabled him to retaliate in kind. His mother's death, his father's peculiarities, and his lack of the wholesome discipline of a large family, may be said to have been his first misfortunes. He succeeded with his profession no better than Voltaire did, but his alternative was very different. Instead of princes and poets, his companions for years were lackeys, servant-girls, miscellaneous vagabonds of all kinds. He wandered about Savoy and the neighbouring districts of Italy and France like a stray animal. Now he had to pass his time in menial service, now to pick up the crusts thrown by religious proselytism, now to wander houseless in the streets of Lyons. The protection of Madame de Warens sheltered him once and again, but he broke loose at last from this haven, and made for Paris. There, or elsewhere, he lived for the next thirty years in the strangest manner, partly on the produce of his literary works and his music-copying, partly on the gifts against which his soul always revolted. His fame and his needs perpetually gave him protectors, of which his extraordinary temper, or his more extraordinary luck, as regularly deprived him.

Few greater contrasts can thus be found than the contrast of the lives of the two men who were thus united in death, and whose union lives in history as something more than this chance one. The life of Voltaire was not indeed one of unbroken felicity. He had his troubles with lackeys and ministers, with rivals in love and rivals in letters, with Frérons and kings of Prussia, with multiform abettors of l'Infame and agents of darkness in every shape. His extraordinary sensitiveness made him feel these troubles quite as keenly as any human being ever felt. But his woes were, after all, only skin-deep. His life was, on the whole, a grand success, a success from the time when his early poems secured what seems to us rather disproportionate admiration, to the crowning triumph of his last hours. His early troubles with his father were only a consequence of the success which attended his efforts to get into the society of the great world in Paris, and to emancipate himself from a hated profession. His unlucky Dutch love, his embroilment with the Chevalier de Rohan, his subsequent sojourn in the Bastille, were but trifles. On the other hand, his visit to England was such a triumph, and so solid an advantage, as perhaps no man of his years has ever yet reaped for purely literary or intellectual merits in a foreign country. From the date almost of his return he was the intellectual king of the country which was acknowledged, rightly or wrongly, as possessing the intellectual hegemony of Europe. The want of pence never vexed him as it has vexed other public men, though perhaps he might have escaped some small annoyances had he been more circumspect in his ways of loading himself with the thick clay. His visit to Prussia did him no serious or lasting harm, and at least enabled him to show that a mere man of letters can possess weapons of offence equal to those of the most absolute, malevolent, and unscrupulous of monarchs. As for the last twenty years of his life, they present a spectacle which is not paralleled in the history of the world. For once the republic of letters had ceased by its own consent to be a republic, and had submitted to a dictatorship. The absolute superiority of Voltaire to every living genius of the writing sort was not questioned by any contemporary, and, strange to say, has never been seriously questioned by any successor. Men who were themselves intellectual princes did not hesitate to do homage to Voltaire, and those who most disliked his real or supposed principles, did not think of questioning or disputing the ability with which those principles were supported and displayed. During this time, too, he had, and availed himself of, the opportunity of adding to his crown of wit, intelligence, and literary skill, the rarer crown of active benevolence. He made himself the champion of the oppressed, the reformer of abuses, the avenger of wrongs. It seemed throughout his whole life that he could put his hand to nothing—save, perhaps, diplomacy—without at once acquiring supremacy in it. He was admitted to be the greatest poet of his time, and even those who care little enough for his style of poetry are forced to confess that, during great part of his career, there was no European poet so clearly master of his own style as Voltaire was of his. That he was the greatest dramatist of his time was and is indisputable. That his prose yields in its way to none even in that century of splendid prose there can be no question. As a tale-teller of the lighter order we must go back to Lucian before we can find his equal, and may go forward to our own days without the chance of similar luck. On graver themes he could write with due gravity, and if his depth was scarcely equal to the smoothness of his surface, it was yet not contemptible. With regard to social matters, what has since been charged against him as a fault was then considered almost as a virtue. While setting his face against individual instances of corruption and oppression, he did not advocate, perhaps did not see the necessity of advocating, any sweeping or revolutionary changes of social order, and thus he earned the gratitude of reformers without incurring the risk of an open breach with Conservatives. In England, and perhaps to a small extent in Germany, he was thought of with some reprobation as a scoffer; but even this reprobation did not, during his life, either blind men to his genius or generate calumny. To sum up all, for the last half century of his long life, he possessed affluence, fame, and power such as no other man of letters from the beginning of history has, without reverses and with steady growth of success, been able to attain.

Very different, as has been said, is the picture of Rousseau's life. In one point indeed, that of literary fame, there may be said to have been some similarity. But Rousseau's celebrity came to him grudgingly and mingled with all manner of annoyance; so late, too, that his power of enjoyment was gone, and the sweetness turned to bitterness within him. In everything else there is nothing but contrast. For the society which early fell to Voltaire's lot and never forsook him, Rousseau had the sordid companionship which, whether its morality be worse or better than that of more polished circles, inevitably leaves on those who have to submit to it a taint in manners, if not in morals. During his whole life he had to subsist either on utterly insufficient earnings, or on the gift-bread which is bitter to all, and which seems to have been bitterest to him. Both of the philosophers suffered, it is true, many things at the hands of many women, but who of those whose admiration for the divine Émilie is weakest will compare her to Thérèse le Vasseur? And who of those who most share Frederic's estimate of Madame Denis would hesitate between her and Thérèse le Vasseur's mother? Voltaire was not overfortunate in his friendships, but his wounds from this source were neither many nor deep, and his position as king of letters gave him in every instance the immense advantage belonging to the superior. Rousseau was all his life in the condition where friend really means dependant, and he knew it only too well. Whatever view we take of any chapter in the long and woeful history of his quarrels makes little difference here, for it is as great a misfortune—perhaps a greater one—for a man to fancy himself the perpetual object of plots and treacheries, as to be in reality plotted against and betrayed. The splendid triumph which closed Voltaire's life does not more strikingly contrast with the sombre and mysterious fate which, in whatever way, befell the recluse of Ermenonville only a few weeks later, than the tenors of the lives which led up to these two ends contrast with one another. The benefits which Shelley enumerates in the famous complaint:

> Alas! I have nor hope, nor health,
> Nor peace within, nor calm around,
> Nor that content surpassing wealth . . .
> Nor fame, nor power, nor love, nor leisure—

cannot indeed be all asserted of Voltaire and denied of Rousseau. Yet if we leave fame and leisure out of the question, hardly one was possessed by Rousseau, hardly one was refused to Voltaire.

In the brief interval which elapsed between the deaths of these famous men and the great assize of God's judgment with which their names and teaching will always be connected, little alteration took place in the manner in which they were regarded in France and by Europe at large. The influence, if not the fame, of Rousseau advanced indeed with more rapid steps than that of Voltaire, inasmuch as the questions upon the solution of which the minds of men were consciously or unconsciously concentrating, were questions upon which Voltaire had less of direct, or at least of apparent, interest to say than Rousseau. But with the outbreak of the French Revolution, the names of its supposed instigators became everywhere, beyond the reach of the Revolution itself, the objects of the most violent onslaughts. People of the stamp of Johnson had indeed already been accustomed to speak of both in a tone in which antipathy was in happy proportion to ignorance. But the general attitude had been perhaps that of George III in his first conversation with Miss Burney. Voltaire was a monster, though a clever monster; but Rousseau was decidedly better. When the Revolution had actually broken out, while there was no limit to the enthusiasm for both, especially for Rousseau, on the side of the innovators, there was no toleration for either left on the side of the party of order. It was then that the greatest orator of Europe employed himself in describing the unquestionable transgressions of Jean-Jacques' private life in the style of Billingsgate. It was then that the extraordinary legends respecting the deaths of the philosophers, which the spite of a certain section of the clerical party in France had embellished or invented, were caught up and made an article of faith, so that they, or at least echoes of them, may be found in works intended for the instruction of youth at quite recent dates. This attitude may be said to have been preserved and intensified in England, during the whole thirty years of the revolutionary struggle, so that even the crimes of the Corsican ogre, of whom it is difficult to say whether Voltaire or Rousseau would have had the most cordial detestation, were in some blind manner charged on their devoted heads. Meanwhile the attitude of the French themselves had been gradually changing towards the two men whom foreigners had so strangely yoked together. The extreme revolutionists never had been—are not, we may add, to this day—in sympathy with Voltaire. They missed in him the sentimental enthusiasm which they wanted, and which they found in Jean-Jacques, and his light-minded wit was not to their taste. So that, oddly enough, the aristocracy being for the time unrepresented as a class or power in France, Voltaire fell into the position of the pet author of the bourgeoisie; the class which, while it clung to the religious *Aufklärung*, dreaded and disliked the complete political development to which that *Aufklärung* led. Still more curious was the counter-influence which tended to produce a similar effect. So potent an Achilles' spear was the genius of Jean-Jacques, that it inspired the reaction against the Revolution quite as much as it inspired the Revolution itself, and was responsible for Châteaubriand at least as much as for Robespierre. So that the sentimental counter-movement of which Châteaubriand himself, de Maistre, Lamartine in his early days, and much later Montalembert, may be perhaps taken as in different ways representative men, while often expressing no lively affection for Rousseau, contributed, in its turn, to exalt him at the expense of his rival. Both these movements culminated in the romantic outburst. In this the ultra-revolutionary and the anti-revolutionary currents met, and, strangely mingled, took a new direction. Never perhaps did a king of letters pay such a tribute to Nemesis as Voltaire did at this moment. As every man's hand had been for him sixty years before, so every man's was against him now. The clerical party revived and asserted its undying hatred. The sentimentalist excited the *fils des Croisés* to arms against the *fils de Voltaire*. The ornaments of young France hurled their most picturesque epithets at the favourite author of national guards and grocers, the composer of classic plays, the enemy of everything *flamboyant* and romantic. Purely literary students turned to Corneille and Rotrou, or went further back still to the great names of the sixteenth century, and if they condescended to pay any attention at all to the *philosophes*, busied themselves with the more sympathetic genius of Diderot. Steady-going friends of order shuddered over the memories attached to the name, and *doctrinaire* republicans shook their heads over it as that of anything but a *Pur*. These noisy classes did not, after all, represent the bulk of the nation, but they certainly took care to represent its voice, and that loudly.

Meanwhile Rousseau fared better. All these sects owed him too much to abuse him very violently, though none cared fully to acknowledge their obligation. But justice and something more than justice had already been done to Rousseau by a foreign poet. Few, I suppose, can now fairly estimate the influence which Byron exercised in Europe from 1820 to 1840, and during that time the famous verses in *Childe Harold* represent the view of Voltaire and Rousseau, which all who were not independent students on the one hand, or religious bigots on the other, were likely to have most frequently in their memory. Every one still knows those lines, and out of proportion as the allowance is which gives page after page of glowing tribute to the one, and a single stanza of not too accurate and utterly inadequate praise to the other, it is perhaps a fair specimen of time's revenges on the life experience of the two men.

But all things pass. The exaggerated idolatry with which Voltaire in his own later years was regarded, the exaggerated obloquy with which religious and political fanaticism took occasion by the French Revolution to requite that idolatry, the sentimental enthusiasm for Rousseau to which Byron gives expression, the temporary disgrace into which Voltaire fell in France, the scorn which transcendentalists and merely historical philosophers felt for him in Germany, all had their day. In England Mr. Carlyle's famous essays on the *philosophes* cleared away at least the grosser calumnies of bigotry, substituted knowledge for ignorance, and gave conclusions which, if they do not satisfy all students as accurate or adequate, were an enormous advance on anything previously accessible in the language. And in England, as in other countries, clearer and independent judgment became gradually possible. Even theological and political intolerance has now for the most part agreed to regard both our heroes as Satans sufficiently extinct to deserve polite treatment; and High Tories and High Churchmen can now treat the author of the Social Contract and the author of the Philosophical Dictionary with historic calmness. The last direct echo of the *Nouvelle Héloise* died ten years ago with Lamartine, the sons of the Crusaders have pretty well relinquished the unequal combat and descended from their prancing steeds, 'Garde National' is a joke and a reproach no more, and *Candide* may be read in France without the slightest danger of any contributor to *Le Parnasse contemporain* brandishing adjectives in the face of the reader. Here and there perhaps some little outburst or survival of spite or ignorance may show itself. A clerical meeting may here and there gravely discuss in England the conduct of a lecturer to young ladies who has hinted that Voltaire was not quite accurately to be described as an infamous and abandoned wretch, and a clerical journal may here and there diligently sum up in France all the hard things he said about democracy, and all his praises of English and Germans as compared with Frenchmen. Or even, which is perhaps most amusing to the impartial spectator, a few monotheistic devotees of Voltaire himself may protest against the association of the citizen of Geneva with their deity. But these are all exceptions hardly of force to be mentioned. The mere volume and variety, to say nothing of the purport, of the works of the two great men we celebrate, must always occasion a wide difference in the comparative estimate formed of their greatness; but that they rank on any admissible system of estimation with the greatest names of the world, is a proposition which I cannot conceive to be rejected by the majority of intelligence and culture in any country, whether for the standard of admission be taken the influence which the ideas they expressed have exercised on human history, or the literary excellence of the forms in which those ideas were expressed.

Some faint protest has been heard against a celebration of this sort, in this case, on the ground of the moral character of the two men whose lives it is proposed to celebrate. No one, I suppose, will attempt to set up either Rousseau or Voltaire for saints. The transgressions of the latter were, indeed, from the point of view of his age and country, far from heavy; and the active and persevering benevolence of his later life might be considered as something of a makeweight. Rousseau's abandonment of his children is a somewhat different matter, and, however we may give him the credit of having painted himself blacker than he really was, it is perhaps difficult to avoid a certain amount of disgust as one reads or thinks of some parts of his character. But we may ask whether it is usual in such case to test men who, in one way or another, may have been notable and eminent in the world, by the conformity of their life to moral laws? A very slight examination will, I think, show that this is very rarely done, and that if it were done, the profane hagiology of the world would find itself singularly curtailed and mutilated. Let us look only at the contemporaries of the very men whose characters are now being discussed. Would anyone object to the commemoration of Frederic the Great for his indomitable courage, his earnest patriotism, his endeavours to do justice to the meanest of his subjects, and his splendid military genius, because his private moral character was in some respects undoubtedly, in others not improbably, one of the worst and most detestable on record? Is it so very certain, again, that the moral character of Goethe stands higher than the moral character of Voltaire? And are we sure that characters which, from the one-sided and imperfect knowledge we possess of them, now appear decorous enough, would bear the frightful strain of being depicted in such an autobiography as the *Confessions*, or the concentrated malignity of the myriad scribblers who hated Voltaire? The general practice in such matters seems to be fair enough. Honour no man for his vices. But let his vices, as in the great majority of cases they do in fact, die with him. It does no mortal any harm now that Voltaire did not always respect the truth, and was sometimes impatient for supper; that Rousseau carried into later life the faults and vices of lackeys and children, and allowed his disease both of body and mind to increase and magnify them. Let these dead things rest with the dead men who did them. They are dead and past, they are not what we celebrate, and thus also they can in no way be of force to interfere with our celebration.

The things that we do celebrate are something very different. I have already in some lame fashion hinted at the practical achievements which may be laid to their account. But there is another side of their greatness, and one which is, fortunately, less likely to be disputed. We have now, at least the wiser among us, arrived at some greater catholicity in literary taste than our fathers possessed. It is no longer a wonder, as Macaulay once admiringly asserted of Leigh Hunt, that a man should be able to adore Shakespeare and Spenser without denying poetry to Dryden and humour to Addison. On the contrary, the man who should openly advance such a denial in consequence of such a prepossession, would now be thought either an eccentric or a very silly person. And if we have thus escaped the fetters of the older criticism as to our own writers, how much more ought we to have escaped them in the case of foreigners, whose names have never, as far, at least, as literary matters go, had the misfortune to serve as shibboleths in England. I know that contempt is wrong and unworthy of the scholar, but I should myself find it hard to avoid despising a man who could not enjoy *Mahomet* or *Zaire*, because of his admiration for *Saint Genest* or *Rodogune* at one end of the roll, or for *Hernani* at the other; who could not like *Le Pauvre Diable* well because he liked *La Légende des Siècles* better, and who felt it necessary to find fault with *L'Ingénu* for fear of wronging Bonaventure des Periers or Théophile Gautier. Whoever is insensible to the charm of Voltaire may take it for granted that his literary organisation is wanting in one and a main faculty. I cannot admit, as Byron and many more would have it, that Voltaire succeeds better in ridicule than in anything else. It would rather seem that his lighter work appeals to a larger circle, and thus the incomparable literary aptitude which he brought to bear on everything is in less danger of escaping notice. It is true that in these lighter works he has caught up the sum of Gallic wit, and uttered it once for all. But the literary charm of all his work is the same. I can remember once borrowing the *Dictionnaire Philosophique*, in some half-dozen big volumes, from a friend (who was so obliging as to lend me his wheelbarrow for their better conveyance), and reading them straight through with immense delight, though such philosophy as I am tinctured with is as far as possible from being Voltairean. I can say the same of the notes on Corneille, with many of which I have the pleasure of being in modest but irreconcilable disagreement. The style of Voltaire is so saturated with lightness and cheerfulness, with reason that gives itself no airs, and gaiety that knows how to keep reason at not too great distance, that it is in itself and irrespective of its subjects an intellectual refreshment and treat.

Certainly as much, though in a different kind, may be said of Rousseau. Few things can be more different from the style of Voltaire than the style of the *Nouvelle Héloise*, of the *Contrat Social*, of the *Confessions*, and of the *Rêveries*; not many such things even can be more different from each other than the styles of these four masterpieces. There is not about the style of Rousseau the unity which characterises the style of his rival. Yet the luscious sentiment of the *Héloise*, the crisp dogmatism of the *Contrat*, the splendid narrative quality of the *Confessions*, the meditative charm of the *Rêveries*, find their expression with equal ease and equal effectiveness at Rousseau's hands. Even a foreigner can discover at once in this style something which is not directly French, which has the strength that a mixture of race sometimes gives, and at the same time the distinctness of savour which such a mixture sometimes destroys. Sir Walter Scott is reported to have said that he could not feel the interest or see the merit of the *Héloise*. Yet the *Héloise*, whether Scott knew it or not, is more than any other book responsible for the romantic movement of which he himself was so doughty a leader. By it an end was put once for all to the *commerce rampant de soupirs et de flammes*, as the heroine of Corneille's *Sertorius*, born before or after her time, calls the love-making of the classical school. By it rather than by any other book were men guided to the discovery of the beauty that is in nature, if not of the beauty that is in art. It revived if it did not initiate the charm felt in:

Le regret pensif et confus
D'avoir été et n'être plus,

as words attributed to the great French poet whom Boileau maligned have it. If in some cases it became the parent of a deplorable family (to transfer an epigram from Diderot to Rousseau), in others it gave us some of the most memorable literary accomplishments of Europe, and but for it the world had wanted many a noble song as well as many an idle one. As for the *Contrat Social*, its philosophical merit, as well as its historical influence, hardly here concern us. But as a literary performance, it may be fairly said of it, that it was almost the first political treatise which was sent home to its mark in a modern language by the feathers of literary power. The *Confessions* have had a more dubious influence. But it may at least be claimed for them that they have helped to overthrow the custom of draping heroes and heroines in the garments of conventional success, and have impressed on not a few readers the tragedy that lies in sordid and undignified failure, no less than failure of the splendid and dramatic order. This truth has become in the last century one far more recognised than at any former time, and curiously enough we may find it even to a certain extent recognised by Voltaire also. *Candide* expresses the ironic side of the matter as fully as *La Nouvelle Héloise* expresses the sentimental one, and so the Heraclitus and Democritus, the Jean-qui-pleure and Jean-qui-rit, of the eighteenth century, lend a hand to each other to influence the literature of the time that comes after them as unwittingly as they have lent a hand to influence its conduct. Literature of *persiflage* and literature of complaint, guerilla warfare against individual abuses and recurrence to first principles that so those abuses may not arise, thus complete each other in a very singular manner. And in literature as in life the question may perhaps be fairly asked, if 1878 differs from 1778 infinitely more than 1778 from 1678, are there any two men to whom the increased proportion of change can be more fairly and in larger measure ascribed than to François Marie Arouet and Jean-Jacques Rousseau?

It is not without hesitation that a mere pawn in the army of letters can speak or write of men of this eminence. To take upon one's self to commend those whose merit has with instructed and competent persons long passed out of the class of debated questions, may seem in all but the few chosen among their successors something of an impertinence. But such an occasion as the present is one of those in which the most insignificant of the living are allowed and indeed expected to show their appreciation of the mighty dead. No fault that I know of is found with those who, with an intention of honour, strew flowers or even weeds on a grave, however small their claim to do so. Yet the commemoration of Rousseau and Voltaire, whatever form it may take in their own country, and whatever support it may receive in other countries, will not add one jot to their merited glory, nor had it been omitted would it detract therefrom. For they are of the order of men of whom our twin dramatists ask in that magnificent epitaph on Pompey:

> Dare you think your pyramids,
> Built to outdure the sun as you suppose,
> Where your unworthy kings lie raked in ashes,
> Are monuments fit for them? No, brood of Nilus!
> Nothing can cover their high fame but heaven;
> No pyramids set off their memories,
> But the eternal substance of their greatness,
> To which I leave them.

Fortnightly Review, May, 1878.

Footnote.—Voltaire was an extremely complicated character; the wonderful diversity of his literary work only reflects this complexity in part, though the one no doubt is the reason of the other. As I can hardly think of any man who displayed so many different forms of the literary faculty, so I can hardly think of any man, whether of letters or of business, who united the capacity and in a way the actual performance of so many different parts. Of his varied ability in practical administrative business there is proof almost as ample as of his varied ability in literary work. If he failed anywhere in what he undertook it was in diplomacy, and it is fair to remember that he had an antagonist to contend with there by whom it was no shame to be beaten. He has not, like Wordsworth, left us explicit intimations that in his own opinion his mission was to be Prime Minister, or Archbishop of Canterbury, or Commander-in-Chief, or Lord Chancellor, or all of them together. But I have no doubt that if the opportunity of any or all of these posts had come in his way he would have accepted it cheerfully, and would have performed the duties on the whole very well. The complementary defect of the quality of Jack-of-all-trades is well known. Voltaire suffered from it less than most people, but he did suffer from it. In no literary style, except in that of satirical prose fiction, or allegory of the social kind, can he be said to have attained the highest mastery. In work requiring research of any kind he was rather rapid than thorough, and he carried to excess the national habit of hasty deduction from insufficiently investigated premises. His moral and intellectual character, with which we are here more specially concerned, shows inconsistencies and blemishes of all kinds. Let us try and sum up what the devil's advocates say against him. He was an unscrupulous liar; he was extraordinarily vain; he was utterly destitute of reverence; he had an impure imagination, which was not checked by the slightest sense of even external decency; he was given to filthy lucre; he was spiteful and revengeful in the extreme towards his personal enemies. This is an ugly catalogue, and it is unfortunately true that no single article in it can be struck out entirely by the most uncompromising defender who knows and respects the facts. Mitigating pleas are all that is possible. His lying, which is a very unpleasant feature to English examiners of his character, has to be taken in conjunction with the fact that it was, so to speak, official and professional lying for the most part. The absurd and iniquitous political and social system of the time and country necessitated and in a manner recognised it. It was little more than the conventional 'not guilty', not so much as the equally conventional 'not at home'. The charge of vanity must be admitted *sans phrase*, but it is not a very damning one. The lack of reverence also is not contestable, though there are some circumstances on the other side, notably the mountain-top story. This was, however, a distinct and inevitable consequence of his peculiar faculty of ridicule, which must also excuse as far as it can (and that is not very far) the uncleanness of his writings. I shall frankly own that that uncleanness is to me the most unpleasant variety of the disease that I know, with the possible exception of Dryden's. His carrying out of the maxim *non olet* is another blot on his character. There is nothing inexcusable, though perhaps there is something rather undignified, in a poet's making money by stockbroking and money-changing; but the Hirsch matter cannot be defended, and the persistent way in which the author of *L'Homme aux Quarante Ecus* and a hundred other protests against financial mismanagement allowed himself to profit by contracts, loans, and so forth, where the profit was due to corrupt administration, is a still greater blot. With respect to Fréron, Desfontaines, et Cie., perhaps the worst thing that can be said about Voltaire is that in point of malignity there is sometimes nothing and generally very little to choose between himself and his adversaries.

All the worst of his faults were emphatically the faults of his time and his education. His merits, on the other hand, were personal and his own, a distinction which, however hackneyed it may be, is almost the only one available in this world of ours. One of the chief of them was an extraordinary kindness of heart and affection for his friends, relations, and, indeed, everybody with whom he was not brought into violent collision. Notwithstanding his occasional fits of ill-temper all his servants and dependants were fond of him, and even the passionate Collini did not find those fits intolerable. Something, perhaps, must be allowed for his love of playing the grand seigneur in estimating his good deeds at Ferney; but even when that allowance is made a solid amount will remain to his credit. Unscrupulous as he was in some ways in the getting of money, he neither spent it unworthily nor hoarded it for the mere sake of hoarding; his object being, as has been said, the securing of independence, which in his time and country no man, who was neither a priest nor a noble, could hope for without a competent estate. (*Fortnightly Review*, August, 1881.)

MANON LESCAUT

EVERYBODY who writes about Manon Lescaut—at least, everybody who is however partially worthy to write about her—must acknowledge that he is not wholly so, though he may be helped by partnership like the companion of a heroine of Mr. Kipling's in a less agreeable adventure—and must also say something about her author. In personality, from what one can make out, sufficiently commonplace in all usual respects, the Abbé Prévost seems to have been the sport of unusual fates in a way which is almost uncanny. About ninety per cent. of his history or chart might be that of any literary hack of his time, passing the ordinary days and years in London, Paris or Amsterdam; producing dozens or scores (Prévost actually got into his second hundred) of volumes; marrying or (as the housekeeper so delicately says in *Old Mortality*) 'doing waur'; and finally dying after a literary quarrel or two, perhaps an arrest, for anything in France, in England for debt, but as a rule ending quietly enough, though as an exception not so, like Gilbert with them, like Chatterton with us. But omitting minor matters, this comparatively blank or commonplace *dossier* of his provides in the rest of it two things of the most different kind, which are of the most extraordinary character and interest. He wrote a masterpiece, and one of a kind which constitutes, even more than most masterpieces do, a species to itself. And the exact fashion of his death became the subject of a story or stories which, after not being heard of for some twenty years, were for the most part accepted for more than a hundred, then strongly but not quite unanimously challenged, the challenge being allowed for the most part since as made good, though perhaps rather in the absence than through the defeat or defect of anybody willing to take it up. As it is, though certainly interesting, a matter which has nothing to do with our main subject, it may be as well to get it out of the way at once. Manon, by herself Manon, is more than sufficient already.

The story of Prévost's death, as accepted not indeed immediately afterwards but, as observed above, for nearly a century after it began to be told, was a sufficiently gruesome one. He had been stricken with apoplexy (this seems to have been actually the case though it may have been aneurism) as he was walking in the Forest of Chantilly. 'Justice' having been quite properly sent for—though it is nowhere clearly stated what person or persons 'Justice' consisted of—it as properly sent for a surgeon to 'constate' the death. The surgeon, considering a *post-mortem* necessary, began one, but in such a thorough-going manner that he at once ascertained that the patient was not dead—and killed him. This story started (about twenty years after the occurrence) in 1763, remained uncontradicted as far as general currency went, and was in a fashion confirmed to Sainte-Beuve in the middle of the nineteenth century by a great-niece of the sufferer. But the modern tendency to rummage into everything could not let such a thing alone: and at last in 1896 M. Henri Harrisse, for his book on Prévost, searched all accessible documents, and treated it very much as it had treated its luckless subject, showing how it had lived and (as has been perhaps generally allowed) killing it. Aneurism is indeed, though more by guess than on evidence, substituted for apoplexy; but the fatal revival disappears. Let us hope this is the case; but a person of sceptical tendencies may not be quite sure yet. In the first place, odd things of new kinds have turned up, especially a singular legend about the possession of the body being quarrelled over and the quarrel settled by money, between the *curé* of the parish and the representative of a local monastery. This M. Harrisse did not altogether reject—for which he was rebuked by a successor of his, M. Schroeder, in 1898. Moreover (and I do not think either of these bionecrographers quite recognised this) the earlier records, though they do not expressly support the myth, by no means exclude it.

Indeed, there are in them some very queer differences: one document alleging death on the spot, another placing it in a *maison presbytériale*; and one putting some excellent and pious observations in the mouth of the moribund, while *apoplexie foudroyante* is apparently assigned by others. For my own part, I am not a lover of 'thrills': I think I like the fictitious one even less than the real. But there is one point about this matter which does not seem to me to have occurred either to M. Harrisse or to M. Schroeder. Suppose, for the sake of argument merely, that the gruesomer versions were true. If so, 'la Justice' and the unlucky and clumsy surgeon would have found themselves in a rather awkward situation: for 'Justice' by its directions, and the surgeon by his execution of them, had undoubtedly killed a man. I do not pretend to know French law in details at that time: but I do know that it was then capable of being set to work in a very disagreeable fashion by persons in authority, or possessing 'interest'. If any such person had got wind of this unlucky *bévue* on the part of subordinate law and medicine, it seems to me that a round fine at least might have resulted, and perhaps something more personally unpleasant still. It would therefore be in the interest of these persons—locally all-powerful but understrappers to those above them—to suppress awkward details. It is hardly necessary to say that it was equally the interest of Prévost's brother to put pious expressions into the victim's mouth, while assigning him a place of actual death quite different from that in the formal *acte de décès*; or to add that the whole set of documents, new and old, is decidedly 'mixed'. I most sincerely hope that the author of *Manon Lescaut* suffered as natural and painless a death as possible, but if I am asked as an almost lifelong critic of documents and a twenty years' practitioner in the study, if only as a journalist, of criminal, accidental, and other 'cases', I am bound to give a verdict of 'Not sufficiently proven either way' or in Latin 'Non liquet'.

Of course this question is not a strictly literary one; but it may justly interest human beings, and still more (to use the elegant old word) 'even Christians'. Some extremely severe censors might also say that the subject of the other literary work of Prévost is irrelevant, likewise: but this, begging their pardon, is absurd. It certainly does not fail to enhance the charm of an oasis (if there are any oases now, and they haven't become mere motor halts) to know something of its surrounding desert. It may be that it has been too much the habit to dismiss, without knowing much or anything about it, the balance of the poor Abbé's enormous work as mere wilderness; but that is no reason for going to the other extreme and cracking part of it up. I do not pretend to have read it all: I rather doubt whether anybody ever has: but I have read enough of the three huge principals—the *Mémoires d'un Homme de Qualité* (matrix of Manon herself but a matrix how far inferior to the turquoise!), *Cléveland*, and the *Doyen de Killérine* (Coleraine), as well as of the smaller *Histoire d'une Grecque Moderne* to be fully entitled to speak of them, and even perhaps to disagree with Sainte-Beuve, but only with the earliest and unripest Sainte-Beuve. *Cléveland* and the *Mémoires*, as indeed the fact that Manon herself is a sort of *enclave* of the latter will show, are rather huge collections of miscellaneous fiction with touches of half-reality in them, than single and consolidated novels or romance. The *Doyen* is somewhat more of a structure and less of a collection; and the *Grecque Moderne* really comes into a kind of specific comparison with Manon.

This rather odd-looking phrase may require explanation. Prévost was a sort of purblind pioneer or harbinger of the historical novel, actually writing books on William the Conqueror and Margaret of Anjou, which are half history, half not: while in his other books classed as fictions, real people come sometimes. The she-Modern-Greek has not been without her admirers: but I have neither admiration nor affection for her. She is bought as a slave and freed by a very sentimental and comparatively virtuous young Frenchman. Then there is a great deal of fine confused love-making, which comes to no particular end, respectable or other. If there is nothing improper, there is also nothing impassioned: if there is some advance in what people have been pleased recently to call *technique* there is no more delicate *Marivaudage* of style than there is indelicate *Crébillonnade* of action. I ventured some years ago to call it 'an exceedingly dull book', and I see no reason to retract the judgment.

The fact would seem to be that—with apologies to those who get so angry with metaphors, analogies, parallels, similes and so forth, which are the farthest advance towards analysis of literature that wise criticism permits itself—Prévost is really a pilgrim of novel-writing, who finds the object of his quest once and once only, but in so finding achieves, for that once, amazingly. He was perhaps less original than his contemporary, Horace Walpole, for undoubtedly he not only imitated his own countrymen, Marivaux and Crébillon, but our people, Defoe, and Richardson, the latter of whom he actually translated (fancy translating Richardson!), while 'Horry', to do him justice, did not exactly copy anybody. But then, grateful to it as we may be, considering its inestimable progeny, we cannot help admitting that *The Castle of Otranto* has no intrinsic merit whatever, except its merit of kind. It is as if in literary biology, Evolutionism and Creationism had combined, and the gorilla had in the very next generation produced a man and all the generations of men since. Now Manon is Eve herself, Eve a little naughtier but almost as charming, and with nothing before in the least like her. For remember, the book is not a romance: there is, strictly speaking, no poetry in it, though there is infinite passion, and abundant incident, such as would make poetry. Character reigns throughout, and character is the novel's subject in both senses, and its sovereign as well.

It would be a banality merely to repeat what has been so often said of *Manon*, that its charm lies in its intense humanity—if it were not that humanity itself in one sense always, in another never, *is* banal. Exactly how he managed to convey this humanity into his book, it is impossible to say. It is certainly the secret of his success:

but the secret of this secret remains unrevealed. In the immense mass of his other books—at least in the large proportion of that immensity, which the present writer has read—there is abundance of that *larmoiement* [1] which was so characteristic of his time and country. But though there is more room for tears in *Manon* than in all the rest of it put together, and though of course some are shed, the book is anything but sloppy or showery with them. The wasting (if love could ever be wasted) of such a love as his; the squandering (there is no 'if' here) of such charm as hers, go deeper than what were once rather well called 'the *accepted* hells'. The very fact that it is possible for somebody, if not for anybody, to say 'What a fuss to make over a fool of a boy, and a baggage of a girl!' is a rather triumphant testimonial to the book itself. That which is not ridiculable is almost always a long way from the sublime, though that which is only ridiculable is farther and hopelessly far. No one worth attending to for a moment would put *Manon* in the latter class.

To what extent this extraordinary intensity is due to the complete freedom of the book from anything Crébillonish is a curious question, but not one to be worked out here. A lesser artist or, shall we say an artist less for the nonce under such extraordinary guidance and guardianship, would probably, would almost certainly, have thrown in for contrast and relief something of the kind. But Apollo and Pallas, for once sitting *in banco* with Aphrodite, thought of another thing and a better, and gave Prévost the power to carry it out.

In the original, *Manon* is hooked or tow-roped on to the main craft by the obvious dodge of a meeting between the Man of Quality and Des Grieux: and I believe some modern students have tried to imagine such an actual meeting on the part of Prévost, and a sub-stratum at least of reality in the story. They would, I believe further, be particularly glad to know that Tiberge was a real person. For my part, Tiberge is the only thing or person in which or whom I see no merit, except that he is a good fellow and does belong to the story, and I extend my utmost commiseration, blended with something that begins with 'con-' if not with 'com-', to people who want novels to have real persons in them.[2] But the same mixture may be extended to them on another count—their obvious ignorance

[1] *Larmoyance* would be much nicer: but the French dictionary admits only the other, and its prudery as to *verba inusitata* must not be violated.

[2] This does not reflect on the historical novel proper. There the real persons have stories attached to them. Which is different.

of, or want of relish for, the facts of literary history. Among these, few are more interesting than the curious discomfort which, when the novel came at last to be born, seems to have attended the birth of the earlier representatives of the family. 'To' romance (as the more recent announcements at the head of the first column of *The Times* put it) its children came quite easily, and with no excuses, though there might be affiliations. The novel, well into the nineteenth century, generally if not always, thought it necessary to assure its readers that it had come specially into the world by being 'told' to somebody or 'found' by somebody or the like, instead of boldly proclaiming that it was simply invention. Even Scott, who has made capital fun of these excuses and pretexts in more places than one, condescends (with very pleasant results) to do practically the same thing in not a few of his Introductions. For our part, let nothing of the kind be required. That there were numerous young persons of more or less discreditable life, who in the earlier part of the eighteenth century were sent to America from France, I have no doubt. That not all their lovers were, as our rough old English used to denominate the male companions of such persons, 'rogues', I think possible. But Manon and Des Grieux the Gods gave Prévost commission or permission to *make*.

The curious supplement, inset, episode, or whatever you like to call it, of the Italian prince and his discomfiture has, I believe, been, as indeed it was sure to be, regarded with disfavour by some critics. It shows no doubt the heroine in a curiously different light from that in which she appears before and after: while either in mere fanciful consequence of this or really, as a twenty years later production, it may seem to be out of keeping in ways not necessarily connected with this. But I think it may be defended even if, or especially when, it is relegated to an appendix, on more grounds than one, though one of these grounds may be a ground of stumbling to my rivals in Manonolatry. In the first place, the author may have wished to show a kind of change in her, which, though it came before a relapse in the matter of the younger G * * M * *, is not impossible, and even psychologically (one begs pardon of the poor word, so misused now, for using it at all) improbable, and which justifies the completer repentance later still. Secondly, it is, if not necessary, certainly useful as a strengthener to Des Grieux in his fidelity, which nearly did give way, and might otherwise have given way altogether, under the crowning trial of such a letter, brought by such a messenger as figures or figure in what we may call the Fourth Act. Thirdly, and here 'the beast goes shrinkingly' (as the poet says in that charming Greek picture-poem in which pedants pick holes), it must be remembered—as it always ought to be remembered, and has not been too often—that Manon is not a 'lady'. She might have been much worse, or not bad at all, if she had been: but she was not one: and her not being one is one of the secrets of her composition. Des Grieux is a gentleman—that is to say, of course, a French gentleman—all through: but Manon, till the final sword of sorrow and suffering has made her one at the last, is not a lady. Victorian? Possibly it is: in fact, it is the absence of this quality which explains and thus in a manner excuses her conduct. Had she possessed it, she might have had quite as many lovers, and been quite as liberal to them, but in a different way. She would almost certainly have been jealous of Des Grieux—for ladies even when polyandrously inclined are not often disposed to tolerate polygamy. In all her earlier affairs there would appear (that with Des Grieux himself excepted) nothing more romantic than there is in a cook or a housemaid exchanging a lower-waged place for a higher-waged one, or making additional profit by taking duty during her evenings out, days off and holidays. The mirror business is symptomatically *un*ladylike: and it is one of the gains to the story which this episode brings that it almost shocks Des Grieux. But the unconquerableness of the girl has a new victory here. Manon, right or wrong, has been, is, and will be the final result of all his deliberations and all his experiences, all his raptures, and all his woes. Of course, somebody may be shocked (though it requires a certain originality to be shocked now) at this view of the Italian's misfortunes, of Manon's conduct, and of Des Grieux's attitude. It was right that the wicked prince should be foiled and insulted; it was, though only a partial, yet a partially partial return, to virtue on the part of Mlle. Lescaut, and the Chevalier Des Grieux, after congratulating (with qualifications) the young person on her correct if uncivil conduct, should have expressed the desire that they themselves should act in accordance with it, and part. Equally, of course, the bringing of ladylikeness, of unladylikeness, into the matter may be the subject of shock or rather scorn. If so, I apologise; but suggest that persons who hold either of those views had better not read any more. Those who take this wonderful dealing of art with nature as such may perhaps like to compare further their views with those of one who has read it at twenty, at forty, at sixty and at eighty, with always fresh astonishment and admiration.

Perhaps:

> To talk too much of Heaven
> Is not well,

(as that true, but I fear little-read poetess Margaret Veley says) and once more, expressions have been made more recently to the effect that it is not well to talk too much, if at all, of gentlemen and ladies. Indeed, about the last time that I remember enjoying a genuine and hearty laugh over anything in a newspaper, it was at reading that to call a woman a lady was 'unequivocal vulgarity'. The vistas opened on the writer's society, experience, taste, and several other circumstances and conditions were too provocative. And I suppose that if to call a woman a lady is bad, to call her not one is even worse, while to avow affection for her notwithstanding this is worst. Yet, if we take the taboo off, and discuss both Manon and her lover, they 'acquire interest' in rather an astonishing degree. Des Grieux, as is proper, acquires the less volume of it, or would do so if his share were not complicated by the contrast of the French and English variety of the species 'gentleman'. To work that contrast out in detail of history and character would be delightful, but here impossible: one can only intimate some lines of the work. In Restoration times, and for some time afterwards, cheating at cards and actual assassination [1] were perhaps possible to gentlemen in England, but in the eighteenth century they became impossible here, though still possible there.

Specially dangerous, as the enterprise may be for one:

> Old as I am, for lady's love unfit,

I do not think it possible to deal with Manon satisfactorily either as book or as heroine of a book, without saying something concerning the most attractive and the most dangerous of subjects, 'love in the *aib*stract', as the lady of Aberdeen was heard saying to the young gentleman in the intervals of the mazy dance.

If Burton has attracted many readers by his title, he has probably disappointed no small proportion by his dealing with 'Heroic' Love.

[1] I mean by assassination (as distinguished from killing in a duel, which is quite a different thing) such deeds as the murder in Lincoln's Inn Fields in which Monmouth took part in fact, or that committed by Vanbrugh's Sir John Brute and his friends in fiction. It requires, I fear, a good deal of special pleading to clear Des Grieux of something like this in the case of the lay brother who blocked his exit, and I do not think that at the same time any Englishman above a Sir John Brute himself would have done it. And he avowedly, though rather unwillingly, cheated at cards.

Exactly what he means by the adjective he never and nowhere closely defines, coming nearest to such a definition, though making it by no means a philosophical one, in the place where at the end of Sub-section Two of his Third Part, he gives 'comeliness of person and beauty' alone for object of the passion, which is termed 'heroical or love-melancholy'. It is indeed probable, if not certain, that 'heroic' is used here in closest connection with, if not absolute dependence on, its use in regard to the heroic poem, the heroic play, and the heroic romance of the period, which even now wait for a thorough and complete examination of the exact range and meaning of the term. Burton himself brings in a good deal which perhaps might have been left out, and leaves out a good deal that might perhaps have been brought in, both as to things of connotation and things of denotation. But he undoubtedly is more or less aiming at what is best called perhaps *passionate* love: the most general, and almost universal theme of poetry, that of nearly all serious and a good deal of comic drama at all times more or less, and certainly the main one of prose fiction, or (latterly) novel writing. It is the present writer's serious and critical judgment that few, if any, more successful embodiments of the motive in the last of these divisions of literature exist than *Manon Lescaut;* and, whether the proposition be a mere truism or a stale paradox, there seem to him to be some things that may without actual impertinence still be said about it.

It is, of course, easy to be virtuous in the old fashion, or clever in the new, and say with scorn or snigger, 'What? You call this impure attachment, or this exaggerated flirtation, love in the abstract?' Well, yes, we do. In the case of Des Grieux, it requires either considerable density or considerable impudence to deny it. In all his dealings with Manon, he has nothing to gain but Manon. She has no money, no interest, no portion, no rank. She is not a 'conquest' (as they said in and after those days in English) that he can win and throw away as he liked, and does accordingly. He has to pay for what she gives him not merely with all his worldly goods but with his fame, his honour, with almost everything—*except* love, that is—that is worth living for.

With Manon of course it is different. She is reckless of money, at least in her ways of spending and getting it—to do her justice one cannot imagine her hoarding, as some persons open to other charges against her have done; while as for 'fame' and 'honour' they are things which for a long time (till love itself has taught her) she does not understand. But she is never out of love with her lover, inconceivable as this may seem to persons who do not, perhaps will not, or indeed possibly cannot understand *her*. It is hardly a paradox that if she did not love her lover quite so much she could not have behaved so badly to him. The passion is a thing apart, intangible and infrangible by ordinary circumstances and experiences. And by a further paradox in appearance, which is not really one in reality, it is probable that her infidelities aggravated rather than lessened the passion of her lover for herself, if they did not even *increase* her love for him. Of course it may be said: 'But do you call all this healthy?' Certainly not: one would be paradoxing and, as too often happens, paradoxing sillily if one held up the book as a gospel of Venus Urania. But it is certainly not one of her sister Pandemos: and in the central spirit of it, if not in the details, perhaps something which is more 'love in the abstract' than elsewhere in the wide range of Erotics can be found.

There are, however, some special points which may be dwelt on with less coming in danger of paradox or extravagance. The virtuous but sometimes rather pragmatical literary activity of modern times has, as one might expect, busied itself with Prévost as with others; and one result of this is the discovery of a great deal more translation certainly, and imitation possibly, in English than had been suspected. Manon herself, indeed, though translated more than once and on one of these occasions by such a more than nobody as Charlotte Smith, exercised little or no influence: for the time *with us* was not yet. And recent critics seem to have pushed the quest of something new too far in trying to make Prévost the father of Romance.[1] It is one of Manon's innumerable uncanninesses that, as was partly shown above, she is not romantic in the very least, while Des Grieux is hardly more so. For though there can be no romance without

[1] But Mr. James Foster in his *Prévost and the English Novel* (Publications of the Modern Language Society of America for June 1927) has collected a mighty list of translations and suggested a mightier one of imitations, inspirations and the like. I confess that I think he has altogether overrated the Abbé's influence on individuals, though perhaps not that on a certain group or period of English novelists. To put the thing perhaps a little too epigrammatically, Prévost influenced those who influenced nobody. I can myself see very little resemblance to him in Mrs. Sheridan's *Sidney Biddulph* and still less in Mrs. Radcliffe anywhere, while he certainly may have any share in Miss Lee's rubbishy *Recess* that anybody chooses to assign to him. I desire not to be in the least impolite to Mr. Foster, but I think that he and all his school are much too fond of assuming direct 'imitation', 'influence', 'origin', etc., when there is merely coincidence or at most *similar* influence of period and fashion.

passion, be it of War, of Love, or of Dante's *Salus*—religious fervour —each of all these passions, even Love, may subsist without Romance.

One of the most curious of the frequent *crevasses*, not so apparently wide as unfathomably deep, between French and English taste is, or until quite recently was, to be found in connection with our book. Indeed, if the width has diminished in appearance only, a point on which I am not in the best position to decide, I should say that the recently covered depths remain as great. This is the old French habit of coupling *Paul et Virginie* with *Manon Lescaut*: and while, of course, admitting the difference of the earlier conduct of the two heroines, finding a special and refreshing similarity in the ends of the two as far as virtuous conduct in different circumstances goes. Now I own that to me, hardly any language—whether that used of old, and doubtless also not of old, by 'our Armies in Flanders', or that admitted quite recently to be only a 'technical dialect' in our Navy—could be too strong for this. Even in itself, long before I read *Manon* and still longer before I knew that anyone had dared to compare the two books, the other always seemed to me a very poor thing combining half-scientific instruction with weak literary *sensiblerie*, and coming to an end partly ridiculous and partly disgusting. Such beauty as the book has is merely description, and such morality mainly copybookish, while in *Manon* the book is alive from initial to colophon and its morality is the morality of life likewise. And the two ends? Manon's has what some have called with no small backing, the greatest of graces, Repentance: Virginie's, whatsoever graciousness may appertain to a not over clean-minded prudery. For though 'purity' is pretty close in spelling to the uglier sham-virtue, I cannot see how it requires or even permits a girl practically to throw away life, that greatest (or greatest but one) gift of God to herself, because circumstances have necessitated in her rescuer's case the discarding of the supplementary gifts of the tailor.

As to Manon's 'repentance' there is, of course, open to the Devil's Advocate the cheapest of cheap rejoinders, quite worthy of *him* but quite ineffectual as regards *her*. One of the boldest and strangest things in the book is the engineering of this. She may be said to be almost at her worst when she despatches that outrageous letter, by a messenger who from some points of view makes it more outrageous still. But this in reality is as it were the thickest and darkest stage of the evil stained-glass barrier through which she has regarded certain things from the beginning. She has never hitherto looked at some feminine compliances as other than trifles: and has never realised the intensity of the agony which they inflict on Des Grieux. Furthermore, the love of mere luxury which has been so fatal to her is here converted into an engine of recovery. The sudden and complete failure of all her own plans: the practical impossibility of restoration to luxurious living and the horrors of the transportation, involving as it at first must seem utter separation from the lover whom in her strange way and with such apparently impossible differences she has really and exclusively *loved*, shatter the veils or screens which have surrounded her; disperse the drop *un*serene that has blinded her eyes, and show her things as they are at last. Her death is no cheap and clumsy way of getting rid of her: it is the only thing that could happen, and the brief interval of happiness cunningly checked at the extreme end is, if not the only, a really artistic way of finish. The worst half of Manon had been bad: but it was too intimately interwoven with the better to be torn away and leave its old companion to flourish indefinitely.[1]

It is not very easy to make up one's mind how much deliberate choice there is in the other 'make-up' of the novel, its incidents and its characters outside of the two principals. There is of course always a danger of seeing too much into things: but there is also a danger of seeing too little. There may be intention in the almost entire absence of anything very exciting in this outside. There was nothing in the least out of the way for the time in the internment of Des Grieux, either to protect him from Manon's fascination or to facilitate others' designs on her. Odd as the suborning of some of the King's servants to defeat the King's justice in deporting Manon may seem, it is quite in the way of the *ancien régime*, and Dumas may have thought of it as well as of still nearer and more historical parallels when he made Rochefort borrow fifty recruits of the 'regulars' to take part in a Fronde attempt at something like rebellion. All the rest is curiously *quiet*. People who are fonder of Tiberge than the present writer is no doubt rely on the contrast he presents to the *furor heroicus* of his friend. Des Grieux's father and brother, though

[1] There have been, as there were sure to be, attempts as idiotic as tasteless, to resuscitate Manon, one I believe making her return to her seductions and involve Tiberge in them. I have always taken the trouble to look up the appendices and suggestions of my reading when they seemed in any possible way likely to deserve it; but I had to draw the line here. For the thing, besides being sacrilegious, is simply stupid.

they—and little shame to them—endeavour to control his madness, can hardly be called tyrannical; the very manslaughter of the unlucky lay brother is slipped over. Even in the final scenes, in a colony where almost any atrocity was in the power of authority to commit, it cannot be said that this authority much abuses its possibilities. It is at least possible to argue, though I do not know that I quite adopt the argument, that Prévost deliberately and as a matter of art flattened and qualified the colours, sounds, outlines of his presentation in order to keep the attention of his readers concentrated always and utterly on this at once human and super-human infatuation of the lovers for each other, and on the torment which one for a time—if not for *all* the time in different ways—inflicts and the other suffers.

One of not the least astonishing things in the book is the quiet pathos of its end. Certain persons—amusing in their way but of whom one soon tires even as amusers—especially after spending some forty years in their desert from 1890 onwards—may call, perhaps even think, it mawkish. Manon probably didn't dress Des Grieux's wound nearly so well as it would have been done at a 'clinic': and arranging your garments so as to make another person more comfortable is almost Victorian. Yet perhaps there may be some to whom things look differently and to whom especially the contrast of this quiet misery and this exchange of charities with the too heedless enjoyments and the bitter disappointments of the earlier book may have a singular charm. And not the least part of this charm will be a continuance of the strange diversity between the persons who have been and are so passionately united. With Des Grieux it is in a way merely continuance—development under fresh circumstances of the unfailing sweetness of his character. With Manon it is apparently—if only apparently, for we have plenty of patterns in hagiography and perhaps out of it—an exchange from debauchery to devotion—from 'wretchlessness of most unclean living' to the very opposite. Perhaps one may admit that the tale had here, taking place and time together, no small advantage in being told by a Frenchman rather than by an Englishman. We might have done it, if we had then begun to tell reasonable and readable tales in prose at all, in the late sixteenth or early seventeenth century. But in the eighteenth we should almost certainly have coarsened the earlier part and possibly made the later, if we did it at all, 'goody', certainly sentimental. That Prévost learnt some things from us is more than probable, but he certainly only learnt what did him good.

As all readers of one of the nearest approaches to a great novel in twentieth century English know, Mr. Compton Mackenzie has made *Manon Lescaut* figure rather largely as a book; and he has done more, Sempronius. He has got into his own book or books something of the same kind of 'heroic love' which Des Grieux displays, though he has thought it necessary to overdo things with that unhappy ending by which the century has tried to evade conventionality, only meeting it afresh at the next turning. Our pair have had their day, or at least not a few—and the last the best—hours of their day: more hours might have been worse. Personally I don't think Des Grieux outlived Manon very long: not for any reason that could be called sentimental or Victorian, but because there was nothing more for him to do or be. He never would have given himself airs or have walked about trailing willows or have done anything of that kind. But there was in the matter what the French *fatalité* perhaps expresses a little more closely than our 'fatality'. I am told that the very latest of the many substitutes for the first chapter of Genesis is an account of how, a few billion years ago, one star jostled another star, and knocked a bit off: whence you see the various forms of *pithecus* and the events called historical and the writing of *Manon Lescaut* would necessarily and scientifically follow. Perhaps because of this jostling, perhaps not, this sort of love does exist: and out of poetry, to which it may be said more properly to belong, there is hardly a better delineation of one of its no doubt innumerable instances than that which is before the reader. Given the characteristics of the two lovers it could hardly come to good—entirely, in any ordinary fashion or for any extensive length of time. Some good people may say 'Ah, yes: if that muddle about the Governor and his nephew hadn't happened, as it very easily might not have happened, there was no reason why Manon and Des Grieux shouldn't have lived, a respectable married couple, in colonial government employ, till their quite timely deaths. They had sown their wild oats; they surely did not want to sow any more; and circumstances, though they looked bad at first, were actually favourable for letting the crop stay no further reaper.' A facetiously minded critic might even suggest without too much chronological difficulty a future meeting with Atala or Réné or both and a contrast of handlings.

But it won't do. The inauspiciousness of the stars, though they may now and then have been in passionate conjunction and have set together not so unkindly, is there and cannot be gainsaid. Burton, as we have seen—more or less—takes it for granted that heroic love *must* be ill-starred—not exactly in the sense of the more famous phrase as to its not 'running smooth'. Indeed the good old-fashioned dictionaries under the words 'smooth' and 'smoothness' will supply easy comments on this. Exactly what set things wrong, it is superfluous to enquire, unless one could get hold of Aphrodite herself. Manon's 'perfidy' is the obvious suggestion. But neither this nor its effects affect though they may bring out the peculiar quality of Des Grieux's love of which we are speaking. Is it not in one of the letters attributed (with whatever truth or falsehood) to Queen Mary and found or put in the Casket of Evil Repute, that the phrase 'black splendour' occurs? I do not believe in the letters: but I rather like the phrase which can be applied in several different fashions. In the fire and flame of Des Grieux's love there was splendour, but there were curious streaks of blackness in it—of blackness ethical a little, perhaps; of blackness of the lower kind of fortune not a little; but of blackness of the higher kind of Fate most of all.

But with all this and all this and twice as much as all this one would never, in one sense, have said enough about this amazing little book and must, in another, have always said too much. Its extraordinary completeness in itself is perhaps the point about it: and certainly supplies some of its chief lovers with their main reason for regarding the Italian prince's business as an afterthought and in a way a 'side-show'—a condescendence to that undoubtedly common if not almost universal but certainly diseased craving of mankind for unnecessary additions. There is here no such excuse—weak but existing—for 'more', as the deliberate unfinishedness of the *Sentimental Journey* and the accidental one of *Edwin Drood* has given to the prurient-minded in one case and to the what shall we say?—minded in both: though one does not like to select any disparaging epithet which would have to fit Henry Jackson and Andrew Lang. So let us say once more, the thing is completely complete, and perfectly perfect.

1931.

A SAINTSBURY SCRAP BOOK

TRIVIA

I. Historians may lie but history cannot.

II. Education means 'bringing out', but it is usually taken to mean 'pouring in', and exceedingly little attention is paid to the nature and capacity of the vessel or the suitability of the influx.

III. Taste, like Style, ought to be the expression of Self; but it is difficult to say in which of the two this is most seldom the case.

IV. Nothing is more curious than the almost savage hostility that Humour excites in those who lack it.

V. Majorities are generally wrong, if only in their reasons for being right.

VI. No person worth much is after childhood 'influenced' by any other person.

VII. Men have buttons on the right side of their garments and women on the left: a fact the reason of which appears inscrutable.

VIII. When people cannot write good literature it is perhaps natural that they should lay down rules how good literature should be written.

IX. Extenuating circumstances are conceivable for almost every crime; but not for writing anonymous letters or throwing orange peel on the pavement.

X. Judicious expenditure on dress is a form of charity; for it pleases an indefinite number of people besides the wearer.

XI. The difference between gourmand and gourmet may be most obvious in eating and drinking, but it practically extends over all the actions and passions of life.

XII. 'It is a wise child that knows its own father' has a further application than that usually assigned to it—to wit: 'It is a wise generation that does not talk foolishly about the one before it.'

XIII. It was once very wisely remarked 'It is impossible to know what will be rubbish tomorrow'. But this is an inadequate excuse for producing what is certainly rubbish today.

XIV. Fanatical and, as it were, monomaniacal efforts to prove a thing true often bring indifference to telling falsehoods about it.

The Book of the Queen's Dolls' House, 1924.

THE 'MODERN' TOUCH IN PHRASE

A HUNDRED and eleven years ago, in July, 1796, Madame D'Arblay, as she had been then for some time, revisited the haunts of Fanny Burney in her old Windsor prison. She brought *Camilla* and she received 100 guineas and a very kind welcome especially from the Princess Augusta, with whom she had always been on good terms. It so happened that the conversation turned on the luckless 'Madame Royale', the eldest daughter of Louis XVI, and the Princess said, 'It's very odd one never hears what sort of girl she is.' Madame D'Arblay adds, 'In her unaffected manner.' But is the manner merely 'unaffected'? Miss Burney's own, especially in the 'Early Diary', is often unaffected enough, though not always; but it seldom if ever has this curiously modern ring about it. Horace Walpole, if 'unaffected' is not exactly the term that one would apply to him, affects unaffectedness with occasionally marvellous success; but I do not think he ever has this tone. Even Cowper has no command of it. It has nothing to do with mere conversational contractions and vernacularities. The free-and-easy writers of the end of the seventeenth and the beginning of the eighteenth century—L'Estrange, Tom Brown, Bentley and Collier, in the horse-play mood of their controversy—are not modern at all; you perceive their date just as clearly as in the most full-dress period of their contemporaries. It has nothing necessarily to do, in one way at least, with vocabulary; that is to say, certain obsolete words would no doubt stand in the way of it, though not quite hopelessly, but it has no need of definitely modern words. Every one of the Princess Augusta's words might be found in English hundreds of years older than her time. Perhaps there is something in the arrangement of the words that does it, but even this is very illusory and evasory. You know it when you see it, but you hardly know the marks by which you know it when you do see it. Only, you can hear the words as if they were said to you at the moment, instead of being a sort of echo of something more or less distant and unfamiliar.

In the very greatest writers, especially in Shakespeare, the tone occurs, sometimes very far back; indeed as far as the modern vocabulary extends. There are phrases in Chaucer which, except for the occurrence of ancient words or forms of words, would be as modern as anything (not merely ephemeral slang) could be, yet their actual archaism is undeniable. But Shakespeare is full of actually 'modern' phrases. For instance, that great answer which Poins made when the Prince repeated to him Falstaff's assertion that he, Poins, had said Prince Hal was to marry his sister. 'God send the wench no worse fortune! But I never said so.' Here in the first half a Poins of the twentieth century would probably (not certainly) say 'girl' instead of 'wench', and 'luck' instead of 'fortune'. But the last part of the phrase is of all time; some would say more especially of modern time. It might have had a slightly more old-fashioned ring even in Miss Austen.

Now, once more, when did this peculiar freedom of speech—this 'disinvolture', to use a word which has been more than once within an ace of establishing itself in English from French and Spanish and Italian—when did it come in, and how, and why? A little later than the Princess's time it is everywhere 'dispersedly', if not everywhere as an established thing. A little earlier it is, except in flashes, nowhere. The popular explanation, I believe (so far as there is any popular explanation of a phenomenon which has not been very much discussed), is that it came from, or at least was much helped by, French, and especially by the study of the great French epistolary authors. In favour of this it may certainly be said that you do not in any other language find it in such perfection and so early as you find it in Madame de Sévigné. It will not do to go back to Montaigne. Not only does the archaic touch interfere there, but there is a good deal of treachery in Montaigne's case; his 'disinvolture' has been very carefully involved to begin with. Of course, people say the same of 'Notre Dame des Rochers' sometimes, but then it does not matter what they say.

No doubt (the very case just cited shows it) a certain carelessness of syntax and other arbitrary restrictions occasionally contribute to the effect, though it is not enough to neglect the syntax in order to attain modernity. Madame de Sévigné herself is notoriously 'incorrect'; so much so that her earlier editors 'buckwashed' her admirable language unmercifully, and even her later—such is the French passion for correctness—are seldom content without showing what she ought to have written, and sometimes making her write it. To Princess Augusta's own speech a precisian might object that a girl cannot be 'a sort of girl', though she may be 'one of a sort'. From which it might be argued that language passes through three stages—one of incorrectness because people have not arrived at the notion of correctness; another where it is artificially cultivated; and a third where it is to some extent deliberately neglected. The earliest and latest stages approximate in good mouths and on good pens; but the changes of the vocabulary obscure the approximation. For instance, the Early English Text Society has within the last few days or weeks sent to its subscribers an edition of the *Festiall* of John Mirk, a writer of the earliest fifteenth century. The book consists of homilies, largely diversified by, and almost composed of, stories of saints' lives, etc., in the usual fashion. Most of these stories are very well known to anyone who has any knowledge of mediæval literature. But Mirk tells them with such admirable simplicity and freshness that there is hardly anything better in Scott himself. You cannot call it 'modern', because the vocabulary is not only archaic, but peculiarly archaic in some respects, and because the substance is as unmodern as possible. But somehow it is fresher, more familiar, more 'unaffected' as Madame D'Arblay would say, than any eighteenth century writing, or most seventeenth and sixteenth.

The mention of Scott may give another 'light'. He was only five-and-twenty at the time when the Princess and her guest were talking; and much later, when he met Madame D'Arblay herself, she was to him as a sort of gracious ghost of another and elder generation. Yet he has not often made his most modern characters talk quite as naturally as the Princess did on this occasion, though he often makes his personages of older times perfectly successful in this respect. From which one might further collect that in order to insure this modernity one must not be too modern in the limited sense—must not let anything merely of the day come in. For that which is merely of the day once will be of yesterday and further back yesterdays ever after; that which is ostentatiously and artificially up to date will of the law of its being become out of date. Which things are no new or recondite allegory. Only they make some contribution to the explanation of the fact that conversation, letter-writing, the less conventional drama (the more conventional is utterly hopeless) when it is written by persons of genius, and the novel under the same rather stringent proviso, supply this really and perennially 'Modern' tone test. And perhaps the best way to prevent securing it is to endeavour to be modern. We, for instance, who lived at the time of composition of the late Mr. T. W. Robertson's plays know that no human being in the society which they were supposed to represent ever talked in the least like their characters. And I should not (supposing myself to be a centenarian) much wonder if somebody, forty years after the present date, repeats this remark of mine about plays of this day which I have not the slightest intention of naming. (*The Glasgow Herald:* 11 April, 1907.)

OF WRITING IN BOOKS

NOT long ago the Librarian of the London Library—that head-agent of Apollo and Pallas *jintly* (as Captain Cuttle would say) in supplying the needs of bookish paupers—wrote a public denunciation of the practice above entitled. Now in differing with Dr. Hagberg Wright on any subject connected with books one would 'go funkingly' as 'the beast did' who 'feared Cytherea' when he was brought to her after he had slain Adonis, and as far as the subjects of his own special province are concerned he could not of course use language undeservedly strong. A person who inscribes anything of his own in a book, *publici* or even *alterius juris*, deserves to have his hand cut off and never read another. I cannot even sympathise with Lamb's allowance of the practice in the case of Coleridge, though I own that if it were not for the extreme danger of allowing *any* infraction, one might be tempted to do so in such a case. But Dr. Wright seemed to extend his disapproval to writing in a man's own books; and here, I confess, I think he went too far.

I do not propose to deal with some correspondence which followed or to give any opinion on Mr. Gladstone's alleged practice of intimating dissent (or at any rate a sort of *distinguo*) by the syllable *ma*, which it seems was not intended for the bleat of an English sheep,[1] but for the Italian equivalent of 'but' itself. The question is best narrowed to its simplest terms, 'May a man write comments,

[1] Which is really much more like *ma—a* than *ba—a*. Sheep *are* Celtic, are they not? and therefore naturally muddle m and b.

criticisms, notes in short of any kind, in his own books?' And, if he may, is the liberty conditional or unconditional?

Some conditions are clearly imposable. Unless the edition is a merely vulgar one he must not *deface* it—in fact one may almost say that except with the aid of interleaving only cheap and, in more senses than one, 'common' editions may be written in at all. Except for *serious* comment, suggestion of really interesting parallel passages, and other things that correspond to the work of an experienced and accomplished *editor* I doubt whether real 'classics', especially poets, should be 'interfered with'. But there is a certain class of book, more often of the novel kind than of any other, which, in a cheap edition with some margin and written by an author good enough to be worthy of critical consideration and not so good as to be above it, invites *marginalia* irresistibly—and which (I speak no doubt as a fool) actually seems to acquire interest from them, not merely in the particular perusal when the (according to Dr. Wright) illicit intercourse takes place, but in subsequent ones.

The author with whose writings I have myself most often 'viciously intromitted' after this fashion is Anthony Trollope:

> His work is not too great and good
> For scribbling censor's daily mood.

The best—that is to say the Barsetshire series with *Orley Farm* and *Can you Forgive Her?*—were most of them first issued either just before or during the time when I engaged most eagerly in and saw most of general society without professional avocations to distract me and put me out of contact. It is the kind of work which presents what people were not then prigs enough to call 'problems', but aspects and situations of character and action with a vividness of actuality which they were again not jargonists enough to call 'technique'. Without being exactly great, it was distinctly good. It as it were invited you to a party of live people who did real things and 'said what they owt to ha' said'. And this made and makes it extremely tempting to join in the conversation and comment on (as you could not actually join in) the actions; to express your opinion as if you had been a man seeing a play, sometimes even carrying the resemblance of condition so far as to hiss or applaud. I am afraid the narrow margins of my 'Bodley Head' copy of the adventures of that most *un*-forgivable Alice Vavasor (her name is almost the only attractive thing about her) are blotched with illegible pencillings of what may be called, in milder and severer senses at once, 'castigation'. Of course Trollope, from his habit of talking directly to his readers, almost asks for something of the reply sort in places; but his characters are live enough to ask for it too.[1]

I suppose no one except some Puritan crotcheteer—certainly not Dr. Wright—would object to interleaving. That preserves the sacred printed matter and its vehicle entirely intact: and the compound can be broken up again and the printed text reinstated without any stain of ink on it; and for my part I like interleaving. If I had been a rich man I should have had quite a large part of my library so treated, though of course not any book of intrinsic beauty or consecrated somehow by special source of possession, extreme rarity, exceptional 'state', and all the other Oldbuckian attractions. But as I have said this is hardly part of the real question. May you inscribe with pen or pencil on the margins of actual books as the publisher sent them out additions of any kind, the same limitations of beauty, rarity, association, etc., being observed as in the case of interleaving?

In a word, I think you may.

Of course there are again limitations other than those just referred to. Good manners require that this annotation should not, especially if there is any chance of any kind of publication, be seriously abusive of the author. You may call him 'an old fool', as you would a live friend on the other side of the library fireplace. But you should not, as the Renaissance critics used to do to each other in print, accuse him of perjury, of parricide, of other atrocious crimes, or of unpardonable ignorance. In cases where such annotations are deserved the authors are not worth 'conversing with'. Good sense, on the other hand, insists that they should not be merely of the Julia Mills kind, for then the commentator merely makes a fool of himself, or herself, not in the amiable fashion above glanced at. (*The Minster*, 1895.)

KIPLING'S 'MANY INVENTIONS'

Many Inventions is not only good, but very good. I am inclined to think it, using words carefully, the best volume that Mr. Kipling has done. It is, of course, unequal; nobody could write fourteen different

[1] Another author who invites or insists upon commentary is Charles Kingsley: his brother Henry does the same but to a less extent. The extreme interest of Charles's stories and characters, and the constant irrationality of his arguments, give 'provocation' in both its senses.

tales of the widest range of subject and style and not be unequal. Of course one reader will like this better than that, and another that better than this. The stories draw nigh with fitful success to that 'True Romance' which Mr. Kipling has celebrated, in verse as heartfelt if not quite as finished as he has ever written, at the beginning of the book, and has not extolled too much. For what is romance but creation? and what is creation if not divine? As for the separate stories, I confess to being in something like the frame of mind of Miss Snevellicci's papa—'I love 'em every one', but as a person of taste must speak with graduated affection, I think I like 'My Lord the Elephant' most as a whole, and 'The Children of the Zodiac' least. The 'Finest Story in the World', which is itself a legend of metempsychosis, has affected me in a very strange fashion, for it seems to me that (in another state of existence, of course) I heard Mr. Kipling tell it, and tell it better than here. 'His Private Honour' is the noblest and most complete; the conclusion of 'Love o' Women' (which seems to me as a whole to suffer from ups and downs) is the most passionate and accomplished. I am too much of a Jingo to be quite a fair judge of 'Judson and the Empire' or 'A Conference of the Powers', but it is to me a blessed thing to think that Mr. Kipling, like Kingsley before him, will breed up Jingos by the thousand. 'Badalia Herodsfoot', though excellent, has been done better before by Dickens and others, with a little less freedom of speech than Mr. Kipling is nowadays permitted to use. I would not wish for a better farce than 'Brugglesmith'; (did Mr. Kipling ever dree the more terrible weird not of being unable to get away from an adhesive drunken man, but of having to look after an evasive one?) And of the more imaginative and ghostly pieces 'The Lost Legion' seems to me to bear the bell. But what a jejune enumeration of personal impressions is this! For the book is to be read and rejoiced over by the reader, not analysed or even pronounced on by the critic, 'which is 'is 'abit', as Mr. Kipling's friend the policeman says. (1893.)

A NOTE ON CRITICISM

IN contradistinction to those of his friend and eulogist, Mr. Arnold, the estimates of M. Edmond Scherer never neglected the historic element, and I cannot but think that this gave him a decided advantage. We all know, of course, what Mr. Arnold meant by his decryings of the historic estimate; and we know also that they were compatible in his own case with much fine criticism and more delightful writing. They were also exceedingly convenient as justifying the somewhat eclectic character of Mr. Arnold's critical philosophy, as enabling him to skip periods, authors, literatures, that he did not care about, and as fortifying him in those secure and extremely one-sided generalisations which he executed with such an incomparable mixture of audacity and grace. To put the thing bluntly and briefly, too many parts of Mr. Arnold's stately pleasure domes of æsthetic elegance would go down in half an hour's battering from the historic estimate, and he showed wisdom in ruling that estimate out. M. Scherer, on the other hand, did not want to build stately pleasure domes; he never wanted, at least knowingly, to do anything but comprehend; and he saw the immense advantages in comprehension which the historical approach gives. Never abusing, never, indeed, accepting without grave modifications the product-of-the-circumstances theory, he always attended to circumstances, to origins, to the filiation of work and of talent in the great literary pedigree.

He had, on the other hand, or fancied that he had, a rather singular repugnance to another great engine of criticism, the comparative method. I say 'fancied that he had', for, as a matter of fact, he sometimes uses it; but he seems to me to have confused two different kinds of comparison—the one a kind as bastard and as mischievous as possible, the other the secret of all really lasting and satisfactory critical judgment. The comparison which says, 'What! *you* like *that*? *I* like *this*,' and justifies its dislike of That because it does not possess the characteristics of This, is as idle, as uncritical, as mischievous, as M. Scherer or anyone else pleases. But the comparison which takes This and That, puts them together, notes what This has and That lacks, observes how This excels That in one way, and That excels This in the other, appears to me to be, on the contrary, the one method by which you can get at really luminous results. These results will not be, as the private impressions even of culture are often, mere will-o'-the-wisps, or, as *a priori* and positive theories are, lights too remote and casting too long shadows to be safely used, but honest hand-lanterns which will lead you about the labyrinth of the world's literature with as few chances as possible of losing your way. (1891.)

SOME THOUGHTS ON THACKERAY

THE art of novel-writing is not old—it is barely at the beginning of its third century, strictly speaking; and already there has fallen, between Thackeray and that one of his predecessors who was most like him in kind and degree of greatness—Fielding—one of those curious veils which Time drops now and then, but at quite uncertain intervals, and through which we can only see darkly, and by a certain effort and calculation. Of the great English dealers with Life through fiction who are this side that veil, Scott, though he is still on the right side of it to all but very poor and unhappy optics, seems to have been partly entangled in its folds to some, and undoubtedly, pioneer as he was, and dealing as he did mainly with romance itself and with past times, gives only partial play to the actually intimate knowledge of pure Life that he possessed. Miss Austen, almost as absolutely lifelike as Thackeray, has, we are told, her lifelikeness obscured by a partly obsolete style, and she certainly limited and 'miniatured' her presentments. Bulwer—our pink friend's 'greatest living novelist'—*did* know Life; but he chose to adulterate his knowledge to an intolerable degree with all sorts of conventions, tricks, fashions. Dickens knew it better—in flashes indeed perfectly; but he, again, chose to subordinate his knowledge, itself very partial, to a perpetual glamour of comic or tragic fantasy—not real at all—as well as to worse things, such as political and social prejudice and crotchet, teasing mannerisms of style, hampering disqualifications of literary and other ignorance. Charles Reade, a genius certainly, never could get that genius into any organic condition, and latterly hampered and choked it by flinging on and into it masses of superfluous information. Charlotte Brontë, a genius likewise, had too short and cramped an existence, too narrow an experience, too little critical faculty, and perhaps a temper none too genial. George Eliot bound herself to the schools and the systems till she became little more than a mere eyeless grinder at the mill with scientific slaves. And the late Mr. George Meredith, himself a novelist, be it remembered, of the 'fifties, handed over in no dissimilar way his subtle and eccentric but real life-knowledge as a familiar spirit to jargon and play to coterie-galleries, and subtle cobweb-spinning to catch the flies of foolish cleverness. It would be absurd to say with the poet that in this case as in another:

> everywhere
> The Knights came foiled from the great quest,

for all these and some others did great things and achieved great adventures. But none of them ever quite mastered *the* problem, *the* quest of the novelist proper—which is the presentation and criticism, without wandering from it or adding to it, of human Life and character by the way of fiction.

Thackeray did. That he saw Life whole is not true. Who has, in the words of the great Platonic conclusion, 'except God'? Not Sophocles, certainly; that, with all respect to Mr. Arnold, is absurd. Of even Shakespeare, near as he has come to it, it is well to remember that Dryden (with that critical finger of his which was unerring when he would let it be so) pointed Shakespeare out as 'the *most* comprehensive soul'. His universality is comparative, is indeed superlative; but it is not absolute. So, and much more so, there are parts of Life which Thackeray does not touch: large parts, some may say; most interesting parts, others; even the best parts, some. So be it; he was human. But the almost superhuman thing about him is that in nothing that he does touch—after he has attained his majority at least—is he ever *un*lifelike, as, from different reasons and in different manners, all the great rivals and contemporaries mentioned above are sometimes. No other writer with whom I am acquainted, save Shakespeare himself, and no other novelist at all, has this infallible and almost divine power of infusing life—life absolute and quintessential—into every human figure that he creates, or that he even touches for a momentary purpose. It is a power which seems specially to belong to ironists—Lucian seems to me to have had more of it than any ancient—yet there is always a danger of their misusing it, as Swift certainly did to some extent. But Thackeray did not. The two parrot-cries above referred to—the old cry of 'Cynic!' and the new one of 'Sentimentalist!'—are actually testimonies to the fact: for those who utter them unconsciously say, 'This cynicism, this sentimentalism, touches us too much on the raw—is too true to life, and therefore too contrary to what we should like life to be.'

Some people hold that the novel, having come late, will complete the old joke by going early—that it has not, like poetry and drama and romance, deep enough roots to last. I do not know; I am a critic, not a prophet. But, as a critic, I know that the greatest things and persons in literature never die and are never excelled in themselves. And whether the novel goes or stays, I am pretty sure that Thackeray will never lose, with those who can see, his position (with only the limits noted above) as the Master of Life in the creation of novel-character. Periods which themselves allow the absolute to be obscured, by the temporary Life may overlook or under-value him; but Time and Life and he will abide together. (*The Bookman*, April, 1911.)

THE PROBLEM OF TRANSLATION

IT is, of course, not at all surprising that the real problem or problems of translation should hardly have dawned upon mediæval translators. They had practically no help from the ancients, the older rhetoric dealing—Greek not at all, and Latin very slightly, with the matter. With rare exceptions, the mediæval translator found quite sufficient to occupy him in the matter of his text and the difficulties of rendering it. Even when a man like Osbern Bokenam did disclaim 'procedyng artificyal' at considerable length, the inevitable humility as to 'Gower, Chaucer and Lydgate' shows how conventional the thing is. And much earlier—when the translator of *Partonope of Blois* very calmly admits that sometimes he understands naught of his author's intent, and at other times finds the labour too great, and must refer the curious to the French book—it would clearly be idle to credit him with any 'theory'. Scarcely at all till the sixteenth century, and then successively in reference to the translation of the Bible, of the classics and of contemporary foreign literature, did theory interpose before or arise out of practice. One is not sure—though naturally *instances* of over-fidelity and over-looseness are as old as translation itself—that any before Chapman had thoroughly realised the opposition of 'word-for-word traduction' and 'aspiring to reach the spirit that was spent in his example'. And it would not be quite rash to claim for Dryden the position of the first English writer and translator of great mark who looked at the thing steadily and as a whole, conceiving and carrying out a theory of what he had to do and meant to do with it.

Whether it was the absolutely right theory is no doubt quite a different question, best answered or parried by the very obvious remark that there are at least three different objects which the translator may have before him, and the attainment of each of which may be satisfactory in its measure and degree. You may wish to set before your reader the nearest possible equivalent, in good English, of what the author actually says in his own language. You may (and this was Dryden's wish and Pope's object) aim at making English readers enjoy as much as possible the gist of what he says. Or you may, taking a hint from Longinus, and aiming highest of all, endeavour to fashion something which, if the author had been an English poet or prose-writer, he might, without diverging at all in spirit or too much in language, have written on the subject. Probably most would accept Davies and Vaughan's *Republic*, Pope's 'Homer', and FitzGerald's *Rubaiyat* as crucial instances of the three methods. Which is the absolutely best of these three it is impossible to say, because the kinds are different. The *phronimos* must decide for himself. (*The Athenæum*, 27 August, 1920.)

SIR WALTER: A FANFARE

. . . THE second person in English literature, the enchanter who could play on every string save one—the string of pure passion—in the whole compass of the instruments of prose and verse, the man whom fools judge to be inferior in this or that kind simply because he was proficient in almost every one, the most inexhaustibly fertile of modern imaginations, the most naturally skilful of modern talents, the hardest worker, the most genial playfellow, the kindest heart, and the largest though the least pretentious brain of two centuries: in other words and to drop a clumsy and useless periphrase, Sir Walter Scott . . . (*Macmillan's Magazine*, December, 1888.)

SEVENTEENTH CENTURY POETRY

NO time is quite barren of those curious objects of the Muse's caprice whom she enables to do one or two charming things and then cruelly turns her back on them. But in the best period of the seventeenth century you can hardly neglect the smallest poetaster without the danger of missing, often detached passages, sometimes whole pieces of 'absolute and earth-born' poetry—poetry such as you may at other times search libraries of quite respectable verse-writers without finding. And what is more, its poetry is as extraordinarily varied in kind: lyric, narrative and dramatic; sacred and profane; melancholy and playful; virtuous and naughty, with not a few other 'excellent differences'. It is thus a province made to the anthologist's hand; and any first lion who has tried it and 'thinks the next a bore' must be not a lion at all, but a cur or at least a curmudgeon. (*The Athenæum*, 9 January, 1920.)

THOMAS CARLYLE AND GERMANY

TO reject the author of *Sartor* off-hand as a favourer of the 'Huns', and therefore anathema, is worthy of no sane creature. The Germans of Carlyle's original enamourment—Goethe, and Schiller, and Novalis, and Tieck, and Jean Paul—had nothing whatever to do with Attila. And if it be argued that his later work on Frederick, and his wholesale partisanship in 1870, did 'something grow to' approval of the worse side of the German nature, it may be delicately suggested that more people speak about the *Frederick* than those who have read it. If (which the present writer unfortunately cannot) one could accept Carlyle's Frederick the Great as the real Frederick the Second, there need not be much cavil at the greatness. As for 1870, Carlyle pretty certainly did not—hardly anybody did—know at the time the rights of that matter; and it may be politely suggested again, on a sure basis of remembrance, that the prejudice in England against the Second French Empire was to a great—not, of course, to the whole—extent as sheer prejudice as anything that has ever been shown or felt in history. It affected the most unlikely people; it is not wonderful that it should have affected a very old man who had 'sworn to the words' of Schiller and Goethe half a century earlier. (*The Athenæum*, 29 October, 1920.)

ON EDUCATION

MOST plain men would agree vaguely—and not a few who have some special knowledge of the subject would agree scornfully or mournfully, according to temperament—with Peacock's more than fifty-years-old dictum that the nonsense talked on education would outweigh all the nonsenses talked on any other subject. And it was only yesterday that one of Oxford's most recent losses—a man hardly to be excelled in scholarship, practical wisdom, and general and special official knowledge—gravely remarked: 'An educational expert is a person whom I regard with the deepest suspicion.' (*The Athenæum*, 20 February, 1920.)

A NOTE ON WIGS

FOR a single object of study one might suggest the physiology and physiognomy of the wig. The wig is—on what one may be permitted to call the face of it—one of the most extraordinary garments —or if the expression be preferred, ornaments—in the history of costume. Its origin may have been traced—but if so I am not acquainted with the tracing—to some early and unrecorded visit to Papua. This is the *most* ultimate thing that suggests itself: the Sudan comes next. It is not, as most garments are in reality or pretence, a protection: for from that point of view it is overtopped and made useless by the hat. It intimates, if it does not actually involve, getting rid of the natural covering; it is, in a way, as though you should have yourself flayed before calling in hosier, shirtmaker, or tailor. And yet there is no doubt that it adds a singular dignity—you might almost call it beauty—to the countenance. That is to say, of course, the full-bottomed wig does: not a 'scratch' or 'tie'. Take, for instance, the portrait of that right reverend toadeater and very indifferent churchman, Bishop Hoadly. The face is not exactly ugly but exhibits an unpleasant combination, when you look into it, of meanness and bullying. Yet, *till* you look into it, the wig (no doubt assisted by splendour of gown, sleeves, collar, et cetera) succeeds to no small extent in carrying off the worser nature; dignifying the meanness somewhat; and allowing the bullying to be not much more than stern. (*The Dial.*)

VICTOR HUGO AND OLD BOOKS

THE only time that I ever 'saw *Hugo* plain' was at a shop in Guernsey where you could buy new and second-hand furniture, second-hand things of most other kinds, and some wine that was neither second-hand nor second-rate, including a certain sparkling white Burgundy, which the Prussians must have drunk dry, for we never could get it after the war. The great Victor was sufficiently recognisable even if the daughter of the shop (who, by the way, was a very pretty girl) had not, with obliging officiousness, whispered his name. He marched, I remember, up to her father and ejaculated, 'Ah! M—— je viens chercher des *books*, des vieux *books*', giving the *ks* a clearness very creditable in a Frenchman, but, of course, pronouncing the *oo* as no Englishman ever would.

Now I do not tell this story (which is nearly as interesting and important in itself as Captain Sumph's immortal anecdote of Byron) in special reference to the oddity of Hugo's putting the only important word of his speech in English, when he was talking to a Guernseyman who, as he was very well aware, spoke French quite as fluently, if not quite as well, as himself. The point a gentle reader may be led to note is that Victor, who could write the best new books of his time and language, evidently shared the reprobate preference for old ones—a preference from time to time passionately deprecated by some of our contemporaries who also produce new books, but, perhaps, books not quite so good as Hugo's. It is not only as they grow older themselves that some people are inclined to this sin; but I suppose growing older never made a man less inclined to it. And what has called to my memory the queer mixture of things in the old shop-warehouse off the steep, narrow street, and the girl's face, and the poet's well-known lion port and the white Burgundy, and all the rest of it, was a reflection upon a reflection of my own.

For in thinking over the books that have interested me most among the productions of the present book season—which is all but half gone—I perceived not at first nor with any malice prepense that they were more or less all such books as would cause sorrow, if not anger, at my preference in the contemporaries above referred to. For they were Mr. Froude's *Erasmus*, Miss Edgeworth's *Letters*, and the Oxford *Dante*—one a new book indeed as far as composition goes, but nearly four hundred years old in point of matter; the next not, I believe, even absolutely new to print, though only just published; and the third endowed with all the virulence, all the unjust attractions, all the temptations to hypocrisy of a classic—a genuine, veritable, undisputed classic. It is such fellows as Erasmus and Dante, such folk even as the gentle Maria, who make Mr. Grant Allen lift an exceeding bitter cry and Mr. James Payn hint in the most genial manner in the world that nobody *does* like classics and that it is only humbug that makes them say they do. (*The Minster.*)

SENSATION NOVELISTS

THERE may, of course be people who read *Nicholas Nickleby* for the squalor, not the comedy, of Dotheboys Hall; *Martin Chuzzlewit* for the murder of Tigg Montague; and *Great Expectations* for Orlick's just prevented smashing of Pip. Probably the same persons would read Shakespeare, if they read him at all, for Cornwall's outrage on Gloucester and the description of the bear eating Paulina's husband. It may even be questioned whether Charles Reade, though he abounds in sensations, can be justly called a sensation novelist. Wilkie Collins, of course, is one, and so is Miss Braddon; and so on the supernatural side is Bulwer in the *Strange Story*. Indeed the last-named novel is in a certain way *the* sensation story, just as *The Notch in the Axe* is the ideal ghoul manifested by parody; and *The Woman In White*, *No Name* and *Lady Audley's Secret* are, again, actual specimens in the non-supernatural kind.

The sensational novel, properly so called, arises (as Aristotle would say) when the novelist—being incapable of attaining, or unwilling to attain, true poetic romance or true plastic character-fiction—aims at and achieves surprise and suspense only or mainly. Both Dickens and Reade had too much *diable au corps* to let them fly at so low a level as this. (*The Athenæum*, 26 March, 1920.)

GEORGE SAND

WHAT made her so fascinating, as she certainly was, is not clear. The numerous descriptions of her face and figure are at no time very attractive, and the portraits are often almost the reverse, with one exception: a pastel with half-shut eyes and a voluptuous smile. Her alternations of schoolgirl romps and silent torpor must have been rather trying; and—though of course there is always a tendency to think that oneself may 'be the magician'—there was such a long, ghastly and notorious list of aspirants to the Dark Tower as might have frighted the most valiant of Childe Rolands. But they came, and they had their trial, and they were turned out; and then they settled down comfortably in the grounds and were kindly invited to afternoon tea. It is rather marvellous—though it is true that she had one spell, of the most potent, in her faculty of letter-writing and the *abandon* with which she used it. There is something very uncanny in the written word of some daughters of Eve. (*The Athenæum*, 15 August, 1919.)

A LETTER TO NORMAN DOUGLAS

February 23, 1921.

Dear Sir,

Permit me to be tedious as well as illegible. I am seventy-five. I have read more novels than a man of seven hundred and fifty ought to have done. For some twenty years I used to review hundreds or thereabouts of English and scores of French as they came out. For another twenty, the first of this so-called age, I have come across just two new novelists who have given me something that I can recommend to a friend. The author of *South Wind* is the second in order of time, not rank.

I am,

Yours very truly,

George Saintsbury.

THE PLACE OF BOILEAU[1]

THERE are disagreeable people who say that the twentieth century, considering that it has almost reached the end of its first quarter, has scarcely contributed anything of the original kind to literature of quality sufficient to enable it to rank with the more distinguished of its predecessors. But no one who has anything like knowledge of past literature as a whole is likely, whether he agrees with the bare assertion or not, to attach very much importance to it. For such knowledge teaches, in the first place, that contemporary *appearance* of literature (on which contemporary estimate of it for the time depends) is apt to be very deceptive; and secondly that, putting possible mistakes from this source apart, you never know, from what is to-day and has been yesterday, what will be to-morrow in this curious other world.

[1] *Boileau and the French Classical Critics in England*, 1660–1830, by A. F. B. Clark. (Paris: Librairie Champion.)

But let all this be as it may, there is one point in which this poor quarter of a century is not so very poor, and that is a not unimportant one—to wit, the serious and profitable study of periods luckier than its own, or less lucky, to keep the impartial attitude. Merely frivolous judgment may no doubt pooh-pooh such a book as that before us. 'Between five and six hundred full-sized octavo pages, not even on the person and work of one certainly famous but after all really second-rate foreign critic and poet (or poetaster) reinforced by others from third-rate to thirtieth, but on the effect produced by them, in another country than their own, at a time when that country's literature was itself not at its most flourishing,' 'Lost labour and not even light—but heavy-minded folly,' says some Pococurante. Well, he is wrong—as the Pococurante of this class, if not also of all classes high or low, is rather apt to be; and it may not be quite idle to speak a few words on the how and the why of the wrongness.

In the first place this book is a very valuable assistance in the task of understanding our eighteenth century literature. It appears to have been a law of nature, if not originally pervading it, certainly called into action ever since the Renaissance, that each period (not necessarily each century) of civilisation should despise its immediate forerunner's ways in manners, in morals, but above all in literature. Savagery does not do this; probably because it has no literature, which seems to be the main irritant. It sometimes eats its ancestors and sometimes worships them; but it generally follows their customs. With us it is otherwise, though the periods of contempt are perhaps shortening—there being even signs of the twentieth already trying to understand (a process well known to be incompatible with contempt except in the rarest cases) the nineteenth. That nineteenth itself was bad in parts about the eighteenth, which in turn had in parts been bad about all older stuff. But it made some good beginnings of intelligence pretty early; and the process has gone on till the present day. Some attempts have even been made to comprehend and expound that curious influence—rather clumsily called Gallo-Classic but certainly consisting in part of classic or pseudo-classic strained or sieved through French, with the strainer giving an undue amount of colour and the sieve unduly contributing things of its own—which affected its criticism hugely, and its creation to a not wholly fortunate extent. But this book is by far the most complete and thoroughgoing of such attempts. The present reviewer has done his little bit in this matter; and he finds it recognised here without any of the not-quite-compliments which frequently attend, and exact payment for, recognition of predecessors by successors. But he confesses quite frankly that his knowledge of detail at beginning the book was considerably extended by the time he got to the end. Professor Clark—a Canadian by birth and now a Professor in British Columbia, but apparently a Harvard student and indebted to scholars and book authorities in the United States and France, as well as in England and Canada—has searched books and periodicals, during the time covered by his title-dates, with a really refreshing thoroughness, never failing, as too many of our 'researchers' do fail, to keep his eye on the exact chronological order of the authors and passages quoted. No one, we think, has pointed out more clearly, and certainly no one has documented quite so fully, the interesting wave-motion of belief and doubt on the subject; the more or less enthusiastic reception of the doctrines not merely of Boileau, but of Rapin, Le Bossu and the rest in the late seventeenth and early eighteenth centuries; the tendency towards revolt in the middle of the eighteenth and—most curious and interesting of all—the rather weak reaction towards the later years which in a manner foretold because it provoked, and was soon overwhelmed by, the great Romantic insurrection.

It is however the easiest thing in the world to make such a demonstration dull; and it is by no means the easiest thing in the world to escape doing this. It will not do to be too gamesome, or you begin to be suspect to Dryasdust. But Professor Clark has had the combined wit and luck to write lightly without making any deliberate jokes, and to put life into his facts without violently jerking their arms and legs. He has given successively a sketch of the reputation of Despréaux himself during the whole period; a careful survey of translations and imitations of his works; another sketch of the minors; a special and specified account of the results of 'Bollevian' influence on English literature itself; and some appendices giving more or less rare texts in illustration and confirmation of his own work, from that most curious epistle of Cutts the valiant to the Duchess of Monmouth about Nicolas, to the queer translations of the 'Lutrin' (one of which may be Oldham's), and including extracts from that very clever and very amusing, if very disreputable fellow, Tom Brown, perhaps our best and worst example of the truth that 'want of decency *is* want of sense', inasmuch as it dooms itself to suppression.

Politics have seldom done much good, and often a good deal of harm, by interfering with literature; but perhaps in this case the interference was not wholly maleficent. Boileau so exactly hit off the rising taste in England for 'correctness', 'neatness', 'wit', 'reason', 'good sense' and what not else of their kind, that he might have done more harm than he did if it had not been for the fact that after all he was a Frenchman and had written that absurd Ode about Namur which our Mr. Prior had burlesqued so delectably. It was however creditably customary to keep his politics and his literature apart when possible; and by the time when the literature itself—at least the critical part of it—was found to be wanting, the politics had become if not insignificant, at any rate capable of being handled coolly. The minors had never made this partial repulsion felt, and there is no doubt that Rapin and Le Bossu did have a bad effect upon some of our men. Bouhours, who historically makes a trio with them, and a quartet with them and Boileau, was a better fellow. But though there are differences of administration in the four, and in others before and after them, there is the same spirit of rule and line, of kind and scheme in all of them. Never is Pegasus allowed his head and his wings; never is the free spirit of poetry permitted to seek, and if possible find, the expression if not the realisation of its dream.

The pleasure which a book of this sort imparts seems to be unluckily hidden from many people, even if they are rather grudgingly prepared to acknowledge some utility in it. This pleasure is closely analogous to that derived (again one fears by the right people only) from looking at maps, or rather picture-charts, of country. You see how the figures and the facts of literature lie in relation to each other. They become all the more alive because of their connection; and this aliveness is utterly incompatible with the 'dullness' which less fortunate folk allege in the history of literature, and above all in the history of criticism. It is curious but true that there are people, and people of no small mark, who confess to this want of interest—in fact who confess further to some contempt, at any rate some surprise, at their fellows who do feel it. The answer is of course that if you take an interest in such things your library ceases to be a collection of *disjecta membra* and assumes the character of a body—a live body. Now wherever there is or has been life there is interest. (*The Bookman*, October, 1925.)

DRUMMOND AND BEN JONSON

IT is very seldom that some people at any rate wish for contemporary editions, with the usual editorial comment, of the literature of old times. Others of course simply hunger for them. But the proudest and haughtiest scorner of gossip must demit his pride, his haughtiness and his scorn at the thought of an edition of Jonson's 'Conversations' with Drummond by someone who knew them both; was conversant with court and literary matters of the time; and had some brains. To wish that we had not got the book at all is easy; I confess that to use a commonly used and rarely noticed bull of quite splendid bullishness I could personally give up whatever knowledge it supplies without the slightest pang or grudge. But we *have* got it: and I think few people who have not definitely set their minds to the matter know how very largely it has influenced our general conceptions of the great period and persons with whom it deals; and yet how extremely difficult it is to test its value as a trustworthy document.[1] If one wanted to show how hard (and therefore rare) really logical criticism is, there is no better text than this. Did Jonson really say these things to Drummond? Did he say them as they are said? or how much colour (as we used to say, camouflage as we say now) did Drummond put on them? If he put any, was it out of positive dislike to his guest? or out of misunderstanding of one kind or another? Are the famous two last paragraphs a more or less faithful shortening of Jonson's general account of himself? or are they Drummond's own exhalation of revenge for his sufferings during the previous weeks? Were there any sufferings at all? These are but a few of the questions that present themselves: and as everybody who knows anything about the matter knows, they have been endlessly discussed.

But when you look into others' answers to these questions, and begin to prepare your own, starting almost necessarily with a sort

[1] As a 'fake' the thing is inconceivable. It is obviously 'took down' with a fidelity which must have satisfied Rogue Riderhood himself; photographed, if not with the 'tricks and frounces' which photography has more recently allowed itself, with the almost clumsy accuracy of its earlier style. To have achieved such a thing as a fake, even to colour and shape something less characteristic into its present condition, would have taken the genius of Fielding or of Thackeray, if not even that of Shakespeare. Now people have as a rule been rather too unkind than too kind to Drummond's original work in prose and verse; but he could no more have invented this than he could have rivalled the three just mentioned in any of their best moments.

of reconstruction of the attitude of host and guest to each other, you perceive that most others have fallen and that you yourself are probably falling into a yawning but insidiously concealed pit. 'How would a fellow like Jonson and a fellow like Drummond be likely to feel and behave towards each other?' we ask. And then you suddenly remember that your own conception of 'a fellow like Jonson' is very largely—more largely than from anything else—derived from this very document, which others have used, and you probably will then use, as a test of itself! Even of Drummond the general notion (so far as there *is* a general notion) rests itself to a far too great extent on another notion—preconceived from this and afterwards applied to it—of a delicate, fastidious, sentimental gentleman confronted with a plebeian sort of genius, much more gigantic than divine. And then you remember that, interesting as all this tangle may be, it has very little to do with the statements of fact here. The peculiarities of Queen Elizabeth's physical construction might be the cause of others in her character and conduct: but the character and conduct after all might quite as probably occasion mere guesses at the cause of them. Were the Muses, in their gifts to Sir Philip Sidney, too frequently reminiscent of their name 'Pimpleides' or not? (remember that Jonson was a boy of only thirteen at the date of Zutphen and that Sidney had been much away from London). The book is a mass of puzzles; but it is full of interest. (*The Bookman*, August, 1923.)

JONSON'S 'DISCOVERIES'

IT is scarcely an extravagance to say that there are two keys or clues which will take you through the whole of Ben Jonson's work from two different sides—the 'Conversations' with Drummond and 'Drink to me only with thine eyes'. The first gives you nearly the whole idiosyncrasy of Jonson's nature; the other the at any rate choicest specimen of Jonson's art. One need not say much of Drummond, and certainly one need say nothing against him. It is of course true that he displays in his report that particular, though by no means universal, foible of his countrymen on which Lamb plays so wickedly in the anecdote about the impossibility of Burns's presence. But this, as it happens, is to our immense advantage. Nor is the other theory of his having put in ill-natured touches much better: noe is indeed sometimes not disinclined to accept the final summary which is generally attributed to Drummond personally, as delivered in reference to himself by Benjamin Jonson—'inglisman' (the Edinburgh authorities were quite right to call him that—for, Annandale or no Annandale origin, there never was a more characteristic example of one kind of John Bull), Westminster boy, bricklayer, volunteer soldier, actor, duellist, playwright, masque-wright, poet, critic, and several other things—but, after all and with all, best described by the famous inscription 'O rare Ben Jonson', one of the cheapest eighteen-penn'orths of history or anecdote.

It is a pity that the lesson of this greatest of all Anacreontics has not been more thoroughly learnt by some students of another of Ben Jonson's works—the infinitely curious 'Discoveries'. Every reader of this curious collection of scores of critical notes or essaykins —tufted with various titles or mottoes, but written as a whole in English—must, if he had the least acquaintance with the 'silver' Latins, themselves Ben's favourite province in his widely conquered domain of literature, have noticed the constant echo of them. And everyone who, knowing the 'Discoveries', read Quintilian or Seneca or even Petronius, must have had similar senses of recognition. But *plagium*-hunting, though a very favourite game with some scholars, is not specially attractive to all; and some of us had early seen that Jonson positively preferred—as indeed many of his contemporaries did—using somebody else's words to express his own thoughts. There was perhaps a little of his native arrogance (people who accept the Annandale pedigree will perceive a heritage of 'lifting' tendency) in this as well as of serious reverence for the classics; but that matters little. Anyhow, if it seems to anyone that the 'Discoveries' are less important as criticism, and their author less noteworthy as a critic, because in an almost bewildering manner he works in the ancients to comment on Shakespeare and Bacon; or because he copies almost a miniature treatise practically verbatim from such a respectable modern as Heinsius—the person to whom it so seems will never understand Jonson himself, and (if one may say so without a too Jonsonian arrogance) is in great peril of misunderstanding whatever literature he takes in hand to criticise, unless Apollo is so good as to preserve him and alter his ways very considerably. As it pleased Ben Jonson to take a handful of scraps of Philostratus in prose and work them to an exquisite filigree of verse, so it pleased him to use these ancients' and moderns' phrase—served up with 'a little of his own sauce', as Mrs. Tibbs would say—for his critical miscellany. And very well he has done it. (*The Bookman*, September, 1925.)

TOBIAS SMOLLETT

I HAVE sometimes wondered, though perhaps idly, what is the exact position of Smollett on what may be called the literary Stock and Share List of to-day? Editions of him still continue to appear—which, after all, is the principal point. The taste for 'strong' things—I purposely use a convenient and widely connoting adjective—which came in with the 'nineties, and has scarcely gone out yet, should have favoured, and in some cases certainly did favour, him. But it seems to me that one does not often, at least as often as formerly, perceive those fragmentary and floating references to him in the literary work of the actual day which are the best test of sempervirescence, and which certainly did appear for more than a century after his death. Scott was born in the very year in which Smollett died; and before Scott's own death both Thackeray and Dickens had begun to write. To all three, and to a very large number of the literary contemporaries of all three, Smollett was evidently *archi-connu*. They had, to something like a certainty, read him early; and Roderick and Strap, Trunnion and Hatchway, Morgan and Lismahago, Tabitha and Winifred—if not, also, the grimmer pictures of *Fathom* and the oddly blended 'interiors' of *Sir Lancelot Greaves*, were members of their mental family and furniture of their spiritual home. I would venture (with all proper fear and trembling before a possible rebuke from my youthful betters) to say that it was not very different with me and with a certain number of my own contemporaries, though perhaps in smaller proportion than had been the case earlier. But does this familiarity continue? I do not say it does not; but *if* it does not I think it is a pity. And let none say, 'Oh! we've plenty of better things, or at least of good enough things of our own.' So, one may again timidly urge, had the earlier generations—or so they might think. 1770–1800 was perhaps worst off in this respect, but, after all, besides the rubbish of the mere Terror School and the Minerva Press, it had Fanny Burney and Mrs. Radcliffe and Mrs. Inchbald, Godwin and Beckford, Moore and Bage. 1800–1830 had Scott and Miss Austen—*quid plures?* And immediately afterwards began the absolute harvest-time of the English novel from Dickens to Meredith. Yet people could read all these all this time and not leave Smollett unread. One at least hopes that it is not otherwise now.

Of course it may be said, not without justice, that fresh accumulations inevitably obscure to some extent the first constituents of the heap. And that historical interest which adds so much to the enjoyment of those who *can* enjoy it, may not reasonably be expected to appeal to many. But it would, once more, be a very great pity if Smollett ceased to be read. That he is one of the very greatest of novelists nobody can contend, save in a freak, or because of some extra-literary partiality. But as it has been confessed by wine-lovers of unblemished orthodoxy that the very greatest growths and vintages are not those one cares to drink oftenest, so a practised novel reader may admit that something similar happens with novels, and that the second growths are here also best suited for repeated consumption. Now in this article of re-readableness Smollett scores. I should myself put Fielding much above him on all intellectual and most æsthetic considerations; I should (to use a common form of expression, which is a nearly perfect example of a 'bull') be more sorry not to have read all Fielding's novels than I should be to have missed any one of Smollett's, even *Humphry Clinker*. But, with the counter-exception of *Joseph Andrews*, I am not sure that for mere re-reading as a pastime, say, in a country inn on a rainy day, I had not rather find one of Smollett's. And the causes of this re-readableness are perhaps worth examining. That he has few or none of the digressions—the *parabases*—which annoy some people so much in Fielding and Thackeray; of the retrospects and recitals which occur in novelists so different in character and date as Scott and Trollope; must undoubtedly be counted in, though not universally. For some of us *do* enjoy the first kind of 'stuffing', and others, or the same, have been gifted by Providence with the invaluable power of skipping with ease what they enjoy with difficulty. A *verior causa*, or at least one of wider application, is his remarkable combination of plenty of incident, well told, and plenty of character sufficiently delineated.

The first characteristic is of course the *sine qua non* of the adventure-novelist, whether his subject is a ride from Paris to Calais in spite of all the force and fraud of a Cardinal Richelieu, or a valetudinarian visit to Bath. But it is comparatively seldom that adventure-novelists have combined with their tale-telling faculty such a gift of characterisation as that which Smollett possessed. And it is perhaps in reference to this last that examination of his genius is most interesting. For sheer narrative power—the gift of telling a tale so that the auditor cannot choose but hear, and has no wish but to hear—is one of the ultimate mysteries of art. It cannot be analysed; and those who have tried to analyse it have, saving their reverences, seldom talked to any purpose. But the different fashions of what we may call life-presentation in fiction are somewhat less 'kittle' to deal with. To schedule them completely here would be of course impossible; but this brief notice would be incomplete without, and may fitly be completed with, a word or two on the fashions which Smollett himself could and could not provide. Of what may be called 'poetical' character—using the adjective in its transferred and common sense, as well as in its original one of 'creative'—he had no mastery, and at this he made no attempt. You are not to look in him for a Hamlet or a Falstaff, a Beatrix Esmond or a Becky Sharp. He did not, and no doubt could not, analyse like Richardson; nor work out a complicated plot with perfectly live characters like Fielding; nor indulge in fugues of eccentric fantasy like Sterne. But he could reinforce that sheer narrative gift which has been attributed to him with a remarkable command of 'humours' in the older as well as the more modern sense of the word—humours national, professional and individual—which seldom offend in either of the two directions in which such humours often sin—that of over-prominence in the particular case, and that of failing to get on with the general business. It is curious how *adequate*—granting the general scheme of the books and not asking them for what they do not offer—this characterisation, slight and superficial as it may seem to some, really is. For an outside and unhackneyed example, take Jerry Melford's letters to his friend at Jesus. Smollett can have had no interior knowledge of Oxford, and the eighteenth century notices of university life are, as a rule, by no means 'convincing', yet, somehow or other, the slight touches here ring sufficiently true.

Now, to tell your story without stammering or boring, and to keep your puppets (even if they *be* puppets) 'never *out*', are accomplishments not precisely attributable to the first-comer, or to many others besides the first-comer, among novelists. But the author of *Roderick Random* showed his possession of them at once, and the author of *Humphry Clinker* left examples of them to posterity in a vastly improved degree. (*The Bookman*, March, 1921.)

LEIGH HUNT AS POET[1]

ONE can never forget in writing of Leigh Hunt that in matter of criticism he showed more catholicity than any of his greater critical contemporaries, Lamb, Hazlitt and even Coleridge; or that in prose he, more than anyone else, turned the Addisonian Essay into the modern miscellaneous 'article'. In verse he revived the enjambed couplet; beat Keats and Shelley hollow in the Nile sonnet competition: and executed that altogether delightful, if not strictly accurate, rondeau which was originally addressed to a 'Nelly', but got altered to 'Jenny', and so started the idea that the heroine was Mrs. Carlyle. And in life—to add that to prose and verse—though he did things which have made those who did not know him find it hard to like him, everybody who *did* know him seems to have found no such difficulty. For Byron does not count: and the abuse of the Tory opponents was in a way Pickwickian by anticipation.

One is therefore really glad to have an opportunity, and an opportunity so well arranged, for revaluing the old balance-sheet and reckoning up any hitherto unentered value in him. Leigh Hunt's serious poetry, or most of it, has always been fairly well known: but Mr. Milford claims, and claims quite rightly, to have put in new or almost new evidence. There is, for instance, and special instance, 'The Nymphs', which the present reviewer quite candidly confesses never to have read *in extenso* till now. It is in a sort of 'Pindaric' measure, the norm being Hunt's favourite enjambed couplet; with lines shortened and lengthened at pleasure, and rhymes, now regular for considerable patches, now involved 'Lycidas'-fashion. For what reason it was so neglected in reprinting—never being given after its first and early appearance in whole, and only once in parts—it is impossible to say: for it is certainly one of Hunt's best. That it is entirely free from his faults—especially those of what can only be called lusciousness turned rancid—one cannot say. One may not have the slightest objection to 'the nude' and yet not rejoice at all in the picture of somebody showing:

> a smooth down-arching thigh
> Tapering with tremulous mass internally.

There are some of his also usual faults of vocabulary—'feel' for 'feeling', etc. But these are few and far between, and the whole is a

[1] *The Poetical Works of Leigh Hunt*. Edited by H. S. Milford, M.A. (Oxford University Press.)

study in dreamy florid description to which the most severe critic can hardly refuse the verdict 'very pretty', and which a more generous one might call really beautiful. It is in fact very like Keats before he came to such maturity as he was ever allowed to reach.

Of the considerable mass of drama—of which *A Legend of Florence* is the best known piece—not much need be said. Among the enormous mass of monographs which modern academic arrangements have fostered, especially in Germany and America, some one may have chosen, and it is nearly certain that some one will again or for the first time choose, the curious subject of the outburst of imitative Elizabethan drama in the first twenty or thirty years of the nineteenth century, as a whole. As far as individual authors and individual plays are concerned there are of course already bookcases full of such treatments. But whether any of their customers has found a third to leash with *The Cenci* and *Death's Jestbook*, remains a question. As far as anything of Leigh Hunt's goes the leash remains a pair. It is, however, or would appear to be on the newly resurrected political verse, that the editor would make at least one of his pleas for reconsideration. Now there is no doubt that Leigh Hunt came at quite the right time for political verse-writing, and nobody who has any critical detachment at all ought to be troubled in judging it by his own political opinions. The staunchest of Tories have applauded the *Rolliad* and 'Peter Pindar' and later, Moore; while if extreme Radicals have sometimes shown sorer withers under the *Anti-Jacobin*, there have been worthy exceptions. One thing, 'The Dogs', which Mr. Milford has recovered for almost every reader who has not been wise enough and lucky enough to provide himself with a copy of that curious periodical, *The Liberal*, is perhaps the soberest and, in more senses than one, the most considerable of Leigh Hunt's attempts at political satire. It has in form the advantage of not being in those floundering and lolloping anapæsts of which Hunt was so fond, and which contrast so strangely with the rush and sweep of 'Young Lochinvar' and 'The Assyrian Came Down': though it is true that its octaves do not come out victors over 'Monks and Giants' or 'Beppo', as Hunt's sonnet did over those of Shelley and Keats. The subject is a stock kind of thing—ill-fed soldiers being set to break and make food for Wellington's hounds in the Peninsula. Hunt of course would not be likely to perceive that the keeping of these hounds was an act of minor strategical genius, to make friends cheerful and show scorn of foes.

It is not violent; it is not positively bad; but there is little point and no sting in it. 'Ultra-Crepidarius', the hitherto unreprinted but (owing to the references of others to its title) not unknown satire on Gifford, *is* in the rickety anapæsts which seldom show worse than when used to convey very bad temper and not very much else. Perhaps the best of all is the little piece (not, it must be confessed, quite undeserved at the time), 'A Hanging We Will Go'. It is only a trifle of course: but Hunt manages to live up to the good old tune the name whereof its title parodies; and keeps clear of the positive silliness sometimes; the triviality in the most kindly word possible; the vulgarity in the least kindly, which so often beset him.

That however there is not a little in him which is neither vulgar nor silly, nor even trivial, is also perfectly true, and it is a reasonable opinion that such cases are exactly those in which editions, as full as possible, are due to posterity. Mr. Milford has not given the 'Juvenilia', and quite rightly so: for the folly of Hunt's father, and not his own, was responsible for a publication one reading of which is sufficient to teach the judicious reader, in the words of another poet well known to and well served by Mr. Milford himself, 'never to come there no more'. But all or as nearly as possible all the verse for which the author can certainly be held responsible is, we believe, here for such readers to read. And we wish every English poet as good as Leigh Hunt or better—nay, very many not so good as he was—were in as fair a case. (*The Bookman*, January, 1923.)

TWO CELLARS

I. A Sentimental Cellar [1]

IT chanced the other day that I had a mind to call on my old friend Falernianus. The maid who opened the door to me showed me into his study, and apologised for her master's absence by saying that he was in the cellar. He soon appeared, and I rallied him a little on the gravity of his occupation. Falernianus, I must tell you, is neither a drunkard nor a man of fortune. But he has a pretty taste in wine,

[1] It would appear from the reference to a 'Queen' that the following piece was written in the reign of Queen Anne, though an anachronism or two may be noted. It must at any rate have been written for one or other of the eighteenth-century collections of Essays.—G.S.

indulges it rather in collection than in consumption, and arranges his cellar (or, as he sometimes calls it, 'cellaret') himself, having no butler or other man-servant. He took my pleasantry very good-humouredly; and when I asked him further if I might behold this temple of his devotions he complied at once. ' 'Tis rather a chantry than a temple, Eugenius,' said he, 'but you are very welcome to see it if you please; and if you are minded to hear a sermon, perhaps I can preach one different from what you may expect at an Oracle of the Bottle.'

We soon reached the cavern, which, indeed, was much less magnificent than that over which Bacbuc presided; and I perused, not without interest (for I had often tasted the contents), the various bins in which bottles of different shapes and sizes were stowed away with a modest neatness. Falernianus amused himself, and did not go so far as to weary me, with some tales of luck or disappointment in his purchases, of the singular improvement of this vintage, and the mortifying conduct of that. For these wine-lovers are curious in their phrase; and it is not disgusting to hear them say regretfully that the claret of such and such a year 'has not spoken yet'; or that another was long 'under the curse of the 'seventies'. This last phrase, indeed, had a grandiloquent and romantic turn which half surprised me from my friend, a humourist with a special horror of fine speech or writing, and turning sharply I saw a smile on his lips.

'But,' said I, 'my Falernianus, your sermon? For I scarce think that this wine-chat would be dignified by you with such a name.'

'You are right, Eugenius,' answered he, 'but I do not quite know whether I am wise to disclose even to you the ruling fancy under which I have formed this little liquid museum, or Baccheum if you prefer it.'

'I think you may,' said I, 'for in the first place we are old enough friends for such confidences, and in the second I know you to be too much given to laugh at your own foibles to be much afraid of another's ridicule.'

'You say well,' he said, 'so mark! For if my sermon inflicts what our toasts call ennui upon you, remember that in the words of their favourite Molière, "You have willed it".'

'I do not, Eugenius, pretend to be indifferent to good wine in itself. But when I called this little cellar of mine just now a museum I did no dishonour to the daughters of Mnemosyne. For you will observe that wine, by the fact of its keeping powers and by the other fact of its date being known, is a sort of calendar made to the hand of whoso would commemorate, with a festive solemnity, the things that are, as Mr. Dryden says:

> Hid in the sacred treasure of the past.

If not the mere juice of the grape (for the merit of the strongest wine after fifty or sixty years is but itself mostly a memory) strong waters brewed on the day of a man's birth will keep their fire and gain ever fresh mellowness to the day when he reaches the psalmist's limit; and in these little flasks here, my Eugenius, you will find a cup of Nantz that was born with me, and that will keep its virtues long after thou and I have gone to solve the great enigma. Again, thou seest those pints of red port which nestle together? Within a few days, Eugenius, of the time when that must was foaming round the Douro peasants, I made mine entrance at the University. You can imagine with what a mixture of tender and humorous feelings I quaff them now and then. When their juice was tunned, what amiable visions, what boyish hopes floated before my eyes! I was to carry off all that Cam or Isis had of honours to profit by, all that either could give of learning. I was to have my choice of learned retirement on the one hand, or of ardent struggle at the hoarse bar on the other, with the prizes of the senate beyond. They were scarce throwing down their crust when that dream faded; they had scarce become drinkable by a hasty toper before I saw very well that metaphysical aid was wanting, and that a very different fate must be mine. As they fable that the wine itself throbs with the early movement of the sap in the vines, so, Eugenius, when I sip that cordial (and truth 'tis a noble vintage) the old hopes, the old follies, the old dreams waken in me, and I am once more eighteen.

'Look yonder again at those cobwebbed vessels of various shapes that lie side by side, although of different vineyards, in the peaceful bins. They all date from a year in which the wheel of fortune brought honest men to the top in England; and if only for a brief space, as I am told, they sang in North Britain, "the de'il went hame wi' all the Whigs before him". (I must tell you that Falernianus, though a loyal subject to our good Queen, is a most malignant Tory, and indeed I have heard him impeached of Jacobitism by ill-willers). But no more of politics.' He paused a moment and then went on: 'I think I see you smile again, Eugenius, and say to yourself, "These are but dry-lipped subjects for so flowing a calendar". And to tell the truth, my friend, the main part of my ephemerides of this kind has been filled by the aid of the goddess who was ever nearest and kindest to

Bacchus. In yonder bin lie phials of the mightiest port that Lusitanian summers ever blackened, and flasks of sack from the more southern parts of that peninsula which our Ben or his son Herrick would have loved. In the same year which saw the pressing of these generous juices the earth was made more fair by the birth of Bellamira and Candiope. The blackest purple of the Lusitanian grape is not so black as the tresses of Candiope's hair, nor doth the golden glow of the sherries approach in flame the locks of Bellamira; but if I let the sunlight play through both, Love with fantastic triumph shows me, as the bright motes flicker and flee through the sack, the tawny eyes of Candiope, and the stain, no longer black or purple, but rosy red, that floats from the Oportian juice on the white napery, recalls the velvet blush of Bellamira's cheek.'

'And this,' I said, pointing to a bin of Bordeaux near me. 'Thou shalt try it this very day,' said Falernianus with a laugh, which I thought carried off some feelings a little overstrained; ' 'tis a light, pleasant wine, and they made it the year that I first saw the lips of Damaris. The flavour is not unlike theirs, and if it should fluster thine head a little, and cause thee what men call heartburn, I will not say that the effects are wholly dissimilar.' It is not like Falernianus even to jest at women, and I turned to another. His face cleared. 'Many a year has passed,' he said, 'since the grape that bore that juice was gathered, and even as it was ripening it chanced that I met Lalage and won her. The wine was always good and the love likewise; but in neither in their early years was there half the pleasure that there is now. But I weary you, Eugenius, and perhaps the philosopher speaks truly in saying that these things are not matters of sympathy, or, as the Scripture saith, a stranger is not partaker of them. Suffice it to say that these imprisoned rubies and topazes, amethysts and jacinths, never flash in the glass, nor collect their deeper body or colour in the flagon, without bringing a memory with them, that my lips seldom kiss them without recalling other kisses, my eye never beholds them without seeing other colours and other forms in "the sessions of sweet silent thought". At the refining of this elixir I assumed the virile gown; when that nectar was fit for drinking I made my first appearance in the field of letters; and this again recalls the death of dear friends and the waning of idle hopes. When I am dead, or if any reverse of fortune makes me part with this cabinet of quintessence, it will pass to heirs or purchasers as so much good wine and nothing more. To me it is that and much more—a casket of magic liquors, a museum, as I have called it, of glasses like that of Dr. Dee, in which I see again the smile of beauty and the hope of youth, in which once more I win, lose, possess, conquer, am defeated; in which I live over again in the recesses of fantasy the vanished life of the past. But it is not often that I preach in this fashion. Let us take a turn in the garden while they get dinner ready, that you may taste,' and he smiled with a smile in which methought passion and satire were strangely blended, 'that you may taste—if you dare—the wine that I have likened to the lips of Damaris.' (*The Yellow Book*, April, 1894.)

II. The Cellar of the Queen's Dolls' House

Great as must have been the consideration required by other apartments of this House, reasons might be put forward for doubting whether any demanded so much as the cellar. And this is said on no idle 'there-is-nothing-like-leather' principle. For he who says it has, in a long and hard-working life, had to give consideration to many things besides cellars—things political, things literary, things educational, things of all sorts, or almost all.

Let us hope that the necessity of a cellar—perhaps not a universal apartment or compartment in Dolls' Houses—was never in actual question. It is not possible to conceive that to persons of such taste and judgment as the original devisers of this edifice there could have been present any doubt of the propriety of such a compartment *ab initio* or of its positive necessity on subsidiary considerations. Resident Dolls would probably—indeed certainly—get married, and would it be even decent for them to have to 'send out' for champagne and probably get wine of the description modestly described in advertisements as 'light and pleasant: suitable for weddings, picnics and other parties'? The Doll of the moment might have influenza—the modern 'English disease', as 'spleen' used to be called. The one medicine for influenza is Burgundy: and the one wine which it is most difficult to be sure of, in casual buying, is Burgundy likewise. I turn to that enlarged copy of the Dolls' Cellar Book with which I have been kindly entrusted, and I find that this fortunate respository has been supplied with five dozen each of 1906 Veuve Clicquot, Pommery 1915, L. Roederer 1911, and G. H. Mumm of the same year, together with two dozen magnums of the last-named shipper's Cordon Rouge for that year likewise. Although a critic of full fifty years' standing in literature, of more than forty in politics, and of nearly as long practice in wine, I cannot better the list; and the notes on the order of use are of the soundest. But will not the butler be offended by the suggestion that he requires them?

Then let us turn to the Burgundy. There is only one entry, and I think properly so; but if I had been consulted, the word which appears at the page-top would have been *my* word—Romanée. They do not add 'Conti', or 'Saint-Vivant', or any other minor localisation, but never mind. With Romanée 1904—two dozen of it—in our cellar we may bid 'flu' fly!

I am not sure, however, that if my profane lips were permitted actually to taste one and one only of the liquors here inscribed, I should not ask for some of the Duke of Penaranda's gift sherry—vintage or solera not dated, but 'shipped by Harvey' as 'Amontillado Duque d'Alba'. Despising sherry was one of the foolishest consequences or instances of that undervaluation of Victorian tastes which seems now to be happily passing; and I have myself recently drunk samples of very admirable quality. But 'Amontillado, Duque d'Alba' is a title that appeals at once to one's palate and to one's historical and literary memories. I daresay the wine with which the Marquis of Steyne resuscitated Mr. Arthur Pendennis was very like this. And whenever I read a newspaper report of that prettiest of all games, polo, wherein the other Duke—the giver—so often figures, I shall imagine the flavour of his gift.

We cannot, of course, go in quite this fashion through all the wines, spirits, liqueurs and malt liquors—for these are most rightly not neglected—which stock this most agreeable apartment. The doll—most fortunate in ever so many sorts of ways—has Montrachet of 1889—the best of all White Burgundies, as I hold Romanée to be of red: while this notable cellar has been supplied with no less than six varieties of Port, including Cockburn's '74 and Taylor's '96, with Warre and Fonseca of various dates, and two dozen *magnums* of 1912 Dow! This is particularly satisfactory, for I once knew a young lady of great beauty, intelligence and charm who after illness was restored to the possession and exercise of all three by the administration of a magnum of Cockburn's '51—not in single dose, it is true—but ingeniously decanted and distributed down to the last drop. Bordeaux supplies Lafite of '75 (I wonder what it is like), Haut-Brion of '88 in magnums (ditto); Margaux (the best of the '99's), and a six-year-old Le Prieuré. One other, however, of the bins deserves a kind of mention which ought to interest even some who regard ordinary wine-talk with indifference if not contempt—for it comes under the head of archæology as well as œnology. This is Bin 12, containing two dozen of 1820 Madeira—'Finest Bual'. Wine of 1820 will, of course, never come again in any case; but wine of the same kind and as good as that of 1820 has, it is believed, actually come in the case of Port, and may have done so in others. Wine, as good as this was at its best, never has recently come from Madeira: and we may say without much rashness never will. Most, if not all, good judges agree that though the vines newly planted after the devastation caused by oïdium three-quarters of a century ago have had that time to make good their footing and flavour, they have never done it with complete success and never will. Only Burke could justly commemorate this addition to the *cimelia* of Windsor Castle from this point of view.

It is impossible also not to spare a special mention to the Château Yquem '74 with which this miniature temple of the Dive Bouteille and its fortunate priestess or priestesses have been endowed: but we must pass to the less dignified but hardly less grateful and comforting contents thereof. Of these the most stately, beyond all doubt, are certain casks of whisky and of beer—for there is a 'cut-and-come-againness', a 'sure stronghold' feeling about a cask which the mere bottle can hardly attain. It is difficult to resist that perhaps deadliest of all deadly sins—envy—when one learns that the deputy-mistress or mistresses to whom Her Majesty may from time to time confide the not at all monstrous regiment of this abode, will have at her disposal two quarter-casks. One is filled with a Scotch whisky—Smith's Glenlivet, which knows no superior if any equal in its own country, and the other with John Jameson—fondly known as 'J.J.'—which corresponds for Irish. Not, of course, that any prejudice or disrespect is intended to other kinds furnished. But the cellar has been, as it were, armed as the entrance of a fortress is guarded by two big guns, with two other vessels. Nor are the remaining spirits neglected except Hollands, the absence of which I regret for a reason to be stated presently. Liqueur brandy of '54 no doubt looks down on two excellent but less ancient representatives of Cognac: and neither rum nor gin fails, while the chief suppliers have consulted what is pretty certain to be the Dolls' chief taste by putting in Chartreuse and Benedictine, Kümmel and Crème de Menthe, with our own two home-made liqueurs Sloe Gin and Cherry Brandy, in decent profusion. And we may close the inspiring catalogue by mentioning that there is no lack of that glorious liquor if not *liqueur* which gives Scotland and Ireland no room for triumph over England in the narrowest sense—Bass! Bass in casks and bottles. Nor is the cellar unfurnished with plant as well as material—thermometers and funnels and cans; bottle-baskets and candlesticks, corkscrews, hampers and case-openers.

Mais c'est artistement complet—not in the melancholy sense in which poor Gautier used that phrase towards the curiously unlucky close of his life.

Many ranges of reflection open out from the point at which we have now arrived. How pleasant it would be to draw up wine-lists from these ample stores to accompany, of course, suitable *menus*—so that there should be no temptation or excuse for the Doll to entertain her friends, as is the deplorable modern fashion, elsewhere than in her own house. How often, one hopes, would she come down and inspect the double-bayed treasury with its bins below and its shelves above! And what a beautiful picture she would make as she gathered up her dress with one hand and reached down as the whim pleased her an emerald flask of Crème de Menthe or a straight ruby bottle of Cherry Brandy with the other! But this sweet picture suggests a reflection of a different kind, severely practical at first, but ending in very artistic matters. 'How,' some businesslike person may say, and be excused for saying, 'how on earth, or under the earth, are you going to get all these things—these casks and cans and baskets—these twenty dozen of Champagne, sixteen of Port, twelve of Claret, and at least twenty or thirty more of oddments in a space measuring what this does?'

Obviously by some process of proportional reduction: and among the results of this process are some of the prettiest things I have ever seen, and not merely prettiest. On taking the liberty to put one of those magnums of Dow's port above mentioned—a beautiful vessel a full inch long and about five-sixteenths across the body—besides one of the my own few most cherished possessions—a 'tappit-hen' (three-bottle flask) of Sandeman's 1904, visions and thoughts came into my mind far too mystical—nothing could be too *great*—for this occasion. Had I been at Oxford in mid-thirteenth instead of mid-nineteenth century I should have written on this text a treatise—folio when printed later—*De Magnis et Parvis*, and Merton College would have counted on its records one more Doctor Profundus!

From this other ruby—actually lighted up by an obliging sunbeam as I write, and so setting off the proper splash of whitewash which marks its position when binned—let us turn to the emerald, really in shape as well as size a fitting eardrop for a doll's mistress, though not for a doll herself. It is, of course filled with Cusenier's *Crème de Menthe*, and with the light showing through its little body hardly emerald so much as aquamarine—real sea-green aquamarine, not the watery blue, almost white, which is allowed nowadays to usurp the name. And a straw-coloured 'Apricot Liqueur', though not exactly the same shape, would make a not at all bad Harlequin pendant. It was partly because of the effectiveness of these out-shapes that I lamented the absence of Hollands. A 'square-face' reduced to scale and showing its blackness among these brightened colours would be very agreeable.

Tantae molis erat ('Such a bother it was', to translate for the benefit of some folk) in this and a hundred other ways to found this admirably representative miniature of a pattern cellar for the present day. The apartment has a vaulted roof—as all cellars ought to have—though I regret to say that none of my own ever possessed one. I do not know whether there will be imitation rats or cobwebs or attempts at the ghastly roof curtaining which comes in so vividly in *No Thoroughfare*. I hope and should suppose not. For the whole principle on which Mr. F. L. Berry, the chief cellarer on this occasion, and his compeers appear to have gone is not imitation or sham, but honest miniaturing—the wines, etc., being the actual wines, and everything genuine though tiny.

No better form or material could, I think, have been employed in providing this little but Joyous Gard of Her Majesty's with one of the most important if not *the* most important department for the promotion of Joyousness itself; and the writer of these humble notes has enjoyed doing them even more than he would have enjoyed partaking of the very liquors they describe. (*The Book of The Queen's Dolls' House*, 1924.)

THE BOUNTIES OF BACCHUS

A MERRY and wise book (*Wine and Spirits* by André L. Simon) on a subject intimately connected with both mirth and wisdom is no small godsend in days when we are rather apt to oscillate between the silly serious and the silly sarcastic. It is an excellent primer; and if Mr. H. A. L. Fisher really wants to earn the praises lavished on him as a great instaurator of education, he should have it cheaply and succinctly reprinted and furnished to his favourite 'continuation schools'. Right principles would then be greatly strengthened throughout the land; and the wrath of the United Kingdom Alliance for Total Suppression of Liquor Traffic and the Church of England Temperance Society would be a joy to see. (*The Athenæum*, 21 November, 1919.)

'THE TALE OF A TUB'

THAT *The Tale of a Tub* is a masterpiece few people of any competence have denied, even when they disliked it; and the only semblance of a reason which Swift's most unfavourable judge alleged for denying Swift's authorship was, in effect, that it was too much of a masterpiece for him. But it has often been observed of Johnson that he never went wrong without coming in some queer fashion right likewise; and one thing that he said of the 'Tale' remains among the best and justest things ever said: 'It is of a mode so distinct and peculiar that it must be considered by itself.' One might, indeed, almost accept likewise the other clause of the sentence, 'What is true of it is not true of anything else he has written', and extend the 'he' to 'anybody'. For the irony of *A Tale of a Tub* is really a species by itself. It is, of course, not absolutely wrong to call it Lucianic in the sense of the great epigram with which Lucian himself (or somebody else) ticketed his work:

> Lucian wrote this, knowing old things and vain:
> For vain is also that which men think wise.

But it wears this mirthful-rueful rue with a most marked difference whether as compared with things before it, like the work of Lucian himself and that of the Preacher, or with things after, like that of Voltaire and Fielding, of Thackeray and Flaubert. It is even different (though the things are rather like the peaches and nectarines that sometimes grow upon the same tree) from the irony of 'Gulliver' or from that of the 'Argument against Abolishing Christianity'. One may thus concede a fraction (though only a fraction) of Johnson's argument without granting his conclusion or even agreeing as to the points of difference alleged within this fraction itself. These, as Johnson thought, were 'vehemence and rapidity of mind, copiousness of images and vivacity of diction such as he afterwards never possessed or never exerted'. The last three words, by the way, are a considerable 'hedge'. The 'vehemence and rapidity' may perhaps pass; they were the natural qualities of youth. But copiousness of images and vivacity of diction never deserted Swift from the *Journal to Stella* to the *Polite Conversation*. (*The Athenæum*, 2 July, 1920.)

DR. JOHN BROWN[1]

IT is not surprising, but it is satisfactory, that the 'Letters' of Dr. John Brown should have reached a third edition in exactly two years. For the book is of the kind that deserves a steady and well-sustained demand. The mere popularity of the author's original work might cause an immediate appetite, but could not maintain it. In fact, anybody who has observed current literature critically for a fair number of years must remember famous instances (which it is unnecessary and would perhaps be unkind to particularise) of such collections, anticipated with eagerness, bought at first freely, and then simply dropped by a not injudicious public. Sometimes the disappointment has been unreasonable, sometimes not; but it has been a fact, and rather a common fact.

It could, and can, need not many pages of reading on the part of a capable person to discover that there is no danger of such disappointment with the letters of 'Dr. John'. One may fancy indeed—but perhaps this is critical vanity—that the very character of his original work guarantees us from it. The persons who as a rule fail as letter-writers are persons of extreme and one-sided seriousness—persons who take immense trouble with their published work and write it under the sense of a mission. Milton's 'Familiar Letters' are in Latin, and their 'familiarity' is of a highly classical description; but we know pretty well what they would have been like in English.

Now nobody would deny that the author of *Horae Subsecivae* could be very serious when he thought it desirable. There is even in his earliest letters a slight strain of what, had it gone wrong, might have become priggishness. But it did not go wrong, and while it was preserved from doing so by the abounding humour and tenderness which accompanied it, these qualities kept each other, and were helped by the seriousness in keeping themselves, from mere triviality or mere sentiment. And the general blend was exactly what is most suitable for letter-writing, as is well seen in almost all good letters and letter-writers from the queen of epistolary quintessence, Madame de Sévigné, downward.

But he had another quality which is almost as indispensable to the best letter writing, what may be called a wise inconsecutiveness.

[1] *Letters of Dr. John Brown:* with Letters from Ruskin, Thackeray and others. Edited by his son and D. W. Forrest, D.D., with Biographical Introduction by Elizabeth T. McLaren.

His own phrenological description of himself, 'great comparison, great ideality of a sort, but no causality or concentrativeness to speak of', is, put in jargon, pretty much of a recipe for making a good letter-writer. With the opposite constitution you may write as 'handsome' a letter as any Mr. Frank Churchill, and beautiful epistolary examples such as are common in the extract-books. But you will hardly have what he himself also calls, though not in relation to himself, 'the rare gift of talking on paper' which in their different ways Madame de Sévigné and Horace Walpole and Cowper had, and which is here.

Almost the only drawback to the book—one made up for as far as possible by excellent and nowise intrusive or excessive editorial links but still existing—is that the letters are very unequally distributed over the life. There are five and twenty pages for the two years or less of his assistantship at Chatham; there are only as many for the eight years between his return to Edinburgh and his marriage, including the time of his establishment in practice, and (as one cannot doubt) his establishment likewise in character and temperament. But the first batch is of curious interest, biographical and external. He is nearly of age; he has been through the High School and the University; he has been apprenticed to Syme; but he is extraordinarily 'young'. Quaint epistolary documents are far from rare, but any future collection of them ought to include that in which he gives to his younger sister Isabella, as to a severe and authoritative auditor, an apologetic account of his expenses at Chatham—the most modest and blameless of budgets, but also the queerest. He has had to buy four pairs of gloves after bringing two pairs with him from an incurable habit like that of the lady in Browning of letting them get 'strayed and mislaid'. He has spent three shillings on 'a piece now and then', which is not extremely surprising when we find that though he had a solid breakfast at 7.30 and a solid dinner at 1 o'clock, the diet for the rest of the day was entirely banyan and at tea consisted of coffee only, without any solid food. He gave twelve shillings for Whateley's *Logic*, 'a good book, but in my circumstances I should not have bought it', and pays eighteenpence for reading *Count Robert of Paris*. With these and other extravagance, especially the books, he's sure his sister 'will be very angry', and begs her, 'if you think I have been very wrong, tell me so'. There's evidently no joke here; the 'triumphant fooling' which is so frequent and so pleasant afterwards has already appeared, but there is nothing of it in this. It's merely that, when already at man's estate and when many men are either wasting their substance, or at any rate thinking themselves quite competent to manage it, he's a good little boy who has spent more than he should, and is very sorry. Yet in a few months we find him grappling single-handed with cholera cases in the great plague of 1832, though still woefully disturbed about ways and means, and explaining painfully that 'Dr. and Mrs. Martin look very queer' at the whiteness of his elbows. So that he has been absolutely obliged to get an extra superfine invisible green surtout at three guineas and a half. Now this kind of small beer chronicle is only despised by people whose contempt is eminently worth having.

Some of the general characteristics of his letters have been indicated already; but, while maintaining them from first to last he is constantly adding to and re-illustrating them. The constant transitions from seriousness to humour, and indeed to farce, remain the principal note; indeed, the resemblance here to Thackeray is so striking that their friendship is little wonder. Of course there are people who do not like this transition, and who especially dislike the pure fooling of slang and misspelling and extravagant pretended romance and rodomontade. To argue with these would of course be fooling of a very different kind; and there's an end of it. But there are others who like it very much indeed in itself and who find that it enhances and relishes in a quite extraordinary fashion the more serious flashes. The great variety of these is itself an added charm. They are very often, perhaps more than anything else, critical of art, of literature, of other things; and Dr. John Brown, more here than in his public writings, where he had to 'artificialise' himself, if ever so little, is full of edification and delight. The worthy wiseacres who insist that a critic shall never contradict himself have plenty of opportunity for puzzlement or triumph as the case may be. You will find if you read the book carefully and have a fair memory, that even on Tennyson, nay, even on Thackeray himself, there are ostensible inconsistencies. Apparently opposite judgments are to be found on the relative excellences of Thackeray and Dickens; while, at any rate at first sight, the fact that so enthusiastic a Thackerayan should be less than lukewarm about *Esmond* may seem inconceivable. At different times (it is satisfactory that the favourable judgment is the later and final one) there may be found two seemingly irreconcilable estimates of *Tom Jones*, the one grudging and almost Philistine, the other pure appreciation.

But do these things come from mere irresponsibility, or from the uncritical waywardness that simply flings out estimates without caring to weigh or check them? Not at all. They are the result of the fact that the writer's mind is genuinely critical, that is is constantly sensitive to impression; but that as the impression is faithfully rendered, and not garbled and corrected to arbitrary standard, it *apparently* varies. The results are all 'true' in the conditions and circumstances, though occasionally large allowances may have to be made for the mood and temperament of the observer—sometimes, though not often, for his prejudices. Of course this kind of criticism is distressing to those who want peremptory and unqualifiable decisions, but they can find plenty of that sort of thing elsewhere.

Dr. Brown's art-criticism, which was one of the first things that brought him into public notice, and which, though not obtruded, is abundant here, is, one supposes, now a good deal out of fashion. Though he never carried the moral-subjective method to the same extent as his friend Ruskin did, and though he was quite alive to Ruskin's extravagant and arrogant paralogisms, it is largely Ruskinian. Nor is it nearly technical enough to please the modern art-critic. Nevertheless one may question whether his æsthetic, both in art and in nature, did not go deeper and spread wider than that of the average discourser on values. At any rate, as he never by any chance preaches, or as the familiar phrase has it, 'pans out', tediously on this or any other subject; as the references to this as to others are seasoning and not stuff—even disagreement with his methods or his results interferes not a jot with the enjoyment of this 'talk on paper'.

But, after all, the chief attraction of letter-writing lies on the one side in the glimpses of persons and incidents, on the other in the illuminating flash of phrase. Both are amply provided here, and with regard to the persons the provision is strengthened by the supplement of letters to Dr. Brown from Thackeray, Ruskin, Lady Trevelyan, and others. But it would have been almost sufficient without them, at least to those readers who have mastered the not very difficult art of looking with the letter-writer through the telescope of his letter at the persons to whom he is writing. Unluckily in some of the most interesting cases, Thackeray's for instance, this cannot be done, for Dr. Brown's letters to him do not appear. But the phantasmagoria is abundant, and it is sometimes not least interesting in the cases of persons who are only names to the reader. The descriptions of travel, always a strong point in good letters, are less elaborate than, for instance, Shelley's, but vivid and sufficient, while the 'small beer chronicle' as it has been called, which is after all not the least refreshing part of the correspondence, is of an admirable tap. And the phrase is not small beer at all. The resemblance, for all their opposition in political and ecclesiastical ideas, between Dr. John and Southey must strike everyone who really knows the two indirectly, as it evidently did strike Sir Henry Taylor, who knew them both in person. Here is the U. P. Liberal on the Anglican Tory: 'What an impudent, pervicacious fellow he was! and yet honest and warm-hearted, and full of ideas—and what a style!' And here is another judgment on Sydney Dobell: 'A fine fellow: *without one particle of knowledge about men or women or anything under the moon.*' And here is one of the best words ever said (and said boldly but politely to Sir Theodore Martin of all men), about translating poetry: 'What would you make of "translating" Burgundy or old Madeira? It would only end in so much dry hot brandy and so much water, the aroma, the bouquet, disappearing into space in transitu.' How could Newman's Apologia be better hit off, from one conceivable point of view at any rate, than as 'strange, sincere, insane, beautiful, painful performance?' And though probably no man ever studied phrasemaking or the purple patch less, one would have to go far before finding anything more perfect as picture and poetry in prose than this of old Lady Dunfermline's deathbed: 'The last thing she did was to give me a glorious bouquet of roses which she had lain in bed holding for me for some hours—roses, and 96, and death!' (*The Glasgow Herald*, 7 October, 1909.)

COMPULSORY GREEK AT OXFORD

To The Editor of THE ATHENÆUM.

SIR, Your Oxford Correspondent has, of course, the amplest right to hold and express his own opinions on the Greek question; but I venture to take exception to his description of those who hold the opposite view. They are not quite always obscurantists from 'country parsonages and seats', who 'do not understand' the matter, who want to 'perpetuate the bondage of the University', and whose interference with 'the teachers' is therefore 'intolerable'. May I put before your readers a few simple facts to show this?

On the last occasion but one when I myself went up to outrage your correspondent's feelings, I travelled in a train with two persons, previously quite unknown to me, who were bent on the same errand.

One of them certainly was a clergyman, but as he had been for a long time, first a member of School Boards, and then of County Educational Committees, etc., he may be perhaps allowed to have had some *locus standi*. The other was a lay schoolmaster, who had been engaged in actual teaching for some twenty years since he left Balliol. When I got to Oxford I met, sat beside in the Theatre, and voted with, a friend who was not only (as I myself then was) a Professor of English, but a much better scholar in half a dozen other modern languages than I can pretend to be in one or two. On leaving the Theatre I met another friend who had also come up to vote for Greek, an ex-official of the very highest class in a Government Department of *general* education. Last year, on that day in June when we once more smote the enemy beside the Isis river, the two non-resident Philhellenists of whom I saw most (except my before-mentioned friend, the Professor of English) were, the one an ex-schoolmaster who, while in his profession, had brought up a famous school from a very low to a very high condition in *all* departments, and had since made himself a reputation in mediæval archæology and other subjects; the other a 'modern' historian whose competence I don't think Mr. Barker himself would dispute.

I venture to think that these half-dozen instances, drawn from part only of the accidental and personal experience of a single individual, make your correspondent's description of our party look rather queer. *We* were 'supporting teachers' too; and, independently of that fact, the vote of each of the persons I have mentioned was surely as well qualified as that of some resident who might for a term or two have been teaching History or Natural Science, and have thought that his pupils were unduly bothered by a subject in which he himself felt no interest.

But, Sir, may I have the boldness (and perhaps the bad taste) to defend my own title (even though I did once rent a disused vicarage in the country for forty pounds a year) to oppose the disestablishing of Greek? I have been learning all sorts of subjects, not merely classics, for some seventy years; and I have been teaching (first as a schoolmaster, later as a professor), examining in, and (as an unmuzzled journalist, author, etc.) discussing many of these subjects for about fifty. I know no subject that even approaches Greek in its possession of that disciplinary and influential character without which all education is worthless. And if anyone says, 'But the amount of Greek required is so small, and there is still no obstacle to anyone studying the subject as much as he pleases', I answer that everything must have a beginning and a basis, and that, from the certain testimony of experience in other cases, obsolescence will follow disestablishment. For these reasons I do not think it 'intolerable' that I should have the opportunity of exercising the franchise in my own University on this matter.

I must, however, add something. The benefits of the unique combination of order and freedom, of beauty and strength, of the amazing marriage of Logic and Magic, in Greek are to be found only in the study of Greek itself. To preserve that, I have before now travelled the best part of a thousand miles, devoted two days of strenuous time, and spent a few pounds of very hard-earned money. To establish in its place the study of *translations* from Greek, I would not walk from one room to another, waste five minutes, or spend half a brass farthing.

I am, Sir,
Your obedient servant,
GEORGE SAINTSBURY.

1, Royal Crescent, Bath.
23 January, 1920.

DIDEROT'S 'SALONS'

A HUNDRED years ago exactly, when the 30th of July came round, it might have been said, in the memorable phrase of an otherwise rather stupid mediæval chronicler, that 'the earth was worse in this year, for that Denis Diderot died'. Only a small part of Diderot's vast work concerns us here; but though small as a part, it is far from small as a whole, and, small as it is in proportion to the other work of its author, no division of that work bears more distinctly the impression of its author's unrivalled personality. In regard to the more notable and important classes of literature the question of origins is hopeless, if not absurd. Nowadays, at any rate, the questions, 'Who wrote the first epic?' or 'Who wrote the first drama?' would be recognised as corresponding to that more immediately comic question, 'Who ate the first oyster?' But in some of the minor and more specialised branches one can prosecute such an enquiry with good hope of at least approximate success, and it is as nearly certain as anything can be that Denis Diderot was the inventor of art criticism as we now understand the term.

The origin of the invention was casual enough. A certain clever person named Grimm, upon whom the whitewashers have been at work with equal vigour and ill success in these latter times, secured (as most people know from Mr. Carlyle, if from nobody else) a lucrative post as correspondent to Catherine of Russia and other potentates, little and big, of the east and north and centre of Europe. They wished to know what was going on in Paris, and Grimm let them know it. Having, however, fully appreciated and practically solved the great problem of profit-making, which is obscurely referred to in the adage, *qui facit per alium facit per se*, Grimm used his friends, of whom he had many, to fill up his correspondence. The most gifted, the most industrious, and the most amiable of these friends was Diderot, and among numerous other contributions to Grimm's private newspaper Diderot charged himself for the year 1759 with the duties of art-critic at the then biennial Salons. Twelve such exhibitions took place between this date and Diderot's death. In 1783 he was already too ill to write; in 1773 he was absent on his Russian tour; in 1777 and 1779 another hand than his did the work, for what reason I am not certain. But on the other eight occasions he was the critic; and his criticisms, after nearly a century, were at last collected in the complete edition of his work which appeared half a dozen years ago. None of them was published in his lifetime, and till 1876 anybody who wished to read them had to hunt up half a dozen different publications. Even now they can scarcely be said to have been finally collected, because in a library edition of the whole works it was practically impossible to give them the commentary and the illustration of all kinds which they especially require. There are nearly a thousand large and well-filled pages of them, and in these days of elaborate books I cannot imagine many things of the kind better worth doing than a separate reprint, annotated by some one who could give the history and whereabouts of the pictures (with some modern touches to aid the reader's comparison from different points of view), and abundantly illustrated. This last point is important because comparatively few of the works and workers dealt with in them have what is called an European reputation (Greuze and Boucher among the painters, Caffieri and Houdon among the sculptors, are the chief exceptions), and it is easy because an extraordinary number of these works were engraved, and because their general character lent itself very well to engraving. Such a work as is here sketched would not exalt the 'Salons' as literature—their rank as such to a capable judge is unmistakable—but it would make them a far more valuable contribution to the history of art, and especially to the history of the criticism of art.

It has been said that these 'Salons' are the first examples of art-criticism as we now understand it, and with the limitations appropriate to all such round statements, it is perfectly true. No doubt from the time that men began to paint or model, other men began to describe what they had painted and modelled. We have admirable descriptions of the kind, as early at least as Lucian, and they are frequent in the Greek romances, not to mention the somewhat jejune examples of the kind to be found in Pliny and elsewhere. Equally of course the revival of art in Italy brought about a revival of description and even of criticism of art. But it would be very difficult to trace the art-causerie—the criticism in which description of particular works, lively illustration of the literary kind, and occasional divergence in the discussion of general points of æsthetics are united—further than Diderot. He was perhaps of all living men best suited to the task. He had an 'encyclopædical head', that is to say a vast store of positive erudition. He had an inexhaustible supply of what may be pardonably called intellectual imagination, the faculty which prevents a man from being merely satisfied with immediate impression, and urges him to trace up its reasons—somewhat fancifully and imperfectly it may be—to general principles. He had a great capacity for taking trouble; always excepting such trouble as makes a man careful about his style and the revision of his uttered thoughts. He was not in the least a recluse, but was always knocking up and down against his fellow-men, and finding out what they felt and thought. He had, as is evident from all his work, a very keen love of art, and if he did not at first know much, technically speaking, about it, the curiosity which made him master of much less interesting details stood him in good stead for learning. Lastly, he knew a great many artists, and (for such knowledge often has drawbacks as well as advantages) was in the habit of indulging in the most beautiful freedom of speech respecting his friends and enemies alike.

At first the defects which are often charged against all criticism of art by those who are not practical artists certainly appear in his work. His criticism is undoubtedly too literary, in the disparaging sense which I believe artists sometimes attach to that word. He is too prone to ask, 'How has this man told me a story?' and to decide that he, Denis Diderot, if only he could paint, would have told the story in a much more poetical and striking way. Also the theories, the ideas, and even the personal prejudices of the artists who were his special friends appear a little too clearly. This latter defect he soon shook off; the former always to a certain extent remained with him. But it must be remembered in his defence that the character of the work which he had chiefly to criticise gave special opening to it. Those were the days of great *machines* for the Gobelins manufactory, of endless scenes from sacred and profane history, of big mythological and allegorical tableaux. Much allowance must be made for a man who is confronted with a thing ten feet long by eight feet high, described as 'A Father Arriving at his Country Estate Where he is Received by His Family', even if he knows that it is only a cumbrous fashion of grouping portraits.

But when the amplest allowance is made for these and other defects, the 'Salons' remain not merely delightful reading, but on the whole most instructive and admirable criticism. From the point of view of the mere reader they have, as no other work of the author's of anything like equal size has, except the letters to Mlle. Volland, the marvellous fulness of life which characterises their author at his best. When he is at this best to read Diderot is like looking down from a balcony into a square crowded with business and pageant and the actors in both. He will begin with a vivid description of his subject, say a sea-piece of Vernet or a 'family-affection' tableau of Greuze. Suddenly he strikes off and gives a string of humorous anecdotes; then he turns to the advantages and disadvantages of drawing from models, then to the discussion of some conventional practice of art. A sketch by a foreign lady who happens to be studying in Paris serves as text for a sermon (decidedly a *sermon joyeux*) on her career and on the careers of foreign lady artists generally, and on the habits of French academicians, and in short on everything and several things beside. Next he sees or pretends to see a friend (who is named) coming towards him, and the friend and Diderot keep up a dialogue quite natural and distinct, like Fred Bayham's bishop and chaplain, for two or three pages. All this may sound as if it were mere trick, easily imitable and often imitated. Often imitated, if any one likes: easily imitable? that depends very much on the reader's faculty of distinguishing.

So far the 'Salons' might be delightful literature without being good criticism, but they are that too. Diderot is not seldom inconsistent—indeed in one or two places he calmly admits that he has said something quite different a 'Salon' or two before, but that he has learnt better since then. On some general and more technical points it is quite possible to disagree with him, and to disagree reasonably. As has been said, he certainly thinks too much of the literary and dramatic effect of a picture. He is too clamorous for movement, story, human interest, and so forth. He sometimes misuses the word *goût* in the way in which all ages have misused its synonyms, but in which the eighteenth century was an especial offender. But on the whole his criticism is extraordinarily just, and he is particularly happy in the least facile of all critical operations, the tracing by cause and effect of the connections between the means used by the artist and the impression produced on the spectator. He has in his 'Pénsées sur la peinture' an excellently expressed thought which is the key to his whole method, as, for the matter of that, it is to the method of all sane criticisms in every art. 'Le goût a prononcé longtemps avant que de connaître le motif de son jugement; il le cherche quelquefois sans le trouver, *et cependant il persiste.*'

That is the 'great word' of criticism, and it is admirably exemplified in Diderot's 'Salons', the most considerable of his critical works. While some critics (more in his day than in ours) proceed on a cut-and-dried method of formulas, applying the foot-rule and listening to the stop-watch; while others (more in our day than in his) exhaust themselves in decoratively describing the immediate pronouncements of *goût* without even endeavouring to connect those pronouncements and render a reason for them, Diderot follows a third course. He asks, 'What is the impression of this work on me?' first. But he is by no means content with that impression. He goes on to ask, 'Why does it produce that impression?' 'What connection has that impression with such and such another?' Sometimes (not very often, because the very habit of such questioning insensibly refines the taste itself) he has to come back upon his impression and ask whether it was a genuine and not a mistaken one.

This, I say, is the method of all good criticism, and there is in relation to the criticism of art no example of it before Diderot which is half so remarkable for combined quantity and quality as Diderot's own. That his method is none the less effective because of the flashing *bavardage* in which he has wrapped it up there can be little doubt; and it may fairly be contended that to some extent at least that *bavardage* expresses honestly and directly enough the course of the very thoughts by which he arrived at his own conclusion. Very few writers think aloud so much as Diderot, and in this is the secret not merely of his charm when he is at his best, but also of his extraordinary inequality and of not a few of his other faults. Certainly there are not many people whose unrevised thoughts and conversation, reported by a kind of shorthand in twenty great volumes, would bear the process as Diderot bears it, especially in the papers now discussed. The comparatively low value of the work which he criticised has sometimes been urged against the 'Salons', but this arises from a mistaken estimate of the true value of criticism. For what the critic, if he is capable, always has his eye on (through the medium of the bad or good examples of art before him) is the art itself, its principles and its powers, its methods and its results. It is the grasp of these things shown in the 'Salons' that gives them their critical value, just as it is the range and variety of sympathy shown in them with subjects beyond art, or only remotely connected with it, that gives them their literary charm. (*The Magazine of Art*, July, 1884.)

A MOMENT TO SPARE—FOR PROUST

I HAVE at last found time, or rather, for it expresses our relations better, Time has been gracious enough at last to find *me*—in regard to *Swann*. It was a new and satisfactory experience. His reality is extraordinary—at least in the main part of the book: I hope for the sake of French upper middle-class society of his day that it is not ordinary in such things as the big dinner scene in vol. II.[1]

Has anybody said that he partakes both of De Quincey and of Stendhal? He does to me, and I'm shot if I ever expected to see such a blend! You see, there is in him on the one hand a double measure of the analytical and introspective power that Beyle's admirers make so much of; with what they also admire, a total absence of prettification for prettification's sake. Yet he can be pretty in the very best sense, while Beyle never can, in the best or any other. Then, too, I at least find in him much less of the type-character which though certainly relieved by individuality in the *Chartreuse de Parme* and

[1] *i.e.*, of *Du Côté de chez Swann;* the dinner at the Verdurins' at which Forcheville is present for the first time with the Cottards, Brichot the painter, Swann and Odette. It is only fair, to both critic and reader, to explain that Mr. Saintsbury had read nothing of Proust save *Swann*, and that only in an inadequate translation. On the other hand, it was as impossible for the editor to contemplate a book of this sort without a promise of collaboration from his old friend and master as it was at the moment, for the doyen of English (if not of European, which is to say the world's) critics to qualify himself for saying more than is printed on this leaf.—C.K.S.M.

other books (especially *Lamiel*), is still always more or less there. But the oddest and to me the most attractive thing is the way in which he entirely relieves the sense of aridity—of museum-preparations—which I find in Stendhal. And here it is that the De Quincey suggestion comes so unexpectedly in. For Proust affects this miracle by a constant relapse upon—and sometimes a long self-restriction to—a sort of dream element. It is not, of course, the vaguer and more mystical kind that one finds in De Quincey, not that of *Our Ladies of Sorrow* or *Savannah-la-Mar*, but that of the best parts of *The English Mail Coach*. In fact, it is sometimes Landorian rather than De Quinceyish in its dreaminess. But, however this may be, the dream quality is there, to me, as it is in few other Frenchmen—themselves almost always poets. Now, the worst of the usual realist is that, being blinder than any other heathen in his blindness, he tries to exorcise dream, though sometimes not nightmare, from life. Such a mixture as Proust's I remember nowhere else. (*Contribution to 'Marcel Proust: An English Tribute' collected by C. K. Scott Moncrieff*, 1923.)

'THE ANNALS OF THE PARISH'

VERY seldom can such a feather have been put, two generations after his death, in the cap of a novelist, never even in his own time ranked as exactly in the first class, as the issuing within a few days of each other of new editions of Galt's *Annals of the Parish* and *Ayrshire Legatees*, by two different publishers of the first rank, Messrs. Blackwood and Messrs. Macmillan, each issue graced with illustrations, introductions by eminent hands, Mr. Crockett and Mr. Ainger, and all possible 'trimmings'. It so happens that the *Annals of the Parish* has been to me one of those books which everybody knows in his own case—books which one is always going to read and never does. You mark the game down early—perhaps from boyhood—but it perpetually eludes you. I have, however, succeeded in running down a fair number of these shy animals before now, and on this occasion I have at last bagged Galt. He is eminently worth bagging, as, indeed, I knew before from other work of his: but none of that work is so good as the *Annals*. And, indeed, a critic given to whimsies might say that it is the kind of book the author of which might be expected never to do anything so good again—a book the goodness of which consists partly in fresh observation of minute local touches and actual human originals, partly in a sort of half unconscious humour. In such cases the observation is apt not to bear a second draft upon it, the humour to become forced or flat when deliberately called upon to exert itself. But the chronicle of the Rev. Mr. Baldwhidder, that unsophisticated Pepys, or diary-writing Parson Adams of Presbyterianism, is the freshest and sprightliest running possible, the sort of thing which reminds us of the fact or fable of the wine-books about liquor that is the result of the mere heaping up of the grapes without any violent pressing or stamping. The *Ayrshire Legatees* is not nearly so good, being a direct and obvious copy, though with some original strokes; but it is quite good enough to be read with pleasure, and sufficiently different to be a foil in subject to its more admirable companion. (*The Minster*, 1895.)

'THE ADVENTURES OF MR. VERDANT GREEN'

THERE are few odder books, if their circumstances and origin be taken into consideration, than *The Adventures of Mr. Verdant Green.* Laymen writing about law and clergy, ladies writing about parliament or clubs, Frenchmen writing about England, Americans attempting to imitate the vulgar speech of England—all these are by-words, and justly by-words, for slips and errors. But it is doubtful whether the unhappiest of them ventures on such a perilous task as a man who is not of the University writing about the University, or a man of one University writing about another. There was once an unhappy novelist who placed his hero at Cambridge and made him 'have a few holidays in consequence of the death of the Greek Professor', an event which might draw forth the tears of the Muses by Cam, or, for the matter of that, by Isis, but which certainly would not bring about anything in the shape of holiday or working day for any man by either. But Edward Bradley, who, in gratitude to Bishop Cosin and Bishop Hatfield (for whom as a Durham man he was more especially bound to pray) called himself Cuthbert Bede, and who never, I believe, paid more than visits to Oxford itself, seems to have had a strange imputation of genius. I myself did not know Oxford till some dozen years after the publication of *Verdant Green*, while the condition of the University had in that time, owing to the operation of the first Commission, altered probably more than it had done in a hundred years earlier. There were no bedmakers, in most colleges at least, any longer; the Proctor was no longer 'plucked', and the very word was giving way to another. Yet *Verdant Green* was true in the really important things still to a very great extent, and the singular fashion in which the author had been able to unite the passing with the abiding features made it more true still.

A good deal of this no doubt was due to the fact that here at any rate Cuthbert Bede takes rank with the real makers; he turns out men and even women, not lay figures. In such other works of his as I have read—*Glencraggan* and what not—he does not display this faculty; he is clever—some of his nonsense verses are very clever indeed—but not much more. But Oxford seems to have touched, stranger within her gates as he was, at once his ears, his eyes, and his lips. His happiest strokes might not have been attained before Dickens; but how few of the imitators of Dickens have attained anything like them, and how seldom did Dickens himself know how to restrain himself to the effect of them! The grave and fatherly admonition of the scout, when Verdant, in his new-born thrift, suggests that the remains of his commons shall be saved, to the effect that fresh bread and butter are far better for his master's health than stale food; the punctiliously exact prescription of the bed-maker as to the sovereign effect of three spots of brandy on a lump of sugar in spasms, and her congratulations to Verdant on his wedding—how these things differ from the tiresome insistence of some imitators on similar characteristics! With what real art are the various episodes wrought together to make a whole! How little padding there is, and how lightly and easily the stock Oxford jokes (some of them almost perennial and, as it has been suggested, concocted by King Alfred in the Brasenhus in the intervals of drawing up the statutes of University College) are brought in, touched off, and left without tedious dwelling!

But undoubtedly the book would not approach positive greatness so nearly as it does without Mr. Bouncer. Dates suggest that Mr. Bouncer may have owed something to another person, that he would not have been quite what he was if Foker had not been. But there is no copying, and I am not absolutely certain that there was complete priority in the heir of the beer-vats. At any rate, Mr. Bouncer is at once himself and also one side of the eternal undergraduate aforesaid. I remember, when I was perambulating Christ Church Meadows in the intervals of an examination for a Postmastership, seeing a small man in a coat and cap, of I do not at this distance of time know what college, struggling to thrust off a punt and ejaculating, 'And they had much work to come by the boat'; and I remember looking into that punt hopefully, but doubtfully, to see whether Huz and Buz were there. They were not; they could not have been; but the soul of their master, which the Reverend Cuthbert Bede had so cunningly fixed, was somewhere about beyond all question. And I should be glad to think that it is there still—still 'very short', still desirous of two ponies, still capable of making practical and agreeable use even of ponies of a different kind from that hoped for, still as full of good fellowship as of mischief, and of not too bookish intelligence as of both.

And Verdant himself is a person too. He is a muff, but not merely a muff. Even the implacable veracity of wine discovers nothing discreditable in him. If the expression be imperfect, the sentiment is undeniable in 'Oxful fresmul, anprow-title!' It is not everyone who in the circumstances would have retained the delicacy which animated his appeal to 'myfrel Misserboucer' for permission to apply that phrase to his new acquaintance; and the appreciation of the 'jollitlebirds' shows soul, just as the indignation which, at a much later and more conventional part of the story, is incited in him by the sight of 'His moustache under Her nose' shows manliness behind those gig-lamps.

In short, to drop falsetto, Cuthbert Bede in this good-humoured extravaganza showed the possession of two qualities which novelists of much more ambitious pretensions have by no means often possessed in the same measure—a remarkable faculty of assimilating and mastering the outward details of his subject, and a faculty not much less remarkable of making his slight and fanciful sketches of persons alive. As he certainly never at any other time showed the first of these faculties to anything like the same effect, and never at any other time displayed any great grip of the second at all, it is not foolish to suppose that there was some singular pre-established harmony between himself and his subject in this particular case, that the hour and the man accorded, as they do too seldom in literature. The thing of course is a trifle, a burlesque, or at best a farcical comedy. One only wishes that the serious things of literature, the epics and the tragedies, were always or often done half so well. They say that close upon a hundred and fifty thousand copies of the book have been sold; would that these dubious arithmetical distinctions were often so justly earned! (*Macmillan's Magazine*, March, 1898.)

SHAKESPEARE AND THE WELSH

'FOR the Honour of Wales' is a good old motto; and no 'seed of the coiling serpent'—that is to say, more politely if less picturesquely, no Englishman—who is a man of honour himself will dream of grudging attempts to carry it out. For one such attempt Shakespeare gives a favourable opportunity. He certainly has no ill-feeling against the Welsh; indeed, there does not seem to have been much, if any, prevalent among Englishmen in his time, despite jokes about 'Taffy's' fondness for other people's beef and his own (or anybody's) cheese. Whether the common attribution of this to the Tudor dynasty is true may perhaps be doubted; at any rate, the results were hardly similar in the cases of the compatriots of the Stuarts or of the Hanover line, even when the actual monarchs had severally become popular. More commonplace causes may have acted. Welsh brigandage had ceased; Welsh girls were pretty; Welsh ale was remarkably good. But these are generalities. As for Shakespeare himself, nobody can deny that Fluellen and Sir Hugh Evans are capital examples of that kindly raillery which is akin to, if it is not one form of, love. And though Welsh touchiness has found something to complain of in Glendower as Shakespeare represents him, few impartial judgements will refuse to accept him as, with Fergus MacIvor for the only dead-heater, the best portrait of a Celtic chief in non-Celtic literature.

But we have touched the rub. *Was* this literature non-Celtic? May not Shakespeare have had a Welsh grandmother? May not she have told him Welsh stories? May he not have been friends with Mr. Jenkins who was not in his time master of the Stratford Grammar School to which he possibly went? May he not have actually visited Wales, the mountains of which, if you are lucky, and are high enough up, and have good eyes or a telescope, you may perhaps see from Stratford? To all which, and to other questions of the same kind, an ingenuous examinee possessing some knowledge of the facts, and some acquaintance with the rules of evidence, can only reply, in most appropriate words, 'Mass! I cannot tell'. But many enthusiastic Cambro-Britons have thought they could tell . . . (*The Athenæum*, 12 December, 1919.)

THE LAURENCE STERNE TITTLE-TATTLE

NOT one of the very idlest dream-problems that one may let wave themselves before the half-shut eye of the mind is, whether Sterne would or would not have liked the idea of his life being written? He had, of course, vanity in plenty; and liked few things (except philandering) better than keeping his name and himself before the public. But he was an exceedingly shrewd person; and knew very well indeed that this particular way of keeping him before the public would have its dangers. Whether there was anything really 'flagitious', and therefore to be hidden, in his actual conduct may be disputed by persons who do not allow mere charity to blind or distort judgment. But he was in the habit of keeping exceedingly doubtful (or not-doubtful) company; and he was in the habit of saying, and still more writing, equally doubtful or not doubtful things. 'Why will fellows write such letters?' said a good-natured critic some years ago, after a scandal of the kind. The question may be difficult to answer, save by the ancient proverb about 'Needs must——' But it is certain that not a few fellows (and those not always bad fellows) seem not to be able to help it, or not to try to help it; and that this particular fellow with whom we deal was most conspicuously of their number. I have always thought that it was much to the credit of two persons who rather require additions to the credit side of their account—Hall Stevenson and Wilkes—that they both refused the solicitations of Lydia Sterne de Medalle, to act as biographers. For they knew, better than anybody, the matter with which they would have to deal; and they knew, as well as anybody, that their hands would scarcely be likely to make any handling of it the better for his memory in the public eye. As for the wretched girl or woman herself, she has long since found her way to the particular *bolgia* of which Ham was the first recorded inhabitant, but which has received some denizens since—the abode of those who expose the weaknesses of their parents. But of late years—indeed for a very considerable time past—large new rummagings have been made into Sterniana; not, it is true, always without furnishing his defenders with some new materials for defence, but hardly ever without increasing the extent of the points where defence is necessary. Besides those who have dealt with such matter as was before them critically, without searching for new—from Thackeray downwards through Mr. Traill and Mr. Henley to the present writer

—Mr. Percy Fitzgerald, Sir Sidney Lee, Mr. Sichel, one or two American investigators, and most recently, Mr. Lewis Melville have added to the material itself. And considering the letter-and-diary-writing and generally gossiping character of the time at which Sterne lived; the nature, manners, and relations in society of the man himself; the various atmospheres in which he lived and the extent to which he was in the French sense 'spread' in this world—one could never feel the least surprise at fresh accessions, if not of knowledge, at any rate of tittle-tattle in the future. Whether the ghastly story of the recognition of his body on the dissecting table be fact or fable, whether the gossip of the footman (not an ordinary footman either) about his last moments be genuine or 'faked'—it is equally clear that here is a memory of a peculiar character, a person and personality to which things happen that do not happen to others. Sterne cultivated the bizarre, during at any rate the latter part of his life, with rather excessive devotion; but this devotion was at least returned, for the bizarre itself attached itself to him, and some of the forms which it took were certainly 'not convenient'. Now these inconvenient things have, in his case, had a nasty habit of reversing the great old dial motto—'*imputantur et* non *pereunt*'. So that one always has an uneasy feeling that, when anything fresh about Sterne leaps to light, he is only too likely to be shamed.

On the other hand, though nothing of any importance has been added, or seems in the least likely to be added, to the 'Works', they require less and less defence as time goes on. It was once, no doubt, a legitimate and to a certain extent useful business to point out the so-called plagiarisms in them, because in not a few cases the books borrowed from were very little known and in some deserved to be made known, because in all cases the filiation of literary matters, if inoffensively dealt with, is of interest. But one of the consolations for pessimists at the present moment is that the dunce's employment of the word 'plagiarism', as a terrible and final sentence of condemnation, has gone a good deal out of use. Some people, at any rate, have come to recognise that most things have been said, and that practically everything has been thought, before in substance; and that the only question is whether the present sayer and thinker has shown due skill and due individuality in his manner of thought and expression. There can be little dispute as to Sterne's having passed this latter test.

We are far removed from any living scandal that Sterne may have given personally, and in an even better position to appreciate his work, disinfected as it is by Time, if we choose. There is indeed a good deal in those last three words, for how few people do really choose to appreciate work as work, without dragging in all sorts of irrelevant considerations! Sterne's work is very small in bulk. The whole of the 'profane'—sometimes decidedly profane—part of it will go into one volume the size of an ordinary novel, though of course with rather thinner paper and with closer and smaller print. The 'Sermons' themselves do not add much, while the *Sentimental Journey*, which practically gives the whole Sterne (except the upper-shelf frippery) in little, does not by itself fill a hundred and fifty by no means crowded pages. Yet, outside of the 'Sermons', there is scarcely a page that is not full, and inside them there are not many pages that are empty, of such an idiosyncrasy of genius as is hard to beat, *as* idiosyncrasy, anywhere. In a certain dubious sense there is no more artificial writer than Sterne in the whole of literature. To some only partially critical temperaments it may seem as if there were no end to the successive strippings off of what Shakespeare calls 'lendings', as if one would never come to the real unadulterated and undisguised quiddity. Perhaps in a certain sense you never do so come. But in the process, if you are a real critic, you discover that there has been a quiddity, nay, a quintessence, saturating all these lendings, and making them, not themselves or their original author's, but Sterne's. Goethe's extraordinarily high praise of Sterne is, as it states itself, taken from such an entirely false point of view, that it has sometimes been merely dismissed as of no value, except as a curiosity, today. Sterne might be important to a German of Goethe's earlier time as an enemy of 'the heresy of instruction' and so forth, but he certainly has never, either in his own time or since, showed himself in that light, or performed that function, to Englishmen. Yet his uniqueness exists, and it has, as a rule, been insufficiently recognised. With him, as has been said, the curtain too often is the picture: you will get at little or nothing behind it. At least for those people who know criticism from both sides—who have conjugated the verb 'to criticise' in its active, passive, *and middle* voices—the famous 'stop-watch' passage is only a superlatively clever rhetorical display, not even enshrining any genuine smart of Sterne himself at criticisms. For some who have not hard hearts, who have felt 'the pity of it' in life and literature keenly and often enough, the Marias and the Lefevres, and even my Uncle Toby himself, though more and more worthy of admiration in the order named, arouse, except in the last case, very little genuine sympathy, and even in that case sympathy which is dangerously mingled with amusement of a slightly satiric kind.

But how superlative the art of it all is! and how extraordinary is the admixture of *some* nature with that art! It may almost be said that Sterne never fails to produce the effect at which he aims. He does not so fail with the stop-watch, or with Maria, or even with the lines of points and the marbled pages. The effect produced may not be wholly pleasing to people today, but it is the effect which Sterne meant to produce, and did produce, on the people of *his* day, and which soon will, or certainly in the usual evolution of things will some day, please again. Elsewhere—in what we, perhaps presumptuously, call his 'greater' efforts because they still please us without allowance—his artistic triumph is not in reality greater. We happen to be at the door when the clock-lock opens it, that is all. And elsewhere, again, he is certainly perennial; no coincidence of hour and audience is necessary.

If we had no tittle-tattle about Sterne; if he had left no letters; if we knew nothing about Kitty Fourmentelle and the 'Bramine'; if he were unsmirched by the society of Wilkes and Stevenson and 'Panty' Lascelles; if we had not that dreadful portrait, with its Asmodean suggestion—how different would the general estimate of him be! There would remain the fie-fie passages in the books; and one might say 'something too much of this', going on to remark that even the something less might have been done in a healthier fashion. But no one except a fanatic of prudery and pudibundity would regard the fault as utterly damning in fact; and no one who knew his Voltaire would fail to detect at least an excuse of pattern in form. The mechanical oddities of typography and general make-up are, after all, but as the farcical or low-comedy element in other compositions; indeed, they are hardly more than properties and costume—the external presentation in which the author chooses to set forth his work, after all, very easily tolerated, and not unsuitable. The very sentimentality—rancid as it is to the novice—readily loses its evil savour when a sufficiently historic sense is brought to bear on it; and indeed can, by anyone who has acquired the most valuable of all critical faculties, be simply neglected and shut out. What remains? Why, such a microcosm of quaint humour; of refreshing contrast to reality where yet the artistically improbable is kept aloof with the cunningest super-realism; of comically presented humanity —as it will be very hard to find in the same compass anywhere else. In this preposterous extravaganza, with all its burlesque, all its horse- (or at least pony-) play; all its doubtful taste; all its not at all doubtful licence; with its shadows and uncompleted characters; its non-existent, or at least, hopelessly flawed and broken stories—there is, somehow or other, something of the Universal. It was this, no doubt, that Goethe saw, though he mistook both its character and its causes when he showered on 'Tristram' the, at first sight, rather amazing epithets and phrases—'finest spirit that ever worked', 'full of freedom and beauty'; 'benefactor of the nineteenth century', 'able to distinguish truth from falsehood', 'possessed of boundless sagacity and penetration.' When one has gasped a little; shaken oneself; got breath, and, so to speak, run under shelter from this storm of panegyric, one sees that what struck Goethe (what, to do him justice, generally did strike him, and made his own greatness by so doing) was the very touch of the Universal which has been mentioned. To use the word 'transcendental' in connection with Sterne may seem outrageously absurd, and yet Sterne does 'transcend' —by the queerest of stairs, no doubt. He is never commonplace, and he is never merely trivial in his attempts to escape commonplaceness. Almost as outrageous may it seem to mention his name in the same sentence with Shakespeare's. Yet, if you take the four great eighteenth-century novelists, though Fielding is of course, the only one who is actually in touch with Shakespeare, Sterne is nearer to the great exemplar of all human 'imitations' than either Richardson or Smollett.

Nor does it require charity pushed to the point of imbecility, or the forcible suppression of our too abundant information about him, or an addiction to the idle art of whitewashing, to improve the conception of Sterne, even as a man, very considerably. If we know too much about him on one side we know, in all fair probability, a good deal too little on the other. There seems to have been no really bad blood about him. *Fatigatus et aegrotus* as he was of his unlucky wife, he seems to have been very liberal to her out of no great means. Except in so far as it furnished him with reading for his miscellany, there could, perhaps, hardly have been a worse life, for such a man as Sterne, than the twenty years of sojourning in a remote country district, with alternation only to the cabals and gossip of a provincial capital and cathedral city. A larger air, a more varied society, the rubbing of shoulders with his equals in intellect, were the very things that Sterne never had till too late, and after the meaner parts of his nature had been fostered and developed, alike by solitude, by 'Crazy Castle' *cochonneries*, and by the most undivine atmosphere of an assembly of average mid-Georgian divines. An early acquaintance with Johnson and a series of the more good-natured bear's hugs (which might quite conceivably have been administered to him by one who tolerated, not only Boswell, but Savage and the Herveys, Cornelius Ford, and Miss Bet Flint herself) would have been a godsend to Sterne, whose faults were after all almost wholly those of a dirty little boy, and for whom, as in the case of other dirty little boys, there could have been no such thoroughly salutary discipline as a good drubbing. The treatment must have been all the more effective inasmuch as Sterne, unlike Goldsmith, had, at least when women were not concerned and he had not a pen in his hand, nearly as much common sense as he had genius, and would have been able to make full profit of this discipline without its making him intolerably uncomfortable at the time. Even short of such a drastic cure as this, larger, healthier, and more varied society could hardly have failed to produce at least a very considerable amendment in the general wholesomeness of his tone.

But we have to take things as we find them: and heaven knows, we might find things and persons much worse than Sterne the man, while Sterne the writer has the one condition of indispensableness—that he is practically unique. Methods so ostentatiously artificial as his may appear to be easily imitable, but who has ever imitated Sterne, not only with the least success, but without the most ghastly and preposterous failure? Now inimitableness is not quite an absolute and exclusive test of genius, for some geniuses have been imitable. But there never has been a not-imitable person who has not also been a genius, greater or less. (*The Bookman*, July, 1913.)

THINGS ABOUT BLAKE

PROBABLY the worst sin of a reviewer, or the worst next to ignorance, is impertinence; and I wish to clear myself of the slightest intention to be impertinent to Mr. Burdett, if I say that I have gathered from more than one or two passages of his book [1] the impression that he thinks such a book not of the most necessary to be written. In one sense, no doubt, it *had* to be written: because the famous series in which it appears would have been still incomplete

[1] *William Blake*, by Osbert Burdett. *English Men of Letters Series*.

without it. There is nothing in the book itself to authorise a suggestion, pertinent or impertinent, that it might have been better written. It is, as a biography, very good. It is as a discussion perfectly sensible, which is very much more than can be said about some other discussions of Blake. But to be plump and plain, is there much good—is there *any* good at all—in *discussions* about Blake? Let him be reprinted as often as he can be. Let him be re-designed (though the 'highbrows' of art assure us that the thing is impossible) and re-coloured as often, as copiously and as well as may be whether as decoratively as in Mr. Binyon's work or as faithfully as in Mr. Hollyer's. Let him have his beauties in art and letters discreetly set forth and praised for ever and for ever. But 'discussion' of him, at least of one kind—manufacture of 'systems' out of him, that is to say, and all the like of it—is rather useless and may more than often be mischievous. To lay down a dictum in his own manner though alas! not with his own power, 'Every man who can understand or enjoy Blake at all understands and enjoys him in his own way.' There is no Guide or Handbook to Blake. In the same words discussion of him *is* useless.

So let us discuss him, and Mr. Burdett's book on him, a little in another kind, whether it be useless or not. For he never ceases to be a tempting subject, and it is always amusing to skate round holes and climb 'pillars'.

There used to be in English nurseries and schoolrooms of the Early and Middle Victorian time a children's game, based upon and intended to stimulate Biblical knowledge, the nature of which can be pretty well guessed from its usual title, 'Prophet, Priest, or King?' Everybody who knows anything about Blake knows that he was 'Poet, Painter, *and* Prophet': and persons of only moderate intelligence who have read books about him must surely have noticed that the triplicity has rather bothered the authors of these books. The artistic specialists have been inclined to regard the poetry as at best a secondary matter, if not as merely a sort of assemblage of mottoes, 'captions', letterpress to the drawings and paintings. The pure—or more or less pure—critics have sometimes seemed as if they were afraid of being accused of not minding their own business if they said much about Blake's work in line and colour: while the propheteers (as we may perhaps be permitted to call them) have forced everything—poetry and painting both—into the service of creating a 'system'—now of philosophy, now of religion, now of a mishmash of both for him. All three sets (as was, one supposes, inevitable) have endeavoured to weave in and spin out the scanty facts of his biography so as to suit their private ends. There are times when Blake-lovers, learning that it was apparently a mere chance that he did not become a practitioner in music as well, have wondered whether they ought to thank Providence or mildly grieve at its ways. It would be something to have, if one could have, a sonata corresponding to the Mad Song or 'O earth! O earth! return' in poetry—to The Ancient of Days or the man who 'wants' to climb to the moon in picture. But this might involve other sorts of creations from the musician and it would certainly involve some very terrible matter from those who write about music. Blake as we have him, though a great treasure and pleasure, is not an easy job: we do not want more handles for its being made still more difficult.

Yet one might add even a fourth P to the initials which, in not *quite* such an alarming fashion as when the angel marked them on Dante have been ticketed on Blake—in this case the initial of Politician. One or two of the commentators, *not* including our present author, have made a good deal of it—things connected with it certainly had to do with his curious experiences in Sussex; and he no doubt did by a piece of judicious advice save Mr. Thomas Paine from a good chance of the gallows. As to the merit of this last action opinions may differ. But it is certain that he ceased, like so many others, to sympathise with the French Revolution: and those who have read his poem upon it (which it must be remembered very few people had had the chance of doing till quite recently) will hardly have found much pure sansculottism therein. There is, however, one point, and a very important point, in which this little fit of actual political measles in him may be taken right profitably with his general character as Poet, Painter, Prophet, Philosopher, and everything else, whether beginning with P or not. It springs from, and is part of Blake's unvarying and essential hostility to Rule. Whether more education—of which he had very little though he had considerable aptitude for it—would have directed his efforts of insurgence more happily in other things, as it actually did in Poetry and engraving, and as Sir Joshua thought it would have done in Painting, nobody can say: and there are some people wicked enough to say that in poetry and painting they don't want him improved at all. Providence had supplied him, in the Elizabethans, with an incomparable place to revolt to in poetry: if our author is right in thinking that his early familiarity with Westminster Abbey Gothicised his tastes in the other art all the more glory to 'the' Abbey. But

Swedenborg and Ossian—who more than anything but the Bible (which they went far to neutralise) served as his tutors in mystical tone of thinking and form of writing—might certainly have been exchanged for the better. At the same time it is difficult even for the most hard-baked advocate of a classical education—and there can be few baked harder than the present reviewer—to agree with Mr. Burdett in wishing that Blake's culture had been more Hellenic and less Hebraic in Literature, more classical and less romantic in Art. In the first place, so robustious and even rebellious a nature as his would in all probability have rejected it, if the chance had been given. In the second, there is just a possibility of the opposition of soil and cultivation resulting in no crop at all, or in featureless and 'fushionless' (as the Scotch say) stuff of no or little value. But in the third place—the most important of all—we don't want a tamed, and managed, and classicalised Blake. There are few greater, and unluckily there are not many commoner mistakes than this desire for something to be, or even attempt to make it, something other than itself. If Blake's own aspirant instead of setting his ladder to the moon and trying to ascend it to the motto-sign of 'I want', had put that ladder neatly away in a barn, and taken a walk to the nearest baker's to buy, or turned into the nearest field to earn, his daily bread he would have been quite a proper and reasonable, but hardly an interesting person.

To set to credit against this (as some may think) mistake, let it be said that Mr. Burdett is sound and sensible though perhaps a little reticent and gingerly on the all-important in one way, quite unimportant in another, question of Blake's mental condition. His conclusion is the pretty certainly right one that Blake was always perfectly sane in his actions and responsible for his conduct, but that in thought and speech and writing and even exercises of manual art he showed symptoms of a state not quite reconcilable with ordinary sanity. There is nothing in this that need in the least offend any reasonable admirer or even in a sense worshipper of Blake: it falls in with the common, and in history and practice well justified, notion about the alliance of great wits and madness; and it can itself be justified from the patent and certain work and the known facts of life without needing the slightest recourse to the legend of the Garden of Lambeth-Eden, or making a mystery of the really quite commonplace squabble with the soldier at Felpham. It is perhaps true that this point of madness which at Blake's first 'resurrection' used to be quite a burning one, has become much less dangerous: but the change may give an excuse for a slight expression of surprise at Mr. Burdett's treatment of the resurrection, or series of resurrections, itself. A person just introduced to the subject—and this excellent set of books has from the first been intended so to introduce people—might, one fears from Mr. Burdett's expressions about the 'hundred years' since Blake's death et cetera, fancy that the discovery of him was one of the glories of the twentieth century certainly, if not even of its second quarter. Of course there has recently been a fresh outburst of interest in Blake evidenced, caused, encouraged, what you like, by the first careful editing of the Prophetic books; the making accessible in completer and cheaper forms of the designs; the discussion of the 'systems' in and out of England and so on. But it is only and barely during the first third of this hundred years that he could really be said to be in eclipse or abscondence: and he was not completely so then. By the sixties Gilchrist's most unusually full account of his life with specimens of the work, and Mr. Swinburne's fulgurous but brilliant and fascinating essay had in no vulgar sense almost 'vulgarised' Blake. It is fifty-three years (more than half the 'hundred') since William Rossetti gave if not a perfect, an extremely useful edition of the Poems: and separate editions of the picture-books began to be issued in facsimile. Even Messrs. Ellis and Yeats's huge Thesaurus of text and comment is a third of a century old and again more also. Add many other dealings with, and some exhibitions of, his designs, and it will not be too much to say that no man not himself a centenarian can say that at any time of his life Blake was ever neglected.

This however may again be said to be a matter of only secondary or even less than secondary importance. More exception to the generally favourable estimate of the book may be taken to the remarks that Blake's 'Writings, exquisite as his lyrics could be, rank below his designs' and that as is elsewhere laid down, you cannot fully appreciate the poetry of the two sets of Songs unless you have before you Blake's original production of them—hand-made and hand-illustrated. It would hardly be a valid criticism to say that this is a sort of petty treason to Mr. Burdett's commission which is to deal with Blake as 'a man of letters': for of course *magna est veritas*. But it *is* a valid criticism to say that the attitude shows an insufficient appreciation of the relation of the arts to each other, and, very specially, of the nature, relative and positive, of poetry itself. To say that The Ancient of Days ranks above or below the Sunflower couplet, for instance, would be, though one does not wish to be uncivil, a mere blunder. The glory of the stars is different not in size or 'rank' but in kind. And though the ornamentation of the Innocence and Experience pieces may add to the pleasure derivable from themselves it *is* an addition—a mechanical and separable addition, not a factor in a chemical compound developing or creating new quality. It is really astonishing how constantly one finds these mistakes about poetry. They are not absent of course in the case of the other arts: but they are there nothing like so frequent. In fact it is the very rarest thing to find poetry criticised as poetry and nothing else. If you so take Blake's poetry you will find that it 'ranks below' nothing of its own kind except in mere quantity and number. In quality and essence it, at its best, never fails: and it is a circumstance rather to its credit than otherwise that when it is not at its best it is generally not poetry at all, but little above doggerel. His wings either raise him to the empyrean: or like those of Baudelaire's albatross pinion him even in walking.

To pass to another part of the subject, when Mr. Burdett quite properly praising Blake's attitude to Chaucer calls it 'his nearest approach [which it certainly is] to orderly criticism' and exclaims, 'How just and yet how like Blake is the following reflection: "The characters of Chaucer's Pilgrims are the characters which compose all ages and nations—as one age falls another rises different to mortal sight but to immortals only the same. For we see the same character repeated again in animals, vegetables, minerals, and men; nothing new occurs in individual existence. Accident ever varies; substance can never change nor decay", ' one thoroughly agrees with him. But would it not have added to the interest if he had pointed out that Blake had evidently been reading an author who was still, in his earlier time, quite as commonly read as Shakespeare or Milton—that is to say, Dryden? The famous passage in the Preface to the Fables which praises Chaucer for incorporating 'the various manners and humours of the whole English nation', and lays it down that 'mankind is ever the same and nothing is lost out of nature though everything is altered,' must almost certainly have been in Blake's mind when he was designing the picture which commemorated the rascality of Cromek and which (perhaps excusably) proved too much for the good nature of Stothard. But there is no doubt that the Catalogue does show in Blake the most curious streaks of criticism and *un*-criticism—streaks which need not in the least trouble those who take a rational view of his rationality—though they may puzzle others.

Let us therefore give thanks unmitigated and undefiled by any rascally comparison with its manifestation in different places, or its utilisation of different *media* and methods—for that 'idiosyncrasy' of

Blake's which Mr. Burdett rightly insists upon, but which seems to be in some respects a sort of trouble to him. If anybody says to me 'But *you* seem rather to neglect Blake as a designer in order that you may extol him as a writer' I pray that he may not be punished for his injustice. If pleasures were comparable, as they certainly are not, I should say that the pleasure given to me by the Mad Song and the pleasure given to me by Glad Day were indistinguishable in amount. I *can* say, that each could not be better in its own way. But I know rather more about the way in which one of these pleasures is produced than I do about the other; my experience of other people's exploits in the one way is far more extensive than my experience of their exploits in the other; I will even be so very bold as to say that I can write verse which is not absolute doggerel and according to different judgments tolerable or intolerable prose, myself; while if I endeavoured to draw an Adam or an Eve the result would be even more deplorable than Princess Angelica's knight's head and helmet before Tomaso Lorenzo (No! it was Betsinda) touched it up. So I may speak more confidently and more by choice, of Blake as a writer than as a designer. But I can acknowledge little less fervency in my admiration of him as either or both. When you come to the third division—the philosophy or the etho-cosmotheology or whatever you like to call it—in not the least agreeable of slang phrases I own that my admiration 'leaves' him, or becomes bare and soon satisfied curiosity, with certain resulting or appended reflections which it is not at all necessary to particularise here. 'Take, read, and enjoy; take, look at, and enjoy' is I think the command in Blake's case—and, for once in a way, I do not think that either as Poet, Painter, or Prophet he would have objected, general objector as he was. (*The Dial*, July, 1927.)

NOTES ON SIX POETS

EDMUND SPENSER: I have frequently been told by persons of good parts that they 'cannot' read Spenser. An otherwise polite and obliging American critic once felt himself constrained to utter a kind of 'Fie! fie!' over a sentence of mine to the effect that the *Faerie Queene* was the only long poem I have ever wished longer. Either the old fear of the allegory biting them, of the elaborate antiquity of the language, or something else, seems to exercise a deterrent effect, which would be more intelligible if we accepted the dictum of the Sadducees to the effect that real lovers of poetry are very few. To me it seems that, to anyone who is such a lover, Spenser is the natural, the quotidian, the unsatiating food.

PERCY BYSSHE SHELLEY: I think myself, and have always thought, that 'A Lament' is the greatest thing in English poetry out of Shakespeare; the greatest thing in the entire poetry of the world out of Shakespeare, Dante, and Aeschylus. Nowhere else, save in some passages of these three poets, has the passionate experience of life (which is a different thing from the 'criticism' of it), been put into such perfectly faultless and flawless verse.

WILLIAM MORRIS: As one passes in mental review the first books of our poets, there are few, indeed, that strike the mind with such a sense of initiation, of a new leaf turned, of a new country opening from a height, as that given by the *Defence of Guinevere*. To have read that book or any such book, at or within a few years of its appearance, exposes the reader, of course, to a disturbing or distracting influence which is very well known in criticism. But it is the business of the critic to allow for that, and to bring himself as near as possible to the condition of those who have read it later, or of those who, speaking paradoxically, might, if it had been possible, have read it earlier. And, after making this allowance, I should myself select Mr. William Morris as the typical poet of the latter part of the century in England. He has nowhere risen quite so high as Mr. Swinburne has; he has nowhere travelled quite so far out of the common as did Rossetti; he has injured his work by extreme voluminousness, and, latterly, by fantastic excursions into regions where, saving his reverence, he talks mostly nonsense. But he was the first to publish, if not to write, of all his school, and no member of it has the combined notes of that school quite so well as he. Mr. Morris chose Chaucer as his master, but it is Spenser, not Chaucer, of whom he really holds; and if anyone has ever revived the dreamy magic of the *Faerie Queene* it is the singer, who at half a full life-time of distance, has sung of Guinevere and of Goldilocks.

THOMAS CAMPION: Of Thomas Campion, till the other day, only a few special students had heard; and widely as the revelation of him has been greeted, I doubt whether even pretty enthusiastic admirers who have critical taste in their composition, would call him a poet of the first order. Campion is possessed almost everywhere of, or by, that extraordinary Elizabethan quality which has been so much, but never too much, talked of. The air and fire that pervade that wonderful division of our verse are his, if not everywhere, yet in a majority of his pieces. It may not be very easy to analyse the secret of this charm. But that is very frequently indeed the case with the best poetry. And Campion has likewise the faculty of making quite commonplace thought and emotion sublime and rare. We may find no very deep, no very pregnant, no very lofty ideas, no very exquisite or uncommon fancy, wedded to the lark-like music of 'When to her lute Corrinna sings', to the sad minor of 'Kind are her answers', to the solemn hymnody of 'Awake, awake, thou heavy sprite', and the rest. But all the thought is just and true, all the fancy is dainty and fresh. And certainly no writer could be more fitted to present or suggest that vast body of minor Elizabethan song which sometimes tempts those who listen to it to prefer it even to the major singers of other times.

SIR WALTER SCOTT: If Scott had not been the greatest of novelists, a novelist who to unapproached synthetic power united analytical faculty enough to make the capital of twenty Psychologues, he would still be regarded by all sound poetical critics as second in English narrative poetry only to Chaucer, and as a master of more than one kind of lyric who is second to none. . . . Wordsworth did not think much of Scott as a poet; what were Scott's complete thoughts of Wordsworth we do not know.

WILLIAM WORDSWORTH: Even in his sublimest poems, even in the great Ode itself, the dull, ruthless drone of the preacher will deafen us to the singer's music; and, in all but his best, this heart-breaking war of sounds is all but universal. How excellent then, by a wise activeness in skipping, to abstract ourselves from the ugly sound and listen only to the beautiful! How much more excellent still to have the exertion of skipping performed for us! (*A Calendar of Verse*, 1892.)

THE PRESENT STATE OF LITERATURE

FOR a man born in the nineteenth century and having had his life spread over a good portion of that and the twentieth to be resuscitated in the twenty-first would be, no doubt, in some respects a bore. Some folk, if one does not mistake, who have imagined things of the kind have thought it necessary or advisable to delete the revived one's memory. But one can imagine some not disagreeable pastime, for a person of literary tastes and knowledge who had not been dememorised, in criticising the literature of the middle period. He would have the advantage of what may be called a double Pisgah sight, forwards and backwards; he would of course retain that knowledge of still earlier time without which all criticism is futile and real criticism impossible; and he would be, if not a very poor creature, almost entirely impartial. There would be of course much interest for him in the literary aspects of the present time: its curious and (begging pardon) surely rather semivirile mania for talking about 'sex'; its amiable anxiety to assure itself and other people that it really *is* cleverer than its grandmother; its devotion to 'psychology' in a sense somewhat different from what had been attached to the word previously; its almost invention—its certainly much increased use—of the Latin equivalent, 'mentality'; its increased valuation of construction and technique. (*The Bookman*, June, 1930.)

A SAINTSBURY BIBLIOGRAPHY

A SAINTSBURY BIBLIOGRAPHY

COMPILED BY W. M. PARKER

I. Literary Histories

PRIMER OF FRENCH LITERATURE. (Clarendon Press, 1880.)

SHORT HISTORY OF FRENCH LITERATURE. (Clarendon Press, 1882.)

HISTORY OF ELIZABETHAN LITERATURE. (Macmillan, 1887.)

HISTORY OF NINETEENTH CENTURY LITERATURE 1780–1895. (Macmillan, 1896.)

FLOURISHING OF ROMANCE AND THE RISE OF ALLEGORY. (Periods of European Lit. Ser., ed. G. S.). (Blackwood, 1897.)

SHORT HISTORY OF ENGLISH LITERATURE. (Macmillan, 1898.)

HISTORY OF CRITICISM AND LITERARY TASTE IN EUROPE. Vol. I. (Blackwood, 1900.)

EARLIER RENAISSANCE. (Periods of European Lit. Ser.). (Blackwood, 1901.)

HISTORY OF CRITICISM AND LITERARY TASTE IN EUROPE. Vol. II. (Blackwood, 1902.)

HISTORY OF CRITICISM AND LITERARY TASTE IN EUROPE. Vol. III. (Blackwood, 1904.)

HISTORY OF ENGLISH PROSODY. Vol. I. (Macmillan, 1906.)

LATER NINETEENTH CENTURY. (Periods of European Lit. Ser.). (Blackwood, 1907.)

HISTORY OF ENGLISH PROSODY. Vol. II. (Macmillan, 1908.)

HISTORY OF ENGLISH PROSODY. Vol. III. (Macmillan, 1910.)

HISTORICAL MANUAL OF ENGLISH PROSODY. (Macmillan, 1910.)

HISTORY OF ENGLISH CRITICISM. (Blackwood, 1911.)

HISTORY OF ENGLISH PROSE RHYTHM. (Macmillan, 1912.)

ENGLISH NOVEL. (Channels of Eng. Lit. Ser.). (Dent, 1913.)

FIRST BOOK OF ENGLISH LITERATURE. (Macmillan, 1914.)

PEACE OF THE AUGUSTANS. (Bell, 1916.)

HISTORY OF THE FRENCH NOVEL. Vol. I. (Macmillan, 1917.)

HISTORY OF THE FRENCH NOVEL. Vol. II. (Macmillan, 1919.)

II. Biographical and Critical Works

DRYDEN. (English Men of Letters Ser.). (Macmillan, 1881.)

SHORT HISTORY OF LIFE AND WRITINGS OF LE SAGE. (Priv. prtd., 1881.)

MARLBOROUGH. (English Worthies Ser.). (Longmans, 1885.)

ESSAYS IN ENGLISH LITERATURE 1780–1860. First Series. (Percival, 1890.)

ESSAYS ON FRENCH NOVELISTS. (Percival, 1891.)

MISCELLANEOUS ESSAYS. (Percival, 1892.)

EARL OF DERBY. (Queen's Prime Ministers Ser.). (Sampson Low, 1892.)

ESSAYS IN ENGLISH LITERATURE 1780–1860. Second Series. (Dent, 1895.)

CORRECTED IMPRESSIONS. (Heinemann, 1895.)

SIR WALTER SCOTT. (Famous Scots Ser.). (Oliphant, Anderson, & Ferrier, 1897.)

MATTHEW ARNOLD. (Modern English Writers Ser.). (Blackwood, 1899.)

COLLECTED ESSAYS AND PAPERS 1875–1923. 4 vols. (Dent, 1923–24.)

CONSIDERATION OF THACKERAY. A collection, with some corrections, of the Introds. to the *Oxford Thackeray* (1908). (O.U.P. 1931.)

PREFACES AND ESSAYS. Ed. O. Elton. (Macmillan, 1933.)

SHAKESPEARE. Reprtd. from *Camb. Hist. of Eng. Lit.*, Vol. V., 1910, with Appreciation by Helen Waddell. (C.U.P., 1934.)

FRENCH LITERATURE AND ITS MASTERS. Ed. Huntington Cairns. Article on French Literature and essays on French writers by G. S., reprtd. from Eleventh Ed. of *Encyclop. Brit.* (1910–11). (Knopf, N.Y., 1946.)

III. Miscellaneous Works

MANCHESTER. (Historic Towns Ser.). (Longmans, 1887.)

INAUGURAL ADDRESS. (Delivered at Edin. Univ. as Prof. of Eng. Lit.). (Blackwood, 1895.)

HISTORICAL CHARACTER OF ENGLISH LYRIC. (Warton Lecture on Eng. Poetry). (O.U.P., 1912.)

SOME RECENT STUDIES IN ENGLISH PROSODY. (Procs. of Brit. Acady., Vol. IX). (O.U.P., 1920.)

NOTES ON A CELLAR-BOOK. (Macmillan, 1920.)

SCRAP BOOK. (Macmillan, 1922.)

SECOND SCRAP BOOK. (Macmillan, 1923.)

LAST SCRAP BOOK. (Macmillan, 1924.)

GEORGE SAINTSBURY: THE MEMORIAL VOLUME. A New Collection of his Essays and Papers. Personal Portraits by Oliver Elton, Sir Herbert Grierson, John W. Oliver, John Purves. Biog. Memoir by A. Blyth Webster. (Methuen, 1945.)

Translations

BALZAC'S 'THE CHOUANS'. Newly trans. with Introd. by G. S. (Nimmo, 1890.)

MÉRIMÉE'S 'CHRONICLES OF THE REIGN OF CHARLES IX.'. Newly trans. by G. S. (Nimmo, 1890.)

SCHERER'S 'ESSAYS ON ENGLISH LITERATURE'. Trans. by G. S. (Sampson Low, 1891.)

MARMONTEL'S 'MORAL TALES'. Selected, with rev. trans., Biog. Introd. and notes by G. S. (Allen, 1895.)

See, for part trans., *Loci Critici* under Introductions, Prefaces, etc.

IV. Introductions, Prefaces, and Edited Matter

ENGLISH POETS. Ed. T. H. Ward. 10 Introds. by G. S. 6 vols. (Macmillan, 1880–1918.)

LE SAGE'S 'GIL BLAS'. Trans. Smollett, preceded by a Biog. and Critical Notice of Le Sage by G. S. 3 vols. (Nimmo & Bain, 1881.)

FRENCH LYRICS. Selected and annotated with Introd. by G. S. (Kegan Paul, 1882.)

CORNEILLE'S 'HORACE'. Ed. with Introd. and notes by G. S. (Clarendon Press, 1882.)

SCOTT'S 'DRYDEN'S WORKS'. Rev. and re-ed. with additional Introds., Notes, and Appendices by G. S. 18 vols. (Paterson, 1882–93.)

SPECIMENS OF FRENCH LITERATURE FROM VILLON TO HUGO. Selected and ed. (Clarendon Press, 1883.)

BEAUMARCHAIS'S 'BARBIER DE SÉVILLE'. Ed. A. Dobson. Essay on 'Progress of French Comedy' by G. S. (Clarendon Press, 1884.)

MOLIÈRE'S 'PRÉCIEUSES RIDICULES'. Ed. A. Lang. Pref. Note by G. S. (Clarendon Press, 1884.)

QUINET'S 'LETTRES À SA MÈRE'. Selected and ed. (Clarendon Press, 1885.)

SAINTE-BEUVE'S 'CAUSERIES DU LUNDI'. Selected and ed. (Clarendon Press, 1885.)

SPECIMENS OF ENGLISH PROSE STYLE FROM MALORY TO MACAULAY. Selected and annotated with Introd. Essay by G. S. (Kegan Paul, 1885.)

VOLTAIRE'S 'MÉROPE'. Ed. with Introd. and notes by G. S. (Clarendon Press, 1885.)

GAUTIER'S 'SCENES OF TRAVEL'. Selected and ed. (Clarendon Press, 1886.)

GOLDSMITH'S 'VICAR OF WAKEFIELD'. With Pref. Memoir by G. S. (Nimmo, 1886.)

RACINE'S 'ESTHER'. Ed. with Introd. and notes by G. S. (Clarendon Press, 1886.)

SWIFT'S 'GULLIVER'S TRAVELS'. With Pref. Memoir by G. S. (Nimmo, 1886.)

MOLIÈRE'S 'ÉCOLE DES FEMMES'. Ed. (Pitt Press Ser.). (C.U.P., 1888.)

POCKET LIBRARY OF ENGLISH LITERATURE. Ed. *Political Verse; Tales of Mystery; Defoe's Minor Novels; Elizabethan and Jacobean Pamphlets; Political Pamphlets; Seventeenth Century Lyrics.* 6 vols. (Percival, 1891–92.)

CALENDAR OF VERSE. Selection with Introd. by G. S. (Percival, 1892.) (In the Pref. to the second edition of Bowyer Nichols's *Words and Days* (1941), Logan Pearsall Smith, on the authority of Messrs. Rivington, reveals that the above book was compiled by G. S., and suspects, on internal evidence, that Nichols had also something to do with the compilation.)

SWIFT'S 'POLITE CONVERSATION'. Introd. and notes by G. S. (Chiswick Press Ed.). (Whittingham, 1892.)

FLORIO'S 'MONTAIGNE'S ESSAYS'. Ed. with Introd. by G. S. (Tudor Trans. Ser., ed. W. E. Henley). 3 vols. (Nutt, 1892–93.)

WORKS OF FIELDING. Ed. with Introds. by G. S. 12 vols. (Dent, 1893.)

POETICAL WORKS OF HERRICK. Ed. with Pref. and Introd. by G. S. (Aldine Poets Ser.). 2 vols. (Bell, 1893.)

ENGLISH PROSE. Ed. Sir H. Craik. 37 Introds. by G. S. 5 vols. (Macmillan, 1893–96.)

JANE AUSTEN'S 'PRIDE AND PREJUDICE'. With Pref. by G. S. (Allen, 1894.)

MARGARET OF NAVARRE'S 'HEPTAMERON'. Trans. J. M. Chartres, with Essay 'On the Heptameron' by G. S. 5 vols. (Soc. Eng. Bibliophilists, 1894.)

MADAME DE STAËL'S 'CORINNE OR ITALY'. [Rev. trans. D. Lawler]. Introd. by G. S. 2 vols. (Dent, 1894.)

WORKS OF STERNE. Ed. with Introds. by G. S. 6 vols. (Dent, 1894.)

NATIONAL RHYMES OF THE NURSERY. Introd. by G. S. (Gardner, Darton, 1895.)

RICHARDSON'S 'SIR CHARLES GRANDISON'. Selected with Biog. Introd. and notes by G. S. 2 vols. (Allen, 1895.)

WORDS AND DAYS. Compiled J. Bowyer Nichols. Introd. by G. S. (Rivington, 1895.)

WORKS OF T. L. PEACOCK. With Introds. by G. S. 5 vols. (Macmillan, 1895–97.)

BALZAC'S 'COMÉDIE HUMAINE'. Ed. with Introds. by G. S. 40 vols. (Dent, 1895–98.)

WORKS OF SMOLLETT. Ed. with Introds. by G. S. 12 vols. (Gibbings, 1895–1900.)

POEMS OF DONNE. Ed. E. K. Chambers. Introd. by G. S. (Muses' Lib.). 2 vols. (Lawrence & Bullen, 1896.)

SIGHTS AND SCENES IN OXFORD. Described by T. Whittaker. Introd. by G. S. (Cassell, 1896.)

BALZAC'S 'HARLOT'S PROGRESS'. Trans. J. Waring. Pref by G. S. reprtd., with additions, from Pref. included in *Balzac's 'Comédie Humaine'* (1895–98). 2 vols. (Dent, 1897.)

STUDIES ON MANY SUBJECTS. By S. H. Reynolds. Pref. by G. S. (Arnold, 1898.)

TEMPLE FIELDING. Ed. by G. S. 12 vols. (Dent, 1902.)

LOCI CRITICI, PASSAGES ILLUSTRATIVE OF CRITICAL THEORY AND PRACTICE. Selected, partly trans., with notes by G. S. (Ginn: Boston, 1903.)

BEST PLAYS OF SHADWELL. Ed. with Introd. and notes by G. S. (Mermaid Ser.). (Unwin, 1903.)

BEST PLAYS OF DRYDEN. Ed. with Introd. and notes by G. S. (Mermaid Ser.). (Unwin, 1904.)

RHYMERS' LEXICON. Compiled and ed. A. Loring. Introd. by G. S. (Routledge, 1905.)

MINOR POETS OF THE CAROLINE PERIOD. Ed. with Gen. Introd., Pref. Notes, and Introds. by G. S. 3 vols. (Clarendon Press, 1905–21.)

BALZAC NOVELS AND STORIES. Introds. by G. S. (Everyman's Lib.). 15 vols. (Dent, 1906–15.)

LONGFELLOW'S 'POEMS'. Selected with Introd. by G. S. (Golden Poets Ser.). (Jack, 1906.)

MÉRIMÉE'S 'NOVELS, TALES, AND LETTERS'. With Gen. Introd. by G. S. 8 vols. (N.Y., 1906.)

PLAYS OF MOLIÈRE in French with Eng. trans. A. R. Waller. Introd. by G. S. 8 vols. (John Grant, 1907.)

SHAKESPEARE'S 'RICHARD II'. With Introd. by G. S. (Renaissance Ed., Vol. XXI). (Harrap, 1907.)

OXFORD THACKERAY. Ed. with Introds. by G. S. 20 vols. (O.U.P., 1908.)

FIELDING. Selections with Introd. by G. S. (Masters of Lit. Ser.). (Bell, 1909.)

FIELDING'S 'TOM JONES'. Introd., reprtd. from Introd. included in *Works of Fielding* (1893), by G. S. (Everyman's Lib.). 2 vols. (Dent, 1909.)

THACKERAY'S 'HENRY ESMOND'. Ed. T. C. & W. Snow. Introd., reprtd. from Introd. included in *Oxford Thackeray* (1908), by G. S. (O.U.P., 1909.)

FIELDING'S 'JOSEPH ANDREWS'. Introd., reprtd. with minor changes, from Introd. included in *Works of Fielding* (1893), by G. S. (Everyman's Lib.). (Dent, 1910.)

SCOTT'S 'LIVES OF THE NOVELISTS'. Introd. by G. S. (Everyman's Lib.). (Dent, 1910.)

THACKERAY'S 'VIRGINIANS'. Introd., reprtd. from Introd. included in *Oxford Thackeray* (1908), by G. S. (O.U.P., 1911.)

STERNE'S 'TRISTRAM SHANDY'. Introd., reprtd. from Introd. included in *Works of Sterne* (1894), by G. S. (Everyman's Lib.). (Dent, 1912.)

RICHARDSON'S 'PAMELA'. Introd. by G. S. (Everyman's Lib.). 2 vols. (Dent, 1914.)

LETTER BOOK. Selected with Introd. on 'History and Art of Letter-Writing' by G. S. (Bell, 1922.)

LONGUS'S 'DAPHNIS AND CHLOE'. Trans. G. Thornley. Introd. by G. S. (Abbey Classics Ser.). (Chapman & Dodd, 1923.)

BORROW: Selections. With Essays by Richard Ford, Leslie Stephen, and George Saintsbury. 'George Saintsbury on Borrow'. Reprtd., with minor omissions, from article on Borrow in *Macmillan's Mag.*, Jany. 1886, and from the republication of it in *Essays in Eng. Lit.*, First Ser. (1890). (O.U.P., 1924.)

HELIODORUS'S 'AETHIOPIAN HISTORY'. Trans. Underdowne. Introd. by G. S. (Abbey Classics Ser.). (Chapman & Dodd, 1924.)

RECEIPT BOOK OF MRS. ANN BLENCOWE. Introd. by G. S. (Guy Chapman, 1925.)

CLEMENTINA BLACK'S 'LINLEYS OF BATH'. Introd. by G. S. New ed., rev. (Secker, 1926.)

GOLDSMITH'S 'VICAR OF WAKEFIELD'. Introd. by G. S. (Constable, 1926.)

WORKS OF FIELDING. Ed. by G. S. 12 vols. (Navarre Soc., 1926.)

TALES FROM BALZAC. Pref. by G. S. (Nash & Grayson, 1927.)

COMPTE DE CAYLUS'S 'COACHMAN'S STORY, ETC.'. Trans E. Sutton. Introd. by G. S. (Chapman & Hall, 1927.)

DE QUINCEY'S 'ENGLISH OPIUM-EATER'. Introd. by G. S. (Constable, 1927.)

TALES FROM GAUTIER. Trans. L. Hearn. Pref. by G. S. (Nash & Grayson, 1927.)

STERNE'S 'SENTIMENTAL JOURNEY' AND 'JOURNAL TO ELIZA'. Introd. by G. S. (Everyman's Lib.). (Dent, 1927.)

WALTON'S 'LIVES'. Introd. by G. S. (World's Classics Ser.). (O.U.P., 1927.)

WORKS OF FIELDING. Ed. by G. S. Illus. G. Cruikshank. 12 vols. (Navarre Soc., 1928.)

FLAUBERT'S 'MADAME BOVARY'. Trans. E. M. Aveling. Introd., reprtd. from *Essays on French Novelists* (1891), which is slightly enlarged from the article on Flaubert in *Fortnightly Rev.* (April, 1878), by G. S. (Everyman's Lib.). (Dent, 1928.)

TALES FROM FLAUBERT. Pref. by G. S. (Nash & Grayson, 1928.)

MAGINN'S 'STORY WITHOUT A TAIL'. Pref. by G. S. (Baskerville Ser.). (Elkin Mathews, 1928.)

MARRYAT'S 'JACOB FAITHFUL'. Introd. Essay by G. S. 2 vols. (Constable, 1928.)

ROUSSEAU'S 'CONFESSIONS'. Pref. Notice by G. S., reprtd. from *Encyclop. Brit.* (N.Y., 1928.)

TALES FROM MÉRIMÉE. Pref. by G. S. (Nash & Grayson, 1929.)

SHORTER NOVELS, VOL. I. ELIZABETHAN AND JACOBEAN. Introd. by G. S. (Everyman's Lib.). (Dent, 1929.)

TRISTAN IN BRITTANY. Trans. D. Sayers. Introd. by G. S. (Essex Lib.). (Benn, 1929.)

FIELDING'S 'AMELIA'. Introd., reprtd. from Introd. included in *Works of Fielding* (1893), by G. S. (Everyman's Lib.). 2 vols. (Dent, 1930.)

FITZGERALD'S 'OMAR KHAYYAM'. Illus. W. Pogany. Introd. by G. S. (Harrap, 1930.)

OLD BOOK: A MEDIAEVAL ANTHOLOGY. Ed. D. Hartley. Introd. by G. S. (Knopf, N.Y., 1930.)

ABBÉ PRÉVOST'S 'MANON LESCAUT'. Trans. Helen Waddell. Introd. by G. S. (Constable, 1931.)

FIELDING'S 'JONATHAN WILD' and 'VOYAGE TO LISBON'. Introd., reprtd., with minor changes and curtailment of Introd. to *Voyage*, from Introd. included in *Works of Fielding* (1893), by G. S. (Everyman's Lib.). (Dent, 1932.)

V. Articles, etc., Contained in Reference and other Works

ENCYCLOPÆDIA BRITANNICA. Ninth Edition. 25 vols. (Black, 1875–89.) Saintsbury's 36 arts. are: 'Pierre Corneille', 'Thomas Corneille', 'French Literature', 'Gautier', 'Joinville', 'La Bruyère', 'La Fontaine', 'Lamartine', 'La Rochefoucauld', 'Le Sage', 'Joseph de Maistre', 'François de Malherbe', 'Marguerite de Valois', 'Pierre Marivaux', 'Clément Marot', 'Mérimée', 'Jules Michelet', 'Montaigne', 'Montesquieu', 'Duchesse de Montpensier', 'Charles, Duke of Orleans', 'Pascal' (in part), 'Quinet', 'Rabelais', 'Racine', 'Cardinal de Retz', 'Ronsard', 'Rousseau', 'Duc de Saint-Simon', 'Madame de Sévigné', 'Madame de Staël', 'Thiers', 'Alfred de Vigny', 'Geoffroy de Villehardouin', 'François Villon', 'Voltaire'.

COMPLETE WORKS OF EDMUND SPENSER. Ed. A. B. Grosart in association with other scholars including G. S. Vol. III. introduces extract from *Short Hist. of French Lit.* (1882) and acknowledges help from G. S. for three papers. 9 vols. (Priv. prtd., 1882–84.)

CHAMBERS'S ENCYCLOPÆDIA. New Edition. 10 vols. (Chambers, 1888–92.) Saintsbury's 8 arts. are: 'Byron', 'Daudet', 'Drama', 'Dryden', 'Flaubert', 'Molière', 'George Sand', 'Zola'.

PARTRIDGE. 'Cookery' by G. S. (Fur & Feather Ser.). Ed. A. E. T. Watson. (Longmans, 1893.)

GROUSE. 'Cookery' by G. S. (Fur & Feather Ser.). (Longmans, 1894.)

YELLOW BOOK. 'A Sentimental Cellar' by G. S. (Elkin Mathews & Lane, Vol. I., April, 1894.)

SOCIAL ENGLAND. Ed. H. D. Traill. 13 arts. by G. S. 6 vols. (Cassell, 1894–97.)

WORLD'S BEST ESSAYS. Ed. D. J. Brewer. 'Voltaire' by G. S. in Vol. IX, reprtd. from review of Jas. Parton's *Life of Voltaire* in *Academy* (July 16, 1881). 10 vols. (St. Louis, U.S.A., 1900.)

ENGLISH MISCELLANY, PRESENTED TO DR. FURNIVALL ON HIS SEVENTY-FIFTH BIRTHDAY. Verses by G. S. entitled 'G. S. to F. J. F.', dated 'Edinburgh, Lammas, 1899'. (Clarendon Press, 1901.)

CHAMBERS'S CYCLOPÆDIA OF ENGLISH LITERATURE. Ed. D. Patrick. New Edition. 3 vols. (Chambers, 1901–3.) Saintsbury's 3 arts. are: 'Dryden', 'Pope' (biog. part by Dr. Carruthers, rev. by G. S., who rewrote the critical part), 'Swift'. These occur in Vols. I. and II.

LIBRARY OF LITERARY CRITICISM. Ed. C. W. Moulton. 8 vols. Contains 43 quotations from G. S.'s criticisms. (Moulton Pub. Co., Buffalo, 1901–5.)

NELSON'S ENCYCLOPÆDIA. 12 vols. (Nelson, 1907.) Saintsbury's 2 arts. are: 'English Literature' and 'Romance', both unsigned.

CAMBRIDGE HISTORY OF ENGLISH LITERATURE. Ed. Sir A. W. Ward & A. R. Waller. 20 chaps. by G. S. 14 vols. (C.U.P., 1907–16.)

MILTON MEMORIAL LECTURES, 1908 (Roy. Soc. Lit.). 'Milton and the Grand Style' by G. S. (O.U.P., 1909.)

ESSAYS AND STUDIES BY MEMBERS OF THE ENG. ASSOC. Vol. I. 'Shakespeare and the Grand Style' by G. S. (Clarendon Press, 1910.)

ENCYCLOPÆDIA BRITANNICA. Eleventh Edition. 29 vols. (C.U.P., 1910–11.) Saintsbury's 38 arts. comprise the 36 contributed to the Ninth Ed., but these are revised and brought up to date, and 2 additional ones on 'Balzac' and 'Romance'.

COMPLETE POETICAL WORKS OF S. T. COLERIDGE. Ed. E. H. Coleridge. (Oxford Eng. Texts Ser.). 'Notes by Professor Saintsbury' to section on 'Metrical Experiments' in Vol. II. 2 vols. (Clarendon Press, 1912.)

ESSAYS AND STUDIES BY MEMBERS OF THE ENG. ASSOC. Vol. III. 'Dante and the Grand Style' by G. S. (Clarendon Press, 1912.)

FAMOUS EDINBURGH STUDENTS. 'Sir Walter Scott' by G. S. (Foulis, 1914.)

BRITISH EMPIRE UNIVERSITIES MODERN ENGLISH ILLUSTRATED DICTIONARY. Ed. E. D. Price & H. T. Peck. 'Versification and Prosody' by G. S. (Syndicate Pub. Co., 1914.)

BOOK OF HOMAGE TO SHAKESPEARE. Ed. I. Gollancz. 'Shakespeare As Touchstone' by G. S. (O.U.P., 1916.)

SONG OF ROLAND. Trans. C. K. Scott Moncrieff. 'Note on Technique' by G. S. (Chapman & Hall, 1919.)

ESSAYS AND STUDIES BY MEMBERS OF THE ENG. ASSOC. Vol. VI. 'Trollope Revisited' by G. S. (Clarendon Press, 1920.)

JOHN KEATS MEMORIAL VOLUME. 'A Reminiscence of "Endymion"' by G. S. (Lane, 1921.)

S.P.E. (Soc. for Pure English) *Tract VI. On Hyphens & Shall & Will, Should & Would in the Newspapers of Today* by H. W. Fowler. Correspondence: 'Idiom, Solecism, and Obscurity' by G. S., followed by Editor's Note on G. S.'s letter. (Clarendon Press, 1921.)

MODERN ESSAYS. Selected C. Morley. 'Beer and Cider' by G. S., reprtd. from *Notes on A Cellar-Book* (1920). (Harcourt Brace: N.Y., 1921.)

I CAN REMEMBER ROBERT LOUIS STEVENSON. Ed. R. Masson. 'A Recollection' by G. S. (Chambers, 1922.)

MODERN ENGLISH ESSAYS. Ed. E. Rhys. 'Scott and Dumas' and 'Henry Fielding and "Joseph Andrews"' by G. S., reprtd. from *Essays in Eng. Lit.*, Second Ser. (1895) and *Works of Fielding* (1893). 5 vols. (Dent, 1922.)

MARCEL PROUST: AN ENGLISH TRIBUTE. Collected by C. K. Scott Moncrieff. 'A Moment to Spare' by G. S. (Chatto & Windus, 1923.)

BYRON, THE POET. Ed. W. A. Briscoe. Addresses and Essays. A Centenary Volume. Part I., chap. vii, 'Byron As A Prosodist' by G. S., reprtd. from *Historical Manual of English Prosody* (1910), preceded by extract from G. S.'s reply to Editor's request. (Routledge, 1924.)

MASTERPIECE LIBRARY OF SHORT STORIES. Ed. J. A. Hammerton and selected by board of eminent critics including G. S. 20 vols. (Educ. Book Co., 1924.)

BOOK OF THE QUEEN'S DOLLS' HOUSE. Ed. A. C. Benson & Sir L. Weaver. Vol. I. 'The Cellar' by G. S. (Methuen, 1924.)

BOOK OF THE QUEEN'S DOLLS' HOUSE LIBRARY (Vol. II. of above). Ed. E. V. Lucas. 'Some Banalities' by G. S. (Methuen, 1924.)

OXFORD BOOK OF ENGLISH PROSE. Ed. Sir A. Quiller-Couch. 'Death of Molière' by G. S., reprtd. from Introd. to *Plays of Molière* (1907). (O.U.P., 1925.)

AUSTIN DOBSON: SOME NOTES by Alban Dobson. 'A Little Necrology' by G. S., reprtd. from *Scrap Book* (1922). (O.U.P., 1928.)

CONTEMPORARY ESSAYS. Ed. W. T. Hastings. 'Mr. William Morris' by G. S. reprtd. from *Corrected Impressions* (1895). (Houghton Mifflin: Boston, 1928.)

EIGHTEEN-SEVENTIES: ESSAYS BY FELLOWS OF ROY. SOC. LIT. Ed. H. Granville-Barker. 'Andrew Lang in the 'Seventies—and After' by G. S. (C.U.P., 1929.)

HUNDRED BEST ENGLISH ESSAYS. Selected by Lord Birkenhead. 'Carlyle' by G. S., reprtd. from *Corrected Impressions* (1895). (Cassell, 1929.)

ENGLISH CRITICAL ESSAYS: TWENTIETH CENTURY. Ed. P. M. Jones. 'Shakespeare and the Grand Style' by G. S., reprtd. from *Essays and Studies of Eng. Assoc.*, Vol. I. (1910). (World's Classics Ser.). (O.U.P., 1933.)

For Product Safety Concerns and Information please contact our EU representative GPSR@taylorandfrancis.com
Taylor & Francis Verlag GmbH, Kaufingerstraße 24, 80331 München, Germany

www.ingramcontent.com/pod-product-compliance
Lightning Source LLC
Chambersburg PA
CBHW071511110726
47908CB00003B/801

* 9 7 8 1 1 3 8 5 6 3 4 9 0 *